Secret Nature of
Devon

Secret Nature of
Devon

Andrew Cooper

GREEN BOOKS

First published in 2005
by Green Books Ltd
Foxhole, Dartington, Totnes,
Devon TQ9 6EB
www.greenbooks.co.uk
info@greenbooks.co.uk

Design by Rick Lawrence
samskara@onetel.com

Printed by Pims, Crewkerne, Somerset, UK

Text printed on Emerald FSC, made from
75% post-consumer waste and up to 25% (at least 17.5%)
pulp from genuinely sustainably managed forests

A catalogue record for this publication
is available from the British Library

ISBN 1 903998 50 6

Photo on page 2: Great spotted woodpecker with young

Contents

Slapton Lower Ley

*To my wife Jeanne, for her encouragement
and enthusiastic support as ever*

Devon

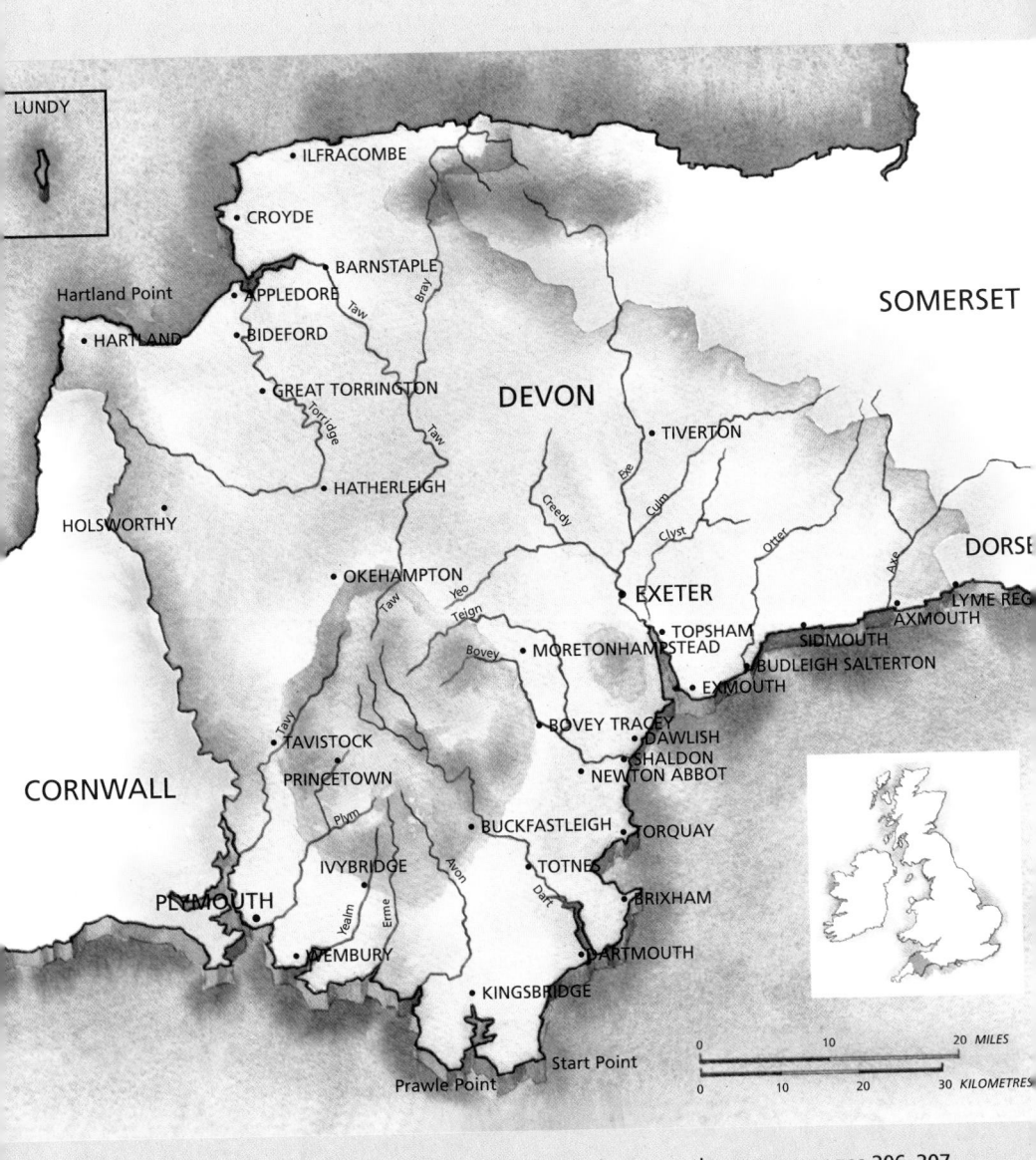

LUNDY

SOMERSET

DORSE

• ILFRACOMBE

• CROYDE

• BARNSTAPLE

Hartland Point

• APPLEDORE

• HARTLAND

• BIDEFORD

• GREAT TORRINGTON

DEVON

• TIVERTON

• HATHERLEIGH

HOLSWORTHY

• OKEHAMPTON

EXETER

• TOPSHAM

LYME REG

AXMOUTH

• MORETONHAMPSTEAD

SIDMOUTH

BUDLEIGH SALTERTON

• EXMOUTH

• BOVEY TRACEY

• TAVISTOCK

• DAWLISH

• SHALDON

• NEWTON ABBOT

• PRINCETOWN

CORNWALL

• BUCKFASTLEIGH

• TORQUAY

• IVYBRIDGE

• TOTNES

• BRIXHAM

PLYMOUTH

• WEMBURY

• DARTMOUTH

• KINGSBRIDGE

Start Point

Prawle Point

0   10   20 MILES

0   10   20   30 KILOMETRES

Rivers labelled: Taw, Bray, Torridge, Taw, Bovey, Creedy, Culm, Clyst, Otter, Axe, Yeo, Teign, Plym, Yealm, Erme, Avon, Dart

For the location of recommended wildlife sites, please see the map on pages 206–207.

Acknowledgements

Many people have generously shared their knowledge and spared valuable time to help me celebrate the wonderful wildlife of Devon in this book. I owe a great debt of thanks to all those who have given their unstinting support and skills during its preparation.

I would particularly like to thank the staff and volunteers of the Devon Wildlife Trust and Devon Biodiversity Record Centre, especially Emma Davies and Jo Pullins for their encouragement and expert help. Thanks are also due to the staff and volunteers of the RSPB South-west office, especially Tony Richardson, Peter Exley and Nigel Hewitt.

Many others have also shared their specialist knowledge and enthusiasm for the wildlife of Devon. I would especially like to thank David Smallshire, British Dragonfly Society; Jeremy Ison, Botanical Society of the British Isles; Dr. Roger Bristow, Chairman and Recorder, Butterfly Conservation, Devon Branch; Roy McCormick, Devon Moth Group; Peter Sutton, Amateur Entomologist's Society; and Dr. David Stradling, Chairman of Whitley Wildlife Conservation Trust, for advice on ants, bees and wasps.

Last but not least, my special thanks go to the Green Books team of John Elford and Amanda Cuthbert for their considerable publishing talents and endless patience.

Yellow flag iris in valley wetland

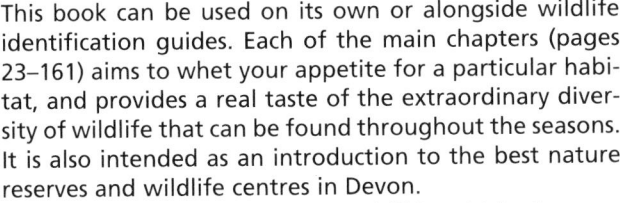

How to Use This Book

This book can be used on its own or alongside wildlife identification guides. Each of the main chapters (pages 23–161) aims to whet your appetite for a particular habitat, and provides a real taste of the extraordinary diversity of wildlife that can be found throughout the seasons. It is also intended as an introduction to the best nature reserves and wildlife centres in Devon.

For tips on **How to Watch Wildlife**, which gives you some of the tricks of the trade of a wildlife film maker, see pages 10–11. For a quick guide to what makes Devon special in terms of its nature, see **Wild Highlights** (pages 20–21), and for more information on individual plants and animals, turn to the **What to See** section (pages 162–205), where you will also find the best month and time to look out for them, their most common habitats, and their status in Devon. Being aware of what each plant and animal needs to survive will improve your chances of finding it, and getting closer to it. The section on **Where to See it** (pages 208–242) will give you a more detailed guide to the best wildlife sites in the county. This information has been compiled with the help and expertise of the principal wildlife conservation organisations in the county: the Devon Wildlife Trust, RSPB and others.

As Devon is a predominantly rural county, urban wildlife is not covered as a separate habitat. Most native wildlife found in gardens can also be found in the surrounding countryside.

While every effort has been made to ensure accuracy in the Secret Nature Guides, wild creatures do not read the books we write about them. Nature is dynamic and forever changing. Also, every season new nature reserves open, and parking, paths and visitor facilities are being built or upgraded across the country. So why not help us to help you. Please let us know what you enjoyed most about this book – send your comments to Wildlink, Church Farm, Haccombe, Newton Abbot, Devon TQ12 4SJ, or email us. You can find our email address and also keep up to date with the wildlife at the author's own farm in Devon by visiting www.wildlink.org.

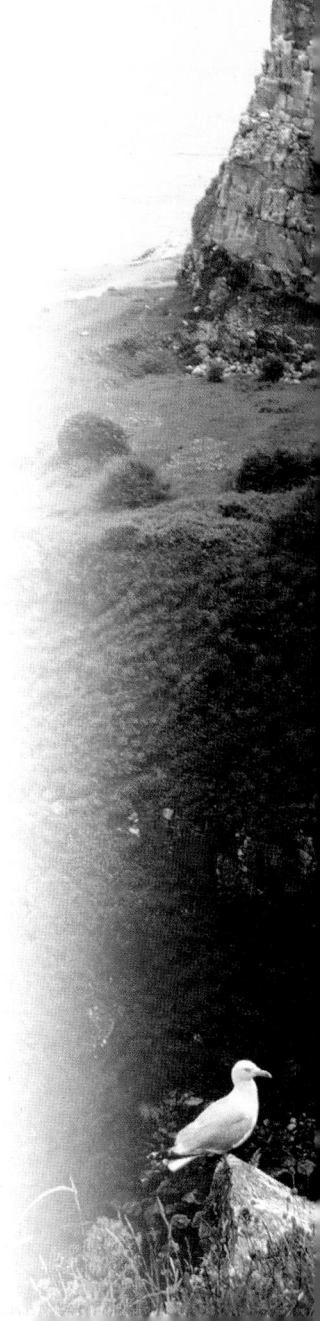

Berry Head quarry

Autumn

Winter

How to Watch Wildlife

Watching any wild animal is a battle of wits – yours against a creature's natural instinct to survive. To enjoy seeing hares boxing, deer rutting or the courting ceremony of great-crested grebe, you do not need to get too close; but it is thrilling to watch a wild animal from just a few paces away, not just on TV. To get close, you may need to use some of our now less used senses. Instinct is a powerful ally: if you are not sure what to do, just follow your natural feelings. Keeping still and quiet is the simplest way to watch wildlife successfully. Many birds and insects are quite easy to approach if you do so slowly and with care. Except for owls, most birds react more to movement than sound. Mammals are more difficult: most have amazingly keen senses of smell and hearing. Deer also have acute eyesight, and bats can 'see' you in pitch dark. Even insects have remarkably good sight – try getting close to a butterfly. It can be done if you approach very slowly, especially when the air temperature is cool in early morning. Just think and move like a chameleon! At first, to increase your chances of success, try visiting places where wildlife is already accustomed to the presence of people – country parks and popular nature reserves. Stay on the paths, and wild creatures will often ignore you. Step off a regular track, and they will be gone.

Timing your visit is crucial. Not all plants and animals can be seen all year round, but every season has its highlights. If visiting an estuary or anywhere on the coast it is important to check the local tide times – both for your own safety and the best opportunity of seeing the most wildlife. The best time for watching many creatures is often early in the day, but wind and weather also play their part. On a lake or estuary in summer, the leeward shore will have the most wind-blown insects, so that is where most birds and fish are likely to be feeding. But if a gale is blowing, most wading birds seek shelter in the lee of reeds or banks.

Some creatures are also rare – indeed so rare that they are protected by law. Bats may not be disturbed at any time. Many birds are fully protected, and others such as the Barn Owl and Kingfisher must not be approached at or near their nest. Check with English Nature or your County Wildlife Trust for a full, up to date list of all UK protected plants and animals.

Early summer
Late summer

When attempting to get close to any creature in the countryside, beware of wood pigeons. They will explode from cover as you approach, alerting every other animal in the neighbourhood. Be aware too of your silhouette and shadow. Stay away from the skyline and keep a bush, tree or hillside behind you to disguise your human outline. On windy days, it is often easier to get closer to a creature than on calm, still days, when sound carries far. Walk into or across the wind. The exception is mist. Many skulking birds, like the rare Dartford Warbler, seem much bolder in foggy weather. Keep to softer ground rather than noisy stones. If you are walking on dry crunchy leaves, try waiting for a gust of wind to disguise the sound of your footsteps. The easiest way is to utilise the increasing number of purpose-built wildlife hides now available country-wide. Some hides even have close circuit television to give you a real bird's eye view.

Wearing neutral coloured clothing, sturdy footwear and using a good pair of binoculars, all adds to your chances of success, and knowing something about the behaviour of wild animals is also helpful. Some creatures are surprisingly curious. If a stoat or weasel crosses your path, try freezing for a few moments – it will invariably come back for a second and sometimes even a third look at you.

There is one last strategy for getting closer to wildlife. If all else fails when you are wearing bright colours on a calm sunny day and there is no way you can conceal yourself, just try pretending you are not remotely interested. Walk casually past without looking directly at it. A wild animal usually only stares at another creature for two reasons – because it is a threat or a potential meal.

Wild flowers are far easier to approach, as they cannot run away, but they can be more difficult to find. The biggest danger with plants is that you may accidentally trample them.

The best tip I can give for successful wildlife watching is to stop, look and listen more often. Just because you cannot see anything, it does not mean they cannot see you. Good watching!

TAKE CARE: Devon has a wealth of tracks and trails criss-crossing the country-side, moors and coastline. Walkers should be careful not to cross private land, and on Dartmoor firing days, keep a wary eye open for military red flags flying.

Notices for MOD Ranges are published in the local press and on moorland notice boards.

LOCAL INFORMATION: BBC Radio Devon (FM 103.4) regularly broadcasts information on Devon weather, travel and tides, as do the evening BBC1 'Spotlight' programme and ITV local news.

Seasons

While plants and most animals broadly keep to the same seasons as we do, birds are different.

SEASONS FOR PLANTS AND MOST ANIMALS

Spring	March – April	(Spring equinox: 21st March)
Summer	May – September	(Midsummer solstice: 21st June)
Autumn	October – November	(Autumn equinox: 21st Sept)
Winter	December – February	(Midwinter solstice: 21st December)

BIRD SEASONS

Spring	(migration)	March – May
Summer	(breeding)	June – July (but some resident birds much earlier)
Autumn	(migration)	August – November
Winter	(surviving)	December – February

The Secret Nature Country Code

- Enjoy the countryside and respect its life and work.
- Guard against all risk of fire.
- Gates – leave them as you find them, if in doubt close them.
- Dogs should be kept under close control at all times.
- Keep to public paths across farmland and marked trails on nature reserves.
- Use gates and stiles to cross fences, hedges and walls.
- Make no unnecessary noise – you will see and hear more wildlife.
- Leave livestock, crops and machinery alone.
- Take your litter home.
- Help keep all water clean.
- Take care on country roads – keep your speed down, especially near horses.
- Cyclists should keep to bridleways, byways and special cycle routes.
- Do not use motorised vehicles on footpaths and bridleways.

And for the most remote areas, I like the simple: 'Take only pictures, leave only footprints'. But personally I do not even like to leave footprints, as they may spoil my next photograph!

Key to Abbreviations used in this Book

CP	Country Park
DBPS	Devon Bird Watching and Preservation Society
DWT	Devon Wildlife Trust
LNR	Local Nature Reserve
MNR	Marine Nature Reserve
NNR	National Nature Reserve
NT	National Trust
Ramsar	European designation for internationally important wetlands
RSPB	Royal Society for the Protection of Birds
SAM	Scheduled Ancient Monument
SPA	Specially Protected Area
SSSI	Site of Special Scientific Interest
VMCA	Voluntary Marine Conservation Area
WT	Woodland Trust

The reason why *Scientific names* are also used in the 'What to see' section is to avoid confusion. Many plants and animals have common local names that may differ from county to county, let alone between countries.

Native species are those plants and animals that were present before the English Channel was finally formed over 6,000 years ago.

Introduced species are those that may have been deliberately released in the wild or escaped from animal collections and gardens. Many plants and animals are now naturalised – living and breeding in the wild.

Dartmoor sunset over Haytor

Introduction

The river Dart flows down through a series of steep-sided valleys, twisting and turning its way south to the sea. It begins its journey on a high windswept and often mist-enshrouded plateau. Dartmoor rises from the midst of Devon like an island towering above a rolling agricultural sea. Combined with the other moors in the region, this massive granite root of the once great Amorican mountain chain now forms the backbone to the south-west peninsula. Down on the south coast at Dartmouth, the lowest reaches of the river valley are so warm and humid that you can grow exotic sub-tropical plants outside all year. Heading upriver, away from the lively port and raucous gulls, the steep wooded banks contain a luxuriance of growth. In early summer the woods are carpeted with bluebells and wild garlic. In their shade, roe deer nervously munch the lush vegetation, while out in the open white egrets stalk the tidal shallows. Here the river is wide and smooth, languid in old age, with broad muddy banks where otters play under cover of night. Here the height of the tide is marked by the cut line of overhanging trees, their branches pruned by the flow of the estuary.

Five miles inland, beneath the first bridge, beyond the bustling medieval market town of Totnes, any influence of the sea is left behind. Above the tidal reach the water now is fresh, and on either side cattle and sheep eagerly graze the bright green flood meadows. A kingfisher flashes low across the river, and a pair of merganser dive in search of fish. As you continue upstream into its middle reaches, the flow quickens. In places the debris of the last winter flood, twisted branches and chaotic bundles of twigs, clings to exposed roots at the woodland edge. In spring, primroses paint the banks pale yellow beneath the old rail line, where steam trains still carry happy bands of holidaymakers. But passing Buckfast Abbey, as you ascend towards the moor, the plant life begins to change. Now the valley grows deeper with steeper sides. The mewing call of buzzards wheeling overhead mingles with the rush of water. Granite boulders begin to line the river. Trees that lower down grew straight and tall, here appear more twisted, adorned with lichen. Some now arch over the narrowing flow, enabling squirrels to cross with dry feet. In the deepest, shady parts, the air is cooler, damper. Ferns festoon the banks, and great lumps of moss-covered granite litter the river's meandering course. Now the Dart divides east and west.

Heading up the East Dart and climbing onto the moor, the native oak wood is soon left in the valley. Steep sided gorges give way to vast bracken covered slopes, divided only by granite walls and then open moor, with a scattering of prehistoric hut circles. Peaty pools, where dashing young trout wait for a passing meal, alternate with fast flowing stretches where bouncing dippers energetically search the currents for food. Here the water bubbles and gurgles with all the vigour of a stream in its youth.

Up on the high moor, the sinuous stream is flanked by heather-clad slopes, dotted with grazing Dartmoor ponies and hardy black-faced sheep. In season, salmon spawn in its gravel bed and the plaintive 'peewit' call of the lapwing carries on the wind. Finally, nearly 600 metres high, the stream that is to become the River Dart starts life as a trickle, emanating from a rain-soaked treacherous bog. Up here among the high tops of ancient weather-beaten granite tors, life is harsh. This is the roof of Devon, almost its highest point. So it is perhaps not surprising to find that on the other side of the ridge, just a short walk away from where the Dart begins, another great river, the Taw, oozes from the bog. But this river heads in the opposite direction, starting its long trek to the North coast of the county. And they are not alone; in all, five of Devon's main rivers start their lives on the high moor.

Follow the Dart, or any of Devon's major rivers, from mouth to source, and in less than thirty miles you can come from a coastline where sub-tropical flowers bloom, to the wind-torn heights of Dartmoor where sub-arctic plants survive. Few places in Britain can boast such extremes, such a rich and diverse nature in such a short distance – Devon can.

Dartmoor

Setting the Scene

The British Isles support a greater diversity of wildlife and habitats than almost any other country of similar size in the world. The natural history of Britain can be just as exciting and stimulating to watch as any big game in Africa – it is just, more often than not, on a smaller scale. There is another world outside our everyday lives, a place where danger and death are common events and survival is only for the fittest. We do not need to travel far to find one of the fastest predators on earth, see herds of grazing wild game or vast flocks of spectacular birds. They lie just beyond our doorstep, for this is the secret side of Britain – its nature.

Geology

In the world of geological time, Devon is world-famous. No other place has given its name to an entire period – the Devonian. Devon is dominated by its magnificent uplands and coastal scenery. At times it seems that wherever you look the views vary from the beautiful to the breathtaking. Yet more astounding is the age and diversity of its rocks and how that influences the world around us. It is the ground beneath our feet that gives rise to the nature of the soil and everything that grows in and on it.

The landscape of Devon is broadly divided in two – uplands to the west, lowlands to the east. While towering sea cliffs form the jagged Atlantic west coast, east of Teignmouth the landscape is much softer. The high ground of Devon is largely composed of hard, thin sediments, slates and shales with a small scattering of hard limestone outcrops. Periodic and extensive volcanic activity across the region has also left its mark. Over time, the mix of rocks has become fractured and twisted, even embedded with the great granite mass that today forms the bulk of Dartmoor. But in a few places, south of the moorland edge, a rare and valuable deposit can be found – ball and china clay. Other clays, marls and limestone, topped by chalk and greensand, can more easily be seen exposed in the eastern cliffs of the county.

In common with most parts of Britain, Devon's geological history is dramatic and extreme. Over 500 hundred million years ago the region that was to be the county of Devon lay closer to the equator, beneath a warm shallow sea. Then a period of monumental mountain building raised the land to the North, through Wales to Scotland. Beneath baking tropical skies, little life stirred. Few plants covered the landscape, and erosion was severe. As the silts washed southward they settled, and eventually became rock.

Wembury rocky shore and coastal cirl bunting habitat

These hard sediments were first discovered in Devon, so the county has given its name to some of Britain's most ancient rocks of their kind. These deposits were formed during the Devonian period, between 345 and 410 million years ago. This was an era when the land was still largely devoid of animal life, where only the first forests of giant tree fern grew. The seas were more dangerous, and life here abounded with monsters of terrifying proportions. The most dramatic outcrops of gritty sandstones formed during that time, creating the wild uplands of Exmoor and the spectacular cliffs of North Devon east of Ilfracombe. But the county contains even older rocks. Down on the southernmost coast of Devon, the picturesque headlands of Bolt Head and Tail, Start and Prawle points, are made from schistose rocks thought to be from the dawn of earth's creation, the Pre-Cambrian period over 570 million years ago.

Elswehere, between the north coast and Dartmoor in deepest mid-Devon, lies a great swathe of grazing land, stretching from the Atlantic west coast eastward to the borders of Somerset. Here the underlying rocks were laid down over 270 million years ago, during the Carboniferous period. They are known as Culm deposits, and the wild flowers of their grasslands are some of the richest in Devon.

Another of the county's significant geological features is a great scar that tears across the landscape. A buzzard's eye view of the county reveals a massive rift. In places the Sticklepath Fault forms a deep valley, rending the county in two from Torquay to Torrington and beyond, passing out across the Bristol Channel north of Lundy.

Yet of all the rocks and sediments, none adds more to the real character of Devon than its bright red soil. The colour is caused by high levels of iron oxide. Today these soils are often some of the most fertile areas for farming and horticulture. So it is ironic that the red soil comes from sandstones deposited over 225 million years ago in the Permian period, when Britain was part of a greater land mass, lying closer to the equator in searing hot, dry desert conditions. Surrounded by mountains feeding debris into a great basin, the deposits of sandstone and breccia gradually grew. Today they are a familiar sight to anyone arriving by train. The railway that winds its way spectacularly along the south coast, between Dawlish and Teignmouth, passes through tunnels cut into this famous red sandstone.

Berry head limestone

Sea and Ice

The landscape has also been shaped by two powerful forces in more recent times. Just take a look across the South Hams, East Devon or the far west cliffs – the skyline of hills is surprisingly level. Over the last few million years, sea levels have dramatically changed. When much of Devon was submerged, the action of waves wore down the island hills to the same height – the sea level, as it was then.

The other great influence on the landscape was just as devastating. Smooth sided valleys, rugged cliff tops and broken granite tors – it is hard to believe that a snowflake could cause such destruction. Yet, over the same period of time, ice and snow periodically covered much of Britain for thousands of years. There have been four major ice ages so far, the last ending over ten thousand years ago. During the coldest periods immense glaciers, some hundreds of metres thick, covered most of the British Isles, except for the south and west. But here the sea was still frozen. Devon was in the grip of an arctic climate. Repeated freezing and thawing shattered exposed rocks, and the resulting rubble mix poured down every slope, smoothing sharp edges and covering cliffs. Today Devon's gently rolling hills hide a remarkable natural history of time.

Climate

The south-west of England enjoys the mildest climate in Britain. Bathed in warm prevailing winds from the Atlantic and ocean currents generated by the tropical Gulf Stream, the region is blessed with a plentiful supply of rain. Most of the moisture falls in the west and on the highest ground. While parts of east Devon receive less than 800mm of rain a year, and the countryside around Barnstaple and Bideford little more, parts of Dartmoor can account in places, for over 2.3 metres. On the coasts of Devon frosts are rare, but Dartmoor has snow most winters. Generally the south-west of England, being a peninsular, does not have such extremes of temperatures as the far north and east of Britain. In Devon, the summers may not be as hot, and the winters are seldom as cold.

Dartmoor in winter, looking towards Newton Abbot

Wild Devon Highlights

Spring

Primrose and wild violets lining a country lane
Walking through a wood filled with wild daffodils
Dipper foraging on a tumbling Dartmoor stream
Paw print of an otter on a muddy bank
Cirl bunting feeding near the coast
Peregrine stooping over a sea cliff or Exeter cathedral
The sight and smell of wild garlic in a wood
Dartmoor hillsides covered in blackthorn blossom
The chatter of the first swallows returning to a farm
A woodland carpet of bluebells

Summer

Nightjar churring at dusk over heathland
Dartford warbler on a gorse bush in full flower
Pied flycatcher and redstart in a Dartmoor wood
Seabird colony at Berry Head
Kittiwakes nesting on Lundy
Basking sharks off Berry Head and around Lundy
Barn owl hunting over a hay meadow
Carpets of orchids on calcareous grasslands
Sea trout leaping from a river at dusk
The looping patterns of bats flying at dusk
Glow worms lighting a lane
Phosphorescence glowing in the sea after dark
Ring ouzel on Dartmoor
Marsh fritillary butterflies on Culm grasslands
Sandwich tern and other migrants at Dawlish Warren

*Cirl bunting feeding young
at nest; Badger drinking*

Wild Devon Highlights

Autumn

Osprey, hobby and honey buzzard on migration
Snow white little egrets stalking an estuary
The sound of rutting fallow buck at Powderham Castle
Salmon & sea trout holding in pools prior to spawning
Late butterflies on remnants of buddleia flowers
Starlings wheeling in winter flocks in red sky at sunset
The North Devon coast in the teeth of an Atlantic gale
Badgers emerging in a golden wood
The mewing call of buzzards wheeling lazily overhead

Winter

Largest flock of avocets in Britain on the Exe estuary
Spoonbill and hundreds of wading birds at Topsham
Brent geese feeding on sea grass at Exmouth
Wildfowl sheltering at Slapton Lee
Thousands of wading birds at Dawlish Warren
Lichen clinging to a wind-blown Dartmoor tor
Dartmoor ponies sheltering behind huge granite boulders
Hazel catkins unfurling in January
Troops of long-tailed tits foraging through the trees
Frogs spawning in an icy Dartmoor pool in January
Snowdrops on the banks of the Dart at Dartington Hall
Flocks of redwings and fieldfares feeding in an orchard
First primroses appear

Buzzard; Primroses

Estuaries

The cacophony of sound and colourful sights at Dawlish Warren, especially over August bank holiday, can be particularly memorable on a hot day. This large sand spit guards the entrance to the Exe estuary on the south-east coast of Devon. On the seaward side, rolling waves and a multicoloured tide of people throng the shore – bathers and sun worshippers, excited children and fraught parents. Yet less than a golf drive away, up and over the sand dunes, tees and greens, is another world, just as noisy and hectic. On the lee side of the Warren the estuary at high tide is calm. The salt marsh and mud flats are flooded, but just offshore a small shingle island gives a passable impression of a busy airport without the scream of jets. The piping calls of several thousand sea birds and waders drown the distant human roar. This wading bird roost is amazing at high tide – a veritable avian leisure island. Thousands of black and white oystercatchers crowd the crest, while flocks of other smaller wading birds, gulls and migrating terns jostle for space, as the incoming tide packs them closer. To see the best action, get to the bird hide at least one hour before high tide.

The fate of most rivers is to empty into the sea. Whether great or small, all at times are murky and much of the sediment they carry is spilled into estuaries worldwide. Britain has around 155 estuaries and most are confined to the coasts of England and Wales. Devon has more than its fair share – twelve, plus the Tamar, which forms the border with Cornwall. The reason is an accident of geology and climate, rather than just a result of its present freshwater flow – a feature of the region is its drowned river valleys. During the Ice Ages, when sea levels were much lower than now, fast flowing melt water cut deep, wide gorges into the coast. Then as sea levels rose they were flooded, and silt began to build up. All around the south-west coast, evidence of drowned forests can occasionally be found. Some winters the tide scours sand from beaches to expose peat deposits and tree trunks that fell several thousand years ago. Yet drowned valleys now form some of our most delightful, picturesque creeks at Dartmouth and Salcombe.

By the time a river reaches the coast it is laden with a microscopic mix of minerals and organic debris. As freshwater mixes with dissolved salts in the sea, particles clump together and begin to drop out of the flow. Over time and tide great banks of mud steadily grow. The fine, sticky silt found in estuaries is also smelly – the result of trapped debris decaying in the ooze. If you have ever struggled across this clinging mud, your boots threatening to

Oystercatcher flock arriving at Dawlish Warren roost

Brent geese flock over the Exe

be left behind, the faint reek of rotten eggs is from the gases released in your wake. Twice daily the vast sand banks, mud flats and meandering channels flood with the incoming tide, and twice daily they are left exposed.

The surface of the mud is a harsh place for any creature to survive. In winter it is bleak, swept by freezing wind and drenched in heavy rain. In summer it is baked hard and dry. Each day, the water that covers the mud changes dramatically depending on the state of the tide. When ebbing it is fresh, when flowing salty, and in between, the mud flats lie exposed to the air. Life does not get much harsher. Yet many creatures live here and thrive as the benefits are great. A plentiful supply of food is delivered to your doorstep twice a day, and competition is limited, so those species that can endure the hardships are often present in huge numbers.

Devon estuaries can be divided into two groups: major and minor. The Dart, Exe, Salcombe, and Teign are the biggest in the south, while the Taw/Torridge form the largest and only estuary on the north coast. On the south coast, the Devon Avon, Axe, Erme, Otter, Plym, and Yealm are relatively small estuaries.

Mud is rich in life, but not all of Devon's estuaries have large areas of it. Some estuaries are deeper than others, and have rather stony shores flanked by steep wooded banks. The best ones for wildlife watching are the Taw/Torridge and the Exe. Both have extensive mud flats and large populations of wading birds during winter, with salt marsh flowers in summer. The Teign also has a good population of birds, and being relatively small, is more easily explored on foot.

ESTUARY PLANTS

Between the muddiest parts of the upper estuary and the great rippled banks of sand at their mouth, beds of grass can be found. This maritime meadow is not produced by a seaweed, but by one of the few true flowering plants that has adapted to marine life: the perennial **Eel Grass** is the only plant to do so in Britain. It grows in some of the most sheltered places. While its long strap-like leaves wave about in the water, its rhizomes help stabilize the mud flats. It even produces flowers underwater, but they have no need of petals. Eel grass beds provide cover for many unusual marine creatures and become an important source of winter food for wildfowl.

Plants are the real power behind the process that turns soft mud into firmer, drier ground. **Glasswort** is one of the principle pioneers of estuary mud. It gets its name from the old practice of burning the plants to get soda ash, once an

ingredient for glass making. Until 1870, glasswort was the only such plant to be found in British estuaries. Then a new hybrid species of **Cord Grass** appeared. It was natural cross-fertilisation between an American and a native species. The result was a plant even more effective and vigorous as a binder of mud.

On higher ground, above the flooded frontier of the mud flats, it is firmer and less salty underfoot. Grey-green swathes of **Sea Purslane** produce yellow flowering spikes in mid-summer. **Sea Lavender** comes into bloom a little later. Further up the shore in July and August, bright clusters of **Sea Aster** buzz with the contented hum of busy insects. Beyond these low growing plants the salt marsh stretches into and real estuarine jungle. Here a broad border of rushes gives way to dense stands of tall, wind-rustled reed that tower above your head. Reed bed is not common in Devon, but where it does occur it is important for some interesting birds, and even harvest mice may occasionally live amongst its leaves.

ESTUARY INVERTEBRATES

In the upper reaches of the estuary where the water is barely brackish, **Sludge Worms** live in the ooze. Hair-thin in diameter, millions can live in just a few square metres of mud. Further down where the water is more salty, large populations of fingernail-sized **Shrimps** build burrows from where they can snatch at passing particles. Yet these are not the most prolific creatures here. Large concentrations of tiny **Spire Shells**, barely bigger than an apple pip, feed over the surface of the mud. Over 42,000 **Hydrobia Snails** have been counted in just one square metre of an estuary. They are consumed in great numbers by some wildfowl and wading birds.

Brent geese feeding on estuary

Nearer the low tide mark, where some sand is mixed with the mud, large **Lugworm** reveal their presence. Numerous small depressions and casts on the surface are produced by their method of feeding. Living in a U-shaped burrow, filtering the mud and sand mix for food, they draw water in at one end and eject the waste from the other, along with indigestible particles of sand. Counting their casts at low tide should give you an idea of their population – often huge.

Ragworm may be even more numerous, and they can also tolerate more brackish water. Yet, they too, spend their lives hidden in mud with good reason. Like lugworm, they appear to feature at the top of the menu for many wading birds. So at low tide, when the mud flats lie exposed, the worms retreat underground. Although dehydration is a real risk for these worms, hungry birds are probably a bigger danger. Such is the threat from ravenous flocks of birds that many creatures living on or close to the surface must rely on armour plating.

Cockles and **Mussels** are bivalve molluscs, commonly known as shellfish. Their two shells are held together by a hinge and closed with a powerful muscle. Different species can all live in the same patch because direct competition is reduced – they do this by living at different depths. **Razor Shells** live near the surface in a vertical hole. These are the ones that retract into the sand, spurting water when you walk past. In contrast the large, hand-sized shell of the **Sand Gaper** can burrow down to half a metre in mud, deeper than the lugworm. However, most shellfish and estuarine worms can be found in the top 150mm, many just within reach of the longest beak.

As the incoming tide returns, carrying fresh supplies of food, the invertebrate life of the estuary comes back to life, fanning, filtering, grazing, siphoning, snatching and scavenging a meal. Hidden at low water, an army of **Crabs** reappear from their trenches as the advancing tide sweeps over them.

ESTUARY BIRDS

Eel Grass Bed

Even estuaries have lawns, cut by gangs of feathered mowing machines – wildfowl. The marine meadows formed by eel grass are special. Only in the most sheltered places can eel grass thrive. Here they are protected from the action of waves that can tear the plants from their beds. And it not just in estuaries that this grass can grow, but also in very sheltered bays. The list of mud- and sand-dwelling creatures in Devon estuaries is long and varied, but where eel grass grows the list gets longer. Eel grass is only exposed at the lowest spring tides. Apart from those creatures already mentioned, those most commonly encountered in these beds include **Edible Periwinkle, Limpet, Northern Lucina, Small Scallop, Chinaman's Hat, Netted** and **Sting Dog Whelk, Tower Shells, Slipper Limpet, Sand Lance, Peacock Worm, Myxicola Fan Worm, Snakelock Anemone, Sponge, Hermit Crab, Sea Potato, Shrimps, Prawns, Sea Squirts, Pipe Fish, Wrasse, Gobies** and **Spined Sticklebacks**. Two of the most intriguing creatures are both types of **Soldier Crab**. Like their

Reed warbler feeding young

Shelduck

Dunlin

hermit relatives, they commandeer suitable discarded sea snail shells for a home. As they grow, they must find a bigger shell. But Soldier Crabs sometimes take their furnishings with them – a **Sea Anemone**. Two types of these crabs live at different depths, and each attach different species of anemone to their shells.

There is one other inhabitant of Eel Grass beds that is even more special. In just a few of the most sheltered locations, one of the rarest and enchanting creatures is occasionally found around Devon's shores – the **Sea Horse**.

Mud and sand flats

The hours birds feed on mud flats is dictated not so much by time as by tide. So hunting is done both day and night, governed solely by the daily rhythm of high and low water. The tip of a wildfowl or wading bird's beak is sensitive to touch. As the bird simply feels for its prey it does not matter whether it is daylight or dark. Large numbers of birds often feed in the same area, but competition is reduced by each species selecting different food or probing at different depths.

Heron and **Cormorant** favour the deeper channels, hunting for one of their favourite foods – **Flounder**. Increasing numbers of spectacular white

Avocet flock on upper Exe estuary

Avocet

Bar-tailed godwit in summer plumage

Little Egrets can also be seen on most Devon estuaries all year. Another equally exotic-looking bird, the **Spoonbill**, is a regular winter visitor along the south coast.

Shelduck consume vast numbers of tiny hydrobia snails whole. **Ringed Plover** feed more delicately, using their short beaks to extract snails singly from their shells with a flick of the head.

In the league of long beaks, curlew win heads down. They can reach the parts other wading birds cannot reach. **Godwit** come second, closely followed by **Redshank** and **Knot**, then **Sanderling** and **Ringed Plover.**

Autumn and winter are the best times of the year to see the greatest numbers of wading birds and wildfowl on an estuary. An incoming tide concentrates the numbers. As the water slowly returns, creeping across the mud, it pushes a noisy ribbon of **Black-headed Gulls, Grey Plover, Godwit, Dunlin** and **Lapwing** towards the shore.

The Exe Estuary is one of Britain's most important places for wintering birds. At peak times it supports over 7,000 wildfowl and nearly 15,000 waders. On a calm day, close inshore at Exmouth it is sometimes possible to see over 3,500 **Brent Geese** feeding on the eel grass beds.

Turnstones feed along the edge of the tide and do what their name implies – they turn stones to look for food. Large numbers gather in flocks from late summer through winter. The best place to see these attractive little waders at rest is Starcross. At high tide the birds cannot feed and so assemble on a favoured roost. While some turnstones can always be seen from the hide at Dawlish Warren, good numbers flock to the small breakwater just offshore by Starcross station.

The most famous wintering bird in Devon visits the Exe Estuary during the coldest months of the year. Britain's biggest flock of **Avocets**, sometimes numbering more than 400 birds with their distinctive plumage and upturned bill, can brighten the dullest December day. Topsham or Turf Lock are both good places to see them, but the best way is by boat. Cruises run from Exmouth. Avocets can also be seen in smaller numbers on the Tamar, where one of their favourite feeding places is near Cargreen. Here they may sometimes be watched from your car!

Mussel banks

Oystercatchers are big, boldly marked birds with black and white plumage and a long red bill. They are expert eaters of mussels. They also feed in two distinct ways, by stabbing or hammering, never both. The technique is either to chisel through a shell or simply stab at a gaping mussel. Young birds appear to follow their parent's predilection and become either a stabber or a hammerer.

Salt Marsh

Winter may find many small wading birds working along muddy channels in a salt marsh. At high tide it is wildfowl, particularly **Wigeon** and **Mallard**, that are the most likely to be seen in any number. Even in summer, the risk of flooding means that few birds attempt to nest in a salt marsh, except for the occasional **Skylark** or **Meadow Pipit** on the higher parts.

Reed Bed

In summer, reed beds come alive with the sound of **Reed** and **Sedge Warbler**. They will build a nest securely hidden amongst the stems, safe from the highest tide. But even here they may still fall prey to the parasitic habits of a **Cuckoo**.

Dawlish Warren Roost

As the rising tide pushes even long-legged birds off their feeding grounds, most seem to head for the roost at Dawlish Warren. There is a really good visitor centre near the car park, run by Teignbridge District Council, and a hide overlooking the birds gives a grandstand view of the flocks. At peak times, over 20,000 birds made up of over 30 different species can be in view all at once. **Oystercatchers**, **Godwits** and **Dunlin** make up some of the bigger flocks, while **Greenshank**, **Little Stint** and even **Ruff** can sometimes be seen. At summer's end, migrating **Common** and **Sandwich Terns**, along with other rarer relatives, add to the spectacle, especially when a **Peregrine** appears and scatters the flock.

Wader roost, mainly Dunlin, at Dawlish Warren

Otter cubs at play

ESTUARY MAMMALS

In some places reed beds back directly onto farmland. Where this occurs, another type of nest may sometimes be found, but this time made by a mammal. The **Harvest Mouse** is Britain's smallest rodent, and is now known to use reed beds in which to build its home. The nest is the size of a tennis ball, and its construction is intriguing and practical. It is so well camouflaged that it actually changes colour with the seasons. So how does it do this? The mouse weaves its home among some close growing stems, tearing reed leaves that are still attached into fine strips. As the leaves are still growing the nest retains its green colour, only turning golden brown as the reeds take on their autumnal hue. Harvest mice must retreat to higher ground before the winter floods return.

   Mink are not uncommon around the mouths of streams, and even the occasional **Grey Seal** finds its way into a Devon estuary every year.

   The **Otter** was once on the verge of extinction, but is now returning to most of its former haunts. Devon always was a stronghold for these delightfully inquisitive creatures. Otters are usually nocturnal, so usually it is only their paw prints or spraint that may be found. Occasionally an otter can be spotted in the early hours of morning, hunting along the banks of a quiet creek looking for fish or crabs on an incoming tide.

Farmland

The simple pleasure of walking down a Devon lane on a sunny spring morning is hard to beat. Flanked by lush green countryside, birds singing, flowers flourishing, nature everywhere bursting into life. It all seems so natural. Yet the British countryside is essentially man-made. Since the first farmers began clearing the ancient wildwood over five thousand years ago, wielding their stone and bronze age axes, the landscape has been ploughed and cultivated, quarried and quartered, measured, counted, traded, and fought over time and again. Today, some eighty percent of Britain is farmland.

Devon has many ancient farms; indeed two-thirds were in existence before the Norman invasion of 1066. Up to the fourteenth century farming expanded further. Then in 1348 the first plague arrived, and Black Death swept through the land. The impact was devastating. Nearly half the population of Britain died and many farms soon reverted back to scrub, then wood. It was not until the sixteenth and seventeenth centuries that rural prosperity saw the rebuilding of many Devon farmsteads.

For thousands of years farming methods had remained virtually the same. Most work was done by hand and the speed of progress on the land was dictated by the pace of oxen and horse. But that was about to be transformed. The Agricultural Revolution really got underway in 1750. Improved breeding of livestock and intensive crop production, using newly invented horse-drawn machines, resulted in larger, more regular fields. In times of war, farming prospered. What followed was a period of unprecedented change for the countryside. The coming of the railways and further improvements of roads saw towns expand and local industries rise – such as the mining of valuable ball clay in south Devon. From 1900, modern times have witnessed the most dramatic transformation. The ending of the First World War also saw the end of cheap labour on the land and the planting of vast tracts of coniferous forests, significantly altering the uplands. Then the revolution moved up a gear. Motorised machinery made short work of the most labour-intensive chores. Faster roads allowed greater and easier movements of people, especially for leisure. The holiday industry expanded to cater for the growing demand. And the last few decades have seen many farms converted into caravan parks and golf courses.

Since 1945 the changes in agricultural practice continued at an almost reckless pace. Bigger farm machines need wider gates, and bigger tractors need bigger fields. At the peak of destruction, over ten thousand miles of hedgerows were being destroyed each year across Britain, and in total over 150,000 miles of hedgerow were destroyed. Even Devon was not immune, but thankfully the rolling hills and steep-sided valleys are not really suitable for intensive arable production. Many parts of the county have, so far, escaped relatively unscathed. Yet new crops, such as vivid yellow-flowered oil seed rape, pale blue linseed, fields of maize and even sunflowers are appearing here and there, while old orchards have steadily declined. In the Teign valley at least, the approach of summer is still heralded by swathes of apple blossom, for this is traditional cider country.

In many parts of lowland Devon, tucked away behind high hedgerows, mature orchards and permanent pastures can still be found. Few places in lowland Britain still boast such a rich and diverse nature as here, and few counties have such contrasts in their agricultural landscapes. The differences can be especially stark in late winter, particularly among the sheep- and cattle-grazed, fertile, red-soiled South Hams. On its northern edge, the slopes of Dartmoor loom above the horizon. Here there is only rough grazing on cold, rain soaked moorland hills, swept by teeth-chattering winds. But low quality pasture is not just restricted to the moors. Poorly drained, cold soils are also characteristic of the Culm measures. These ancient pastures, found across a large part of mid-Devon, and traditionally grazed by Red Ruby cattle, remain in parts a haven for wild flowers.

Early in the year, long shadows and the coolness of early light find a dairy herd plodding back to the farm, their breath gently rising in clouds over their black and white backs. The arrival of a warm spring day brings out **Bumble Bees** and **Orange Tip Butterflies**, feeding on **Primroses** now crowding lanes and wooded meadow. The first **Swallows** arrive, swooping low over the farm yard; their excited chatter soon bursts from every cattle shed and stall. Great wooden doors and barns built from local stone have weathered well over the centuries. **Robins** and **Wrens** quietly investigate any open buildings, just as they have done over millennia, poking their beaks into every nook and cranny, looking for food or places to nest around the farm.

Within a few weeks **House Martins** dive in to cling beneath the eaves of the old farm house; they seem thrilled at finding their mud nests from the previous year. Down below, a gang of **Sparrows** squabble over spilt grain, before

Farmland hedge with wild rose

rising in a flurry of feathers as the farmer roars into the yard in his tractor. **Song Thrushes** and **Blackbirds** eagerly await the morning clearance of dung. The movement of a steaming heap reveals a feast of worms – and breakfast is served. High above, the raucous call of **Rooks**, busy building their nests, mingle with the sounds of the farm – white **Pigeons** cooing, contented cattle and mechanical pumping as morning milk pulses into tanks. It is a scene repeated as the seasons pass, come rain or shine, year after year, up and down the county, generation after generation.

So the landscape of Devon is rich in the remains of earlier lives. Over thousands of years our ancestors scythed and shaped the countryside, leaving a legacy of farming that brought with it countless wild animals and plants. It is a nature that survives along with medieval field patterns, historic houses and ancient woods – these features make the British landscape one of the richest and most varied on earth. In Devon they are still linked by hedge banks painted with colourful wild flowers, winding their way through centuries-old sunken lanes.

Hedgerows

Devon is the hedgerow capital of Britain. With a staggering 33,000 miles of hedge, it contains more than any other county; and that is not all. If a hedge contains five woody plants in a 30-metre stretch, and supports one special creature such as a **Dormouse** or **Cirl Bunting**, it is considered to be species-rich. Devon has over a fifth of all such hedgerows in the country. But the hedge is not unique to Britain. They can also be found across the English Channel in Normandy, elsewhere in Europe, and even in North America. Hedgerow trees may grow from ground level or along the line of a ditch; some, like many in Devon, consist of banks of earth or granite boulders. Watching a skilled farm worker repair an old Devon bank makes it look deceptively easy.

It is thought that at least a quarter of Devon's hedgerows may be more than 800 years old, and a good number considerably older. Many Bronze Age fields survive in the county. But the first peak of hedgerow growth lasted for two hundred years, starting around 1150. During this time the bulk of the county's boundary banks, sunken winding lanes and crazy network of small fields were formed.

Hedgerow flowers: red campion and bluebell

Orange tip butterfly

Small tortoiseshell butterfly

There are, it seems, three ways a hedge can be created. The first involves hard labour. Many hedgerows are built from local stone, others of turf. More are just planted in the ground, and countless prehistoric ones survive in the south-west of England. Even the Romans were hedgerow fans, often preferring a living fence to one that would slowly rot in time. By the ninth century, different counties had established different traditions of hedge building, and the custom remained virtually unchanged for a thousand years. Then came the revolution – agricultural, that is – and the Enclosure Acts. New laws from 1750 made the fencing of fields and other lands mandatory. Over the next century an amazing 200,000 miles of new hedgerows were planted across Britain. What followed was a period of great unrest, as waves of conflict raged across Europe and around the planet. But from 1850 until the end of the Second World War, little changed on the hedgerow front.

The second way a hedge can be born is by neglect. Growing naturally along the line of an ancient hazel wattle or more modern barbed wire fence, nuts and seeds buried and lost by forgetful squirrels and absent-minded jays soon begin to grow. In time, if not cut back or nibbled by foraging sheep or mice, a line of young saplings simply arises by default.

The third origin of a hedgerow is far more intriguing and rich. When the first fields were carved out of the original wildwood, some trees and shrubs were often left to form a boundary. But the real value of such ancient hedgerows is not just in their trees; woods are made up of far more than just standing timber, they are strips of surviving primeval woodland that contain spectacular and diverse plants – a real vestige of old England.

Over hundreds of years generations of farmers have cut and trimmed, laid, repaired and even restored entire sections of hedge. But hedgerows are only as good as the hands that maintain them. Their prime purpose is to keep domestic stock in or out. In the past, landowners used to allocate a hedge to each farm worker; if kept in good shape, they provided tool handles and firewood, as well as fodder for livestock and fruit for the family. But a good thick hedge, carefully maintained – cut not too early or hard – supports a wealth of animal life. Countless insects, birds and mammals of woodland edge have made themselves at home in the hedge. Hedgerows are vitally important as corridors linking woods large and small, and contribute immensely to the diversity of country life.

Comma butterfly   *Great green bush cricket*

HEDGEROW PLANTS

Some 600 different plants have been identified in hedgerows across Britain, but usually only half that number can commonly be found. The location of a hedge partly determines its plant community. On the most exposed coastal cliffs where pasture gives way to cliff, hedgerow trees are often stunted and bent away from the prevailing coastal winds. Here low-growing cushions of **Western Gorse** may be the dominant vegetation. Throughout spring and summer these maritime hedges burst with colourful tufts of pink **Sea Thrift**, yellow **Kidney Vetch** and white **Sea Campion**. Between these taller plants, hugging the face of this wind-buffeted rock garden, smaller flowers can thrive – **Milkwort**, **Wild Thyme**, **Bird's Foot Trefoil** and **Violets**. Bramble is tough; its thorns enable it to scramble and climb over walls and other shrubs. Yet for countless wild creatures, from exposed cliff tops to the most sheltered inland valley, bramble is a rich source of food and shelter. An abundance of flowers in mid-summer is followed by the annual glut of juicy blackberries.

Away from the effects of salt spray but still exposed to the wind, other hedgerows may be dominated by **Hawthorn** and **Blackthorn** shrubs. In more sheltered parts, mature trees become the dominant growth – **Oak**, **Ash** and **Holly** or even dense stands of young **Elm**. Beneath them bloom banks of **Primroses** and **Bluebells** with **Red Campion**, **Foxgloves**, **Betony**, **Yellow Toadflax**, **Greater Stitchwort**, **Arum Lily**, **Wood Sage**, **Golden Rod**, **Valerian** and **Herb Robert.** Even in mid-winter, fronds of ferns and leaves of **Wall Pennywort** still peek from between the stones.

A variety of trees and shrubs grow in hedgerows. For a definitive list and guide to dating a hedge, see pages 40–42.

HEDGEROW INSECTS

The insect life of a hedge is not dissimilar to that of a woodland edge; it is just richer, as there are usually two sides to a hedge. Over 1500 insects are known to live in hedgerows. In early spring **Orange Tip Butterfly** can be seen patrolling along their banks. So too can the occasional **Brimstone**, especially where there is plenty of ivy for it to hide in. As the flowers of summer bloom in succession, many more butterflies and other insects are attracted to the hedge, but not all spend their entire lives within this rich border. Some, like the **Gate**

Hedgehog young   *Weasel*

Keeper, may spend their entire lives within just a few hundred metres of a hedge. Others, like the **Wall Butterfly** and **Meadow Brown**, **Peacock**, **Small Tortoiseshell**, **Comma** and visiting **Red Admiral** butterflies, may only frequent the flowers of a Devon hedge from time to time.

HEDGEROW BIRDS

Some 65 birds live in, on or around hedgerows in Britain, and almost half actually nest in them. The bird life of a Devon hedge is impressive in full song, especially early in the morning on a warm summer's day, when the air is still and insects hum. Then the wheezing call of the **Yellow Hammer** – *'a little bit of bread and no cheese'* – carries far along the lanes. In winter these bright little birds become more social, roosting together at night.

Elsewhere, along a narrow strip of the South Devon coast stretching just a few miles inland, lives a much rarer relative of the yellow hammer – the **Cirl Bunting**. In the coldest months they may easily be overlooked as they flock with **Linnets** and **Chaffinches**. They all feed extensively on the seeds of arable weeds, foraging amongst the winter stubble of spring planted barley. In summer they nest in the hedgerows, where the cirl buntings also raises its young on a regular supply of grasshoppers. The success of these birds over the last decade is exciting. Once numbering just over a hundred pairs, the population of these attractive, mainly Mediterranean birds has more than quadrupled in recent years. This startling achievement has been achieved through careful study and management by the RSPB and Devon Wildlife Trust with the cooperation of local farmers, and facilitated by DEFRA conservation schemes.

HEDGEROW MAMMALS

Half our native mammals, 20 in all, have been recorded living in hedgerows. Devon is rich in hedges and their hogs. The **Hedgehog** is one of the most common and widespread creature of the countryside, and it is not just found in hedgerows. It mainly forages for insects and snails at night. By day it hides in any suitable size hole in a wall, or in a nest of leaves under a bush or pile of cut

Bank vole   *Woodmouse*

branches. Active for only part of the year, throughout the warmest months, it hibernates during winter when its food is hard to find.

The **Common Shrew** is a close relative of the hedgehog but is active all year, and around the clock. Shrews lead short, frenetic lives. Eating and sleeping in short shifts of twenty minutes or so, they must consume their own body weight every 24 hours just to survive.

Bank Voles and **Wood Mice** are common mammals of the hedgerow. They feed on a variety of nuts and berries, whatever is in season. Both are mainly nocturnal, but the Wood Mouse is by far the best climber and will forage high in the branches of small trees searching for food. Only one other rodent is more at home in the tree tops – the **Common Dormouse**. No longer common, today the dormouse is the rarest rodent to be found in a hedge. It is a most attractive little creature with chestnut colouring and furry tail. Although unlikely to be seen, signs of its activity can be much easier to find. Dormice nibble open hazel nuts in a distinctive way. They will strip the bark from wild honeysuckle stems in spring to make new nests, and in autumn their ball-like homes can occasionally be found after a hedgerow has been trimmed.

Where a hedgerow borders a field of wheat or more commonly in Devon, barley and oats, a very different rodent may be found. The **Harvest Mouse** is the smallest of its kind in Britain, and the only one to exhibit a prehensile tail. It is also becoming rare. A large healthy hedge, regularly trimmed rather than ruthlessly flailed, is the best place to look. Once, when wheat and barley crops were harvested late in summer, the nests of harvest mice could be more frequently found among their ripening stalks. Today, modern strains of crops are cut much earlier in the season, so harvest mice have adapted by breeding in adjacent hedgerows or in the tall growth of ditches between fields.

Both **Stoat** and **Weasel** hunt along hedge banks. The stoat looks mainly for rats and rabbits, the weasel for small rodents. Indeed, so small is the weasel it is said that its skull can pass through a wedding ring. They are both endlessly curious and highly entertaining creatures to watch, especially in a family group. If you surprise some, just stand quite still. At first they dive for cover. Then when curiosity gets the better of them, they will come back out to see why you have not moved – it works almost every time!

Common lizard on stone wall

ESTIMATING THE AGE OF A HEDGEROW

A hedgerow can be roughly dated by counting the number of different trees and shrubs found in a 30-metre stretch (pacing is accurate enough). Research suggests that each species of woody shrub represents about 100 years, so if a section contains hawthorn, oak and hazel, that hedgerow should be around 300 years old. This is based on the work of Dr Max Hooper and others – it is known as Hooper's Rule. It can be surprisingly accurate, apart for the Elm exception (see below).

For accuracy, it is best to avoid hedgerows adjacent to woods. Some trees are good indicators of a very old hedgerow. **Spindle** and **Field Maple** will only grow when a hedge is thick enough to shelter their delicate saplings. Often there will already be three or four other trees and shrubs well established. So if you find either spindle or field maple in a hedge, you can presume that it is at least four to six hundred years old.

Estimating the age of a hedgerow is a fascinating pastime, especially in Devon where ancient hedgerows are common. Although not always accurate, it is intriguing to imagine the historical events at the time a hedge started its life.

LIST OF TREES AND SHRUBS FOR THE PURPOSE OF HEDGE-DATING

Alder   *Alnus glutnosa*
Apple   *Malus sylvestris*
Ash   *Fraxinus excelsior*
Beech   *Fagus sylvatica*
Blackthorn   *Prunus spinosa*
Briar (or wild rose)   *Rosa arvensis*
    R. canina
    R. rubiginosa

Broom	*Sarothamnus scoparius*
Buckthorn	*Rhamnus cathartica*
Cherry	*Prunus avium*
Cherry-plum	*P. cerasifera*
Dogwood	*Cornus sanguinea*
Elder	*Sambucus nigra*
Elm: wych	*Ulmus glabra*
English	*U. procera*
East Anglian	*U. minor*
Cornish etc	*U. stricta*
Dutch, Huntindon *	*U. x hollandica*
Furze/Gorse	*Ulex europaeus*
Guelder-rose	*Viburnum opulus*
Hawthorn: hedging	*Crataegus monogyna*
woodland	*C. laevigata*
Hazel	*Corylus avellana*
Holly	*Ilex aquifolium*
Hornbeam	*Carpinus betulus*
Lime: ordinary	*Tilia x vulgaris*
small leaved (pry)	*T. cordata*
Maple	*Acer campestre*
Oak: pedunculate	*Quercus robur*
Sessile *	*Q. petraea*
Pine	*Prunus domestica*
Poplar: aspen	*Populus tremula*
black	*P. nigra*
white	*P. alba*
Privet (wild)	*Ligustrum vulgare*
Rowan	*Sorbus aucuparia*
Sallow	*Salix caprea*
	S. cinerea
Service	*Sorbus torminalis*
Spindle	*Euonymus europaeus*
Sycamore	*Acer pseudoplatanus*
Wayfaring-tree	*Viburnum lantana*
Whitebeam	*Sorbus aria*
Willow: crack	*Salix fragilis*
White	*S. alba*
Yew	*Taxus baccata*

* Including hybrids

The elm exception!

English elm can be very invasive in a hedge, suckering profusely, and will soon dominate most other species of tree and shrub. So although elm may be the only tree present, the hedgerow can be far older than 100 years.

ESTIMATING THE AGE OF A HEDGEROW TREE

The best way to estimate the age of an individual tree is by cutting it down and counting its growth rings, but that is rather drastic! Far easier, although only a rough guide, is to measure its girth. Trees grow bigger and faster on the out-side of a wood where there is less competition for nutrients and moisture. So some allowance must be made for a tree's situation.

A general rule of thumb is that 25mm (1") of girth, at chest height for an adult, is equivalent to one year's growth for a free standing tree. But for a tree growing inside a wood, you can only allow 13mm (½") of girth to be equivalent to one year's growth. Nature, however, is never that simple. Whilst this guide can be applied to uncut trees such as oak in middle age, it is of limited value for much older trees. Any trees that have been pollarded or undergone natural crown loss are impossible to age by girth, because these factors will have influ-enced its growth.

Hay Meadow and Culm Grasslands

Traditional hay meadow is today a real rarity in lowland Britain. Many survived up until the Second World War, when they were ploughed and planted for food. Since then, most of those that remained were harrowed, re-seeded, weeded and sprayed with chemicals or improved with artificial fertilisers. Now they are more often cut twice yearly for silage – grass that is rolled up and wrapped, then left to ferment and form nutritious cattle feed. Such practice may be better for agricultural efficiency, but it wreaks havoc with a wildlife that evolved over centuries of traditional farming. Yet ancient hay meadow does survive. It is also being revived from more recently improved pasture by various government schemes and on nature reserves.

One type of ancient grassland was once common across a large part of Devon but rare elsewhere in Britain is 'Culm', which is the Devon name for a type of poor quality, sooty coal that has given its name to a dark damp soil. The Culm sedimentary deposits, on which these soils form, occur across a wide area of central Devon. They can be found from the Exe valley in the east to the far west coast, covering over 1,200 square miles. In appearance they form rather undulating, hilly ground with a series of ridges. Yet much of their wildlife value is now lost. Since 1905 nearly 90% of Culm grassland has disappeared – ploughed or improved. Thankfully, most that remain are now protected as nature reserves by the Devon Wildlife Trust.

CULM GRASSLAND PLANTS

Plant communities of the Culm can broadly be can divided into two types: rush pasture and purple moor-grass.

Rush pasture is usually a rather wet or damp meadow, where soft and sharp-flowered rushes grow, with **Marsh Bedstraw, Greater Bird's-Foot Trefoil, Lesser Spearwort, Water Mint** and **Meadowsweet.** By contrast, purple moor-grass dominates its plant community, allowing less opportunity for other

plants to grow. Moor grass often forms a tussocky, fen-like character, where **Wild Angelica, Tormentil** and **Devil's-Bit Scabious** can flourish. Elsewhere, moor grass can be found with **Bog Asphodel, Cross-Leaved Heath, Common Cotton Grass** and **Sedges**. In other places it may be so wet as to become bog, dominated by mosses with **Marsh St. John's-wort, Bog Pimpernel, Bog Pondweed, Marsh Pennywort,** and **Round-Leaved Sundew.**

Alongside rivers and streams, particularly where the ground is waterlogged, tall fen vegetation is more common, with **Ragged-Robin, Meadowsweet, Wild Angelica** and **Yellow Iris**. Sometimes even more interesting plants may be found, including **Southern Marsh-Orchid, Heath Spotted-Orchid, Lesser Butterfly Orchid, Saw-Wort, Bogbean, Pale Butterwort, Marsh Thistle, Petty Whin** and **Marsh Lousewort.**

Other plants typically found in Culm grassland may include **Lesser Skullcap, Marsh Ragwort, Pale Butterwort, Bell Heather, Creeping Forget-me-not, Heath Bedstraw, Lousewort, Marsh Thistle, Slender St John's-wort, Sneezewort** and **Whorled Caraway.**

CULM GRASSLAND INSECTS

Butterflies abound in these pastures, with some nationally uncommon species such as **Marbled White** and **Small Pearl-Bordered Fritillary**, and even the rare **Marsh Fritillary.**

CULM GRASSLAND BIRDS

The Devon Culm grasslands contain many common birds, but also some that are becoming nationally rare. The **Grasshopper Warbler** and **Willow Tit** both breed well on the grasslands, along with **Tree Pipit** and **Reed Bunting**. In winter, **Woodcock** and **Snipe** may often be encountered.

The **Green Woodpecker** is known in Devon as the 'yaffle' because of its manic cry. It is also called the 'rain-bird', as it seems most insistent when showers are due. Whatever its name, it is a handsome, striking bird that feeds extensively on ants in grasslands. Its long sticky tongue probes quickly through the ant's tunnels, collecting adults and eggs alike. It nests in trees, hollowing out a hole in the trunk situated in a hedgerow or on the edge of a copse.

Marsh orchid, ragged robin, buttercup; Cottongrass

Cultivated Fields

Devon boasts some of the oldest fields to be found in Britain. The remains of many Bronze Age enclosures can still clearly be seen on Dartmoor. In the lowlands, most evidence of prehistoric hedge banks and field ditch has long since been ploughed back into the ground. When the Romans first arrived in Britain large areas of farmland were already parcelled and ploughed: a fact that can be seen in other parts of the country, as their long straight roads often cut across older field systems. From medieval times, the combining of long narrow cultivated strips into furlongs, then into fields, was more subject to fashion than improving technology.

Only about ten percent of Devon is arable land, and of that, over two-thirds is cereal, the rest fodder crop or horticulture. Many birds and mammals forage in fields throughout the year, but the most interesting ones must surely be the **Brown Hare**, **Skylark**, **Grey Partridge**, **Corn Bunting**, **Cirl Bunting** and **Turtle Dove**. Sadly, with the exception of the cirl bunting, none are as common as they once were, although some are making a good comeback.

CULTIVATED FIELD PLANTS

Any plants found naturally in a cultivated field are referred to as arable weeds. Their annual appearance can provoke extreme passions – love and hate. Modern farming methods have virtually eliminated some of the most beautiful flowers from our fields, while other plants have become serious and persistent weeds. The highly efficient cleaning of seed, and chemical sprays, have caused the **Corn Poppy** and **Corn Marigold** to decline, while the **Corncockle** has almost disappeared. But some less significant plants produce abundant quantities of tiny seed with an importance out of all proportion to their size. Arable weeds enable many seed-eating birds of farmland to survive the winter months, especially in the stubble fields left after the harvesting of spring barley. There is one plant, however, that is found nowhere else in the world than in some arable fields in the south-west of England – the **Purple Ramping Fumitory**.

CULTIVATED FIELD INSECTS

The use of powerful pesticides on farmland has adversely affected the numbers of beneficial insects as well as pest species, but thankfully this is not universally true. Some farms have never made use of sprays, while others have done so with care.

The biggest bush cricket in Britain can be found in Devon, particularly the south. The female **Great Green Bush Cricket** when full-grown can reach up to 42mm in length. They can be found on cultivated farmland as well as the wayside and even in gardens from July to October. Harmless to humans, they should be seen as a friend of the farmer or gardener as they feed mainly on other insects – caterpillars and beetle larvae.

Field poppy

Woodlark   *Grey partridge chick*

CULTIVATED FIELD BIRDS

The distinctive song of the **Skylark** pouring out of a clear blue sky is one of summer's more memorable sounds. Devon is fortunate in still having a good population of skylarks, although they are not as common as they once were. They tend to nest out in open fields, more often among crops than just grass, especially where a good breeze will help keep them aloft. Hovering and singing at the same time is quite a talent.

The **Woodlark** has a more mellow, liquid song than its better-known cousin. Although a bird primarily of lowland heathland, acidic grassland and recently felled plantations on sandy soils, there is a small population in Devon which breeds on low intensity mixed farmland. They feed in areas of short vegetation with bare ground on well-drained soils where tree cover is sparse. Eating invertebrates during the summer, they switch to arable seeds in winter. Some trees for singing posts and areas of longer vegetation for nesting are also important to the woodlark. Found also on land cultivated for cereal crop, they are now confined to the extreme south of England. Historically the Erme and Teign valleys were strongholds, but the bird is now considered rare.

Grey partridge can still very occasionally be heard in fields of barley or wheat, but you are more likely to see its introduced French relative, the **Red-legged Partridge**.

Winter can be a particularly good time to visit cultivated land, especially in coastal areas. This is when many more birds move inland. Flocks of **Lapwing** and **Oystercatcher**, even **Curlew** and **Golden Plover**, along with large numbers of **Black-headed Gull**, **Herring Gull** and the occasional **Common Gull**, can all be seen during the coldest months.

In recent decades modern farming methods have had a huge impact on our wildlife, especially on cultivated ground. The reasons are both complex and simple. One easy explanation is that stubble fields went out of fashion. Now as soon as a cereal crop is harvested the next is sown within a few weeks. For wildlife geared to follow the seasonal cycle of farming over centuries, the resultant crash in bird numbers resulted in an increasingly silent spring. The introduction of a new agricultural conservation scheme, encouraging farmers to

Goldfinch feeding young   *Hornet on apple*

leave fields of winter stubble, is now reaping its rewards. Many small and rare birds rely on the seeds of arable weeds for winter survival. Along the coastal strip of south Devon especially, stubble fields are once again becoming a more common sight. Further inland too, large flocks of other birds, chiefly made up of finches and thrushes, forage ploughed fields for weed seeds, worms and insects. Often these flocks consist principally of seed eaters, **Greenfinch**, **Goldfinch**, **Chaffinch** and **Linnet** with the occasional smaller numbers of **Redpoll**, **Siskin** and **Brambling**. **Meadow Pipit** move from their summer homes on the moors, to feed in lowland fields. **Magpies** are also much more conspicuous along with gangs of **Jackdaws**, **Rooks** and a few **Carrion Crows**, but these can all be outnumbered by larger flocks of squabbling continental **Starlings** that spend the winter months here.

One of the most unusual sights, which is often seen in Devon, is 20 or more **Buzzards** collecting on ploughed land. Despite their image as solitary, free wheeling, high flying hunters of rabbits and rodents, buzzards often feed on smaller prey – earthworms – especially when thrown up by the plough. Another tactic of this big bird of prey is much craftier. In frosty or very dry weather when worms are scarce, a buzzard may simply wait by a mole hill, not for its builder to emerge but for earthworms, escaping from the little black digger below.

CULTIVATED FIELD MAMMALS

In mid-winter the activities of the industrious **Mole** may be the only sign of a wild mammal on farmland; the creature itself is seldom actually seen. They create a network of passages underground as a trap for earthworms burying through the soil: the worms simply just fall into the tunnel. A regular patrol by the mole is then all that is needed to find a wriggling meal. Every so often the mole extends its system of runs by pushing more soil out of the ground. The result is a new rash of freshly excavated mounds littering the fields, much to the annoyance of farmers and gardeners.

Recently ploughed and harrowed land also offers rich pickings for the **Fox**. **Mice** and **Voles** disturbed by a tractor working the soil enable foxes to find an easy meal – especially when the farmer has quit for the night. After dark is

Mistletoe berries   *Red admiral butterfly*

when most mammals visit the fields. Principally nocturnal, the **Badger** is common in Devon, foraging across farmland for worms and grubs. **Hedgehogs** snuffle along the borders. **Red Deer** also graze out in fields, especially around Exmoor. **Roe Deer** are more widespread, and even the little **Muntjac** is becoming common in some places.

Orchards

A vast fruit-bearing forest once grew scattered across much of lowland Britain. In full bloom this planted parkland was famed worldwide as a glory of the English countryside. Pears, plums and cherries can be found in many parts of Britain, but it was an apple orchard that once grew alongside every farmhouse in the land. Devon is still rich in traditional farms, and many still retain their old orchards.

Today more than four thousand different varieties of apple are known, all of which owe their origin to the humble wild crab apple tree. The modern apple is a product of patience. Over two thousand years, people have sought to breed the most succulent, sweet fruit they could find. The apple provides food and liquor, and so was a valuable asset for any farmer. Devon is famed for its rough cider, called 'scrumpy'.

The parkland-like setting of an orchard attracts many creatures, and provides a home to some interesting plants. Yet few birds and mammals spend their entire lives among its fruit trees.

ORCHARD PLANTS

Lichens can commonly be found festooning the branches of old apple trees in Devon, but they do no damage, merely living on the surface of the bark. However, it is doubtful that a parasitic plant, which invades its host's tissues, would be tolerated on such a valuable tree, were it not for pagan custom. The **Mistletoe** is still considered to be a mysterious plant. Growing in a tangled ball of green branches and leaves, it produces distinctive white berries during the winter months. Few birds can cope with their sticky flesh, but those that do

Blue tit: young fledgling in apple tree nest hole   *Song thrush*

seem to thrive on its seasonal fruit. As its name suggests, the **Mistle Thrush** consumes large quantities of the berries, and is the plant's main means of dispersal. Although the birds do wipe their beaks on the branches, occasionally leaving a sticky seed, most germinate from their droppings. Considering that a seed will pass through a thrush in the astonishingly short time of 30 minutes, it is no surprise that the distribution of mistletoe is just locally common.

ORCHARD INSECTS

Bees are often the most obvious insects of the orchard, especially at blossom time – and not just **Honeybees**. A multitude of other communal **Bumble Bees**, **Solitary Bees** and **Wasps** all play their part in helping to pollinate branch loads of blooms.

Butterflies are best seen on sunny days throughout the spring and summer. Some will survive into autumn and even over winter, hiding in nearby sheds. The **Small Tortoiseshell Butterfly** emerges from its barn or outhouse shelter in early spring. They can commonly be encountered feeding on thistles and other flowers in the orchard. But the big **Red Admiral** is the one to watch in late summer. When apples over-ripen and fall to the ground, they soon begin to rot. This is when red admirals arrive to imbibe their favourite liquor: cider. When cool and full of fermented juice, these handsome butterflies can easily be approached quite closely, as they seem slow to get up and go. Cider seems to have the same effect on people as butterflies.

Wasps and **Hornets** may also be attracted to windfall apples, so it pays to be wary when walking through an orchard at summer's end.

ORCHARD BIRDS

The Mistle Thrush was named after what was thought to be its staple diet. We now know they eat just as many earthworms as other fruit and berries. It is the largest and loudest of our thrushes, as well as being one of the earliest birds to breed each year. Its ringing song can even be heard in the teeth of a January gale.

The **Lesser Spotted Woodpecker** is much less common than its Great cousin (and surprisingly not much bigger than a sparrow), and is more typically found in the orchard. By hammering into a tree it makes a new nest each year. In subsequent seasons the hole is then exploited by a succession of other small birds. **Blue** and **Great Tit** commonly nest in holes in trees, and **Starlings** will also often breed in old orchards.

The combination of relatively undisturbed permanent grassland and rough old bark on gnarled and twisted branches, offers sanctuary to many insects. These in turn are eagerly sought by the **Green Woodpecker**, **Tree Creeper**, **Nuthatch** and **Tits**.

One of the most charming birds of the orchard chooses to nest out on the thinnest apple branches it can find. The **Goldfinch** is common wherever it can source enough thistle seeds in nearby fields. In contrast, the **Bullfinch** will feed in the orchard but nest in a nearby hedge. Although beautiful to watch, their presence is often not welcomed by the farmer as they literally nip young apples in the bud.

During the coldest months of the year, some orchards seem very popular with birds. An old neglected orchard is best, where windfalls litter the ground. After a fall of snow these orchards can become the focus of attention for hundreds of noisy migrants – **Redwings**, **Fieldfares** and starlings flocking in from northern Europe. **Blackbird** and **Song Thrush** may join the fray, but it is a spectacularly short-lived feast. As the rotting apples are greedily devoured, the flocks soon move on to the next orchard.

Barns and Buildings

An old neglected barn standing in the corner of a field, with roof tiles slipping and walls crumbling, is today often no more than a sad monument to a bygone age. Once used to shelter farm stock or bales of hay for winter feed, buildings such as these used to play an important part in the seasonal work of the farm. But many now have a life of their own.

BARN INSECTS

Besides over-wintering **Small Tortoiseshell** and **Peacock Butterflies**, **Spiders** and **Harvestmen**, **Wood Boring beetles** and a myriad of other tiny creatures, one group of insects literally make a bee line for barns. A wild **Honeybee** colony only requires a tiny gap between outer stones to gain access. Inside, any space in the wall is soon filled by their beautifully constructed wax comb. These will either be dripping with honey or packed with growing grubs – replacement workers or the next generation of queens to maintain the buzzing life of the colony.

Devon has many ancient barns made from local mud. Known as cob, it has been used by people as a building material for thousands of years. Its durability and strength comes from the ingredients that help bind the mud together – gravel, straw and cattle dung. Raised on a stone foundation with a good roof, plastered in lime render and lime washed with colours mixed from milk or local

Little owl in nest hole
at base of apple tree

Ruby-tailed wasp

soil, barns are as much a part of Devon as rolling hills and moorland tors. But where exterior render falls away to reveal softer mud wall, it soon attracts the attention of solitary bees. The hairy-legged **Mining Bee** is just one of some sixty different species of solitary bee found in Britain, though only a few actually nest in walls. On a sunny, south-facing section of exposed cob, each bee excavates a short tunnel leading to a little cell. Here it lays an egg. Hundreds may make their holes in the same patch. The **Red-tailed Bumble Bee** will also dig its own nest in a cob wall, but bees do little damage and many of these loose colonies may be decades old.

Wherever solitary bees live, a parasitic wasp can usually be found. The tiny, iridescent **Ruby-tailed Wasp** has the habits of a cuckoo. It creeps inside the nest of a mining bee and lays its own egg alongside. The wasp grub hatches before the bee and turns it into its first meal.

BARN BIRDS

In the past, one creature was so familiar to farmers that it was named after its favourite haunt – the **Barn Owl**. On silent wings, and with the ability to see in near dark and pinpoint the slightest sound, it is no surprise that they were said to possess supernatural powers. As their principal prey consists of field voles, rats and mice, they were considered a friend of the farmer and encouraged to nest in their buildings. When barns were built of stone or cob, a hole was often constructed at one end, known as an owl window. Mid-summer is probably the best time to catch a glimpse of these elusive birds, hunting out over the meadows, beating gently along hedgerows and quartering the fields. At this time of the year they may well have young, and so may even be seen hunting in late afternoon on undisturbed ground. Due to changing farming practices and the disappearance of suitable old buildings, the barn owl is now sadly a rare sight, but Devon still appears to have a healthy population.

The **Kestrel** is more commonly seen hovering alongside roads and motorways but it is also a farmland bird. They too will nest in barns, and sometimes even share the same roof as a barn owl. Although eating similar food, they tend to avoid competition – the kestrel takes the day shift while the barn owl is more active at night.

The only other bird of prey that may nest in the wall of an old barn is another nocturnal hunter, but one that lives entirely on different prey. The **Little Owl** feeds largely on earthworms, beetles and moths. Originally introduced into Britain during the 19th century, it soon spread across much of England's farmland; but then it already had an ally here – the mole. Little owls can often be found where moles are active underground, flying from mound to mound looking for their favourite food.

Other birds choose to nest closer to the centre of farm life. Stables and barns built around a busy farmyard are a favoured place for our summer herald – the **Swallow**. Wintering in South Africa, the British population of swallows arrives in April to breed throughout the summer months. And they are not alone. Besides resident **Wrens** and **Robins**, the **Spotted Flycatcher** is a summer migrant that will also nest inside open-fronted barns and in the walls of old buildings.

BARN MAMMALS

Wherever there is animal feed, rats and house mice are never far away. They are considered a pest, eating crops and carrying disease, although many fall victim to natural predators – fox, stoat, weasel and owls.

Bats are more welcome. **Long-eared** and **Pipistrelle bats** are commonly found in the lofts or walls of old farm buildings. Even **Lesser** and **Greater Horseshoe Bats**, which can live in large colonies, will sometimes use old deserted buildings as summer roosts.

Swallow feeding young at nest   *Long-eared bat in farm loft*

Fresh Water

Nothing can compare with the fascination of sitting by water on a fine day. Whether it is a bubbling stream in spring, a mirror-smooth pond in summer, or a fast-flowing autumn river, water is essential for life. But some creatures need more than others. In the first week of January, high on a Dartmoor bog, frog spawn can already be found beneath a protective layer of ice. By the end of February on the edge of the moor, dippers are constructing their mossy nest which is hidden beneath the cascading curtain of a waterfall. Soon squabbling moorhens can be heard on ponds across Devon, as the vibrant colours of spring sweep across the shire. Summer brings swallows swooping low, skimming the surface for a drink or feeding on small insects attracted to water. House martins, seeking material to build their nests, stuff their beaks with mud from the edge of a pond; dragonflies hawk over it and, providing the water is still, white water lilies may bloom in it. As the weather warms, the drab tangled fringes of ponds and rivers come back to life, rising in a fresh green growth of reed. Now warblers sing from their depths and the wind rustles their strap-like leaves. Ducklings frenetically follow their mother, herons wade purposefully, intent on finding another fish, and a family of mute swans, mum, dad and gangly grey youngsters, swim serenely by. All too soon, autumnal mists rise above the water. Now is the season to watch golden leaves floating gently down stream. Salmon and sea trout appear in the deeper pools. Streams that only a few months before were reduced to dry beds, are once again flowing fast and high in the cool of a winter's day, and rivers turn from crystal clear to chocolate brown.

Devonshire mizzle, that soaking blend of mist and drizzle that falls so softly over the county, is like rain the world over – both a destroyer and giver of life. On Dartmoor in summer it trickles harmlessly over bare rock. Seeping into cracks and crevices, it soon disappears into the ground, only to reappear in tiny streams lower down. In winter it can freeze overnight. Ice expands as it forms, splitting huge boulders and shearing great slabs from sea cliffs. Such powerful forces were responsible for the great 19th-century earthquake in east Devon, more of which can be found on pages 123–126 (on the Undercliff).

Five of Devon's major rivers begin life on Dartmoor's high tops. Small streams soon merge on the moors, tumbling headlong over rocks. Squeezing between boulders, the burgeoning torrents rush down through the woods. As they come together they grow into rivers, increasing in size and power as they reach the lowlands. A flood is a powerful force, undermining embankments, toppling

*Lake flora: water lily,
reed and alder tree*

bridges and eroding the foundations of railway lines. Yet, laden with silt and bursting their banks, pouring across open fields, marooning sheep and drowning roads, they are also agents of dispersal. Fish and other aquatic life can be spread from pond to pond by the deluge. Within a few days the water subsides. Only the jumbled branches, hung high and dry on a barbed wire fence, leave any trace of its sudden surge.

The prevailing south-west winds bring moisture laden air across the region. Each raindrop is almost pure water, containing a little carbon dioxide and oxygen absorbed as it falls through the atmosphere. Soaking into the ground, the water picks up tiny quantities of minerals and organic matter, eventually gaining enough nutrients to sustain and support life. Most streams and rivers eventually empty into the sea, but sometimes their progress is stopped and the water forms a lake. With a perennial nutrient-rich flow, these bodies of water can become exceedingly rich in wildlife, but they are rare in Devon.

Indeed, so much rain falls on parts of Dartmoor that the visitor may be forgiven for expecting to see great lakes and a landscape sprinkled with pools, but on the moors permanent ponds are scarce. The granite bedrock is highly fractured and porous to rainwater. The lack of glacial action in the south-west of England during the last ice age also means that there are no suitable basins or dammed valleys to form large lakes inland. But sometimes on the coast, shingle banks are created by the action of wave and tide, which can prevent streams running straight into the sea. Here a lake can form – Slapton Ley on the south coast is one of these. All other lakes in Devon are man-made.

Ponds and Lakes

For animals and plants, living in a pond or lake may seem a much more leisurely affair than fighting for your life in a fast-flowing river – but a casual look can be deceptive. It's true that pond plants do not have to adapt to the perpetual pull of the current or constantly shifting sands and gravel, and so life in a pond can take on a different form. Rooting in the thick, nutritious ooze, broader, bigger leaves can grow to the surface. Here they will capture more light. From a depth of over two metres, deep **Water Lilies** will send up soup-plate-sized leaves to lie on the surface, soon followed by large, elegant white flowers inviting insects to pollinate them.

Flooded wood and lake edge

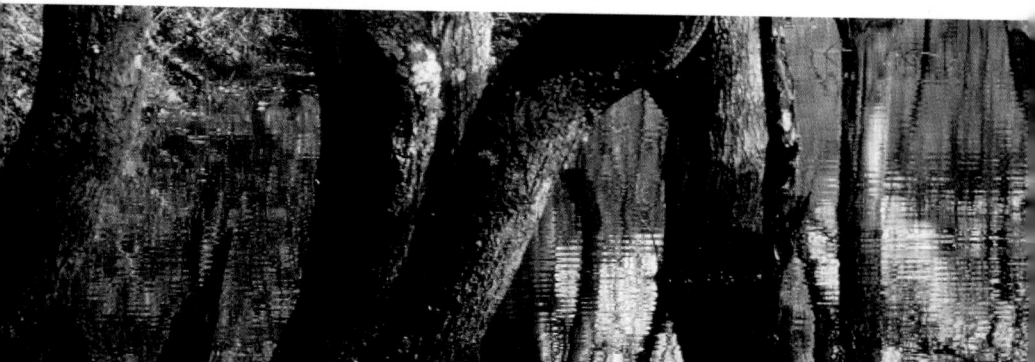

The plant life of a pond can be zoned according to the depth of water – from the deepest parts to the shallowest margins and damp surroundings. Some ponds are natural, but many more are man-made. Farm and dew ponds, ditches, village and garden ponds all served a purpose in the past – to provide a source of water for domestic stock or villagers, and also for fire-fighting, or raising fish. Others were built to be ornamental. Whatever the reason, a freshwater pond is a magnet for wildlife.

The **Yellow Water Lily** can live in water deeper than the larger **White Water Lily**, and may grow from a depth of three metres. In Devon it is largely confined to the east of the county. But while the majority of plants cannot take root in such deep water, a few are not so limited.

POND AND LAKE PLANTS

Essentially, freshwater plants can be divided into different types according to how they grow. Some have their feet in water and heads in the air, while others may live their entire lives completely submerged.

Free-floating Pond Plants

The highly invasive, tiny-leafed **Duckweed** is a free-floating plant capable of colonising the parts that others cannot reach. But perhaps the most bizarre and intriguing aquatic plant of all free-floaters is the **Greater Bladderwort.** They live submerged just below the surface, and sometimes produce small golden yellow flowers that rise above the water surface. But it is the parts growing underwater that sets this plant apart from the rest – it eats animals. Not big ones but small creatures such **Daphnia**, better known as the water flea. The plant produces little bladders along its stems, each one just a few millimetres in length, which are miniature traps. The devious device has an aperture at one end surrounded by tiny, stiff, sensitive bristles forming a kind of funnel. These are the trigger. When a water flea touches a bristle, its trap door opens in an instant; water rushes in to the bladder and the hapless victim is carried inside with the rush. The door snaps shut again. Here the creature dies and slowly decomposes, releasing nutrients which are absorbed by the plant. It is not a common plant in Devon, but can often be seen at Stover Lake near Newton Abbot.

Common frog

Swan mussel and tadpole

Submerged Pond Plants

Some plants have completely taken to life in freshwater: these are the submerged plants. **Stoneworts**, **Green Algae** and the increasingly common **Canadian Pondweed** all live beneath the surface. Others, like the water milfoils and willow moss, while remaining largely submerged, and only raise their flowering and spore-bearing parts into the air. **Common Water Starwort** hedges its bets: it is a widespread, adaptable pond plant surviving mainly underwater, but with the ability to be pollinated both above and below surface.

POND ZONES

Floating Leaf and Emergent Zone

Apart from the water lily, many aquatic plants need to raise their flowering parts above the surface to seed or shed their spores. One of the most ancient groups of plants, little changed since before the age of dinosaurs and the appearance of modern flowering plants, grows prolifically in standing water – the **Water Horsetail**. Several species can be found in Devon, but the most common can reach over one and a half metres in height

The **Amphibious Bistort** is a more adaptable plant. As its name implies it is quite capable of growing in or out of water – a great asset where ponds are prone to drying out. **Water Mint** is widely distributed across the county. So too are *Potomogeton* species, known more commonly and collectively as pondweeds. Several different ones can be found in Devon, but not all are common. The most frequently encountered in moorland pools is the **Bog Pondweed**, while the **Broad-leaved Pondweed** is more common around Exeter.

The **Water Plantain** produces a tall, stately flower stalk from its rosette of large basal leaves. Its delicate pink flowers are produced throughout the summer months but only open in the afternoon. In contrast, the **Common Water Crowfoot** forms a carpet of white flowers with yellow centres, from spring through summer.

Greater diving beetle underwater *Great crested newt courtship – male and female*

Swamp Zone

Swamps are normally wet throughout the year (whereas marshland can dry out during summer seasons). Tall upright plants, which are seldom branched, and have long narrow leaves, reduce any damage that could be caused by a flood. Hollow stems and tough, fibrous leaves also enable them to be buffeted by wind; they are supported by long, creeping rhizomes which infiltrate the mud in a dense tangle. Besides producing seeds, the **Common Reed**, **Bulrush** and the **Common Club Rush** also spread from buds on their rhizomes to quickly colonise large areas. Extending into open water, silt gets trapped between the stems, and the swamp steadily grows. Other plants can then take advantage of the conditions created. **Water Dock** can be found in south and east Devon. More common are the spectacular great flowers of **Yellow Flag Iris**, which can be found across the county.

Freshwater can contain a wealth of tiny creatures, some almost invisible to the human eye. They are the start of a wonderfully complex food chain. A whole host of water fleas, lice and shrimps that provide food for larger fresh-water animals.

POND MUSSELS AND SNAILS

Animals that live in shells are all grouped together as Molluscs. Two of the most common forms are snails and bivalves. The **Swan Mussel**, the biggest fresh-water shellfish, is a bivalve reaching up to 150mm in length. A bivalve mollusc has two shells joined by a hinge, which can close tight using powerful muscles. The tough shell of an adult mussel renders it virtually immune from any preda-tor, but youngsters, which swim freely by clapping their two valves together, may readily be eaten by fish. However, this food chain is two-way: up to three months of age, young mussels lead a more predatory life, parasitizing large fish by burrowing into their skin to feed on blood. As adults, they live half buried on the pond or lake bed. They feed and breathe by using a siphon to move water through their body, filtering out microscopic food and absorbing oxygen. Their hard shell is made up of three layers, but it is the inner one, consisting of glistening 'mother of pearl', that is only revealed when the animal dies and the shell is empty. Occasionally a speck of sand or dirt may be encapsulated in the same substance, and it can sometimes form a freshwater pearl.

Pond snails are commonly found in most unpolluted freshwater pools. They can arrive at a new pond in various ways, perhaps by flood or even on the feet of a visiting duck. Their names are often descriptive – **Ram's Horn**, **Wandering**, and the **Great Pond Snail**. Although they live underwater for most of their lives they breathe air, so must return to the surface to refill their tiny lungs. Pond snails differ from their land-living relatives by having their eyes at the base of their tentacles instead of at the tip.

POND INSECTS & SPIDERS

POND INSECTS Dragonflies are the most conspicuous resident insect life of any pond. They are divided into two groups – the more delicate **Damselflies** and the fast-flying, more robust **Dragonflies**. Both are harmless to humans and are easy to distinguish. While damselflies fold their wings vertically over their backs, dragonflies hold them horizontally out away from their body. Their flight differs too. Damselflies are weaker and daintier, while dragonflies are the Ferraris of the insect world – their speed and acceleration is legendary. Dragonflies can also be divided into two groups – hawkers and darters. The hawkers are bigger and tougher-looking, and they hold a larger territory which they regularly patrol or 'hawk' while watching for their smaller insect prey. The more stout-bodied darter dragonfly tends to wait on its favourite perch – a suitable stick or leaf – for insect prey to fly pass, before darting out to seize it.

The adult flying stage of the dragonfly is just a small part of its life, often no more than a few weeks. Much more time is spent underwater as a predatory nymph. Here it relies on stealth and camouflage to catch its prey – anything from a water flea to small fish or a tadpole. Nymphs can take a couple of years to mature before emerging as adults. Early morning in mid-summer is the best time to catch sight of this extraordinary event. Usually under the cover of dark, mature nymphs crawl out of the water up a plant stem, where they rest a while before their drying skin splits open to release the fully formed adult inside. Soft and vulnerable at first, their wings slowly unfurl and expand. It can take several hours before they are dry and hard enough to fly. Perhaps even more amazing is how little dragonflies have changed over hundreds of millions of years. Watching the emergence of a dragonfly is to glimpse a lost world, an event that would have been familiar to a swamp-grazing dinosaur.

POND SPIDERS The female of a small type of **Wolf Spider** typically carries her egg cocoon from her spinnerettes, tucked under the end of her abdomen. The **Raft Spider** is much bigger and more spectacular in habit. It will sit on a floating leaf waiting for its prey, perhaps a small fish, with its legs splayed and dangling, just touching the water's surface, enabling it to detect any tell-tale ripples. But there is a more extraordinary creature of its kind – the **Water Spider**. This one is capable of diving. In spring the water spider creates a bell of air underwater, caught beneath a beautiful little canopy of silk. Throughout the summer, it then periodically embarks from its sub-aquatic home to hunt

Southern hawker dragonfly, newly emerged

through the waterweed. It will catch tiny fish or seize small insects caught in the surface film. During winter it hides in a tougher, specially constructed diving bell, built in deeper water.

POND FISH

The second smallest fish in Britain is the **Three-spined Stickleback** or 'tiddler' commonly found by children in ponds. Generally, the bigger the pond the more species of fish are likely to be found. **Pike**, **Perch** and **Carp** can often be found in larger ponds. The carp especially is quite capable of surviving where other fish do not have enough oxygenated water. Living for up to fifty years, it can grow to a considerable size – easily reaching 10 kilos, and occasionally even more.

POND AMPHIBIANS AND REPTILES

Eight species of amphibians and reptiles today live wild in Britain, although two of these have been introduced and can only be found in the South. Most amphibians must return to freshwater to breed, and they spend all or part of their lives in and around water. In Britain they are divided into two groups that differ in body and habit from each other – those with tails, and those without. The first comprise frogs and toads, the second newts.

FROGS AND TOADS Two species of toad and one frog are native to Britain, but only one toad can be found in Devon. So how do you tell the difference between a frog and a toad? At first glance they can appear very similar. We all learn as children that the **Common Frog** hops and the **Common Toad** walks, but that is a generality, and they do not write the books! It is however, a reasonable guide. At least their spawn is very different. Frogs produce a mass of eggs that stay together in a clump between January and March. Toad spawn is found later, more like a string of black pearls wound around pond vegetation.

The rare natterjack toad is absent from Devon. Outside the breeding season, frogs and toads can often be found far from water. They also tend to hide by day and emerge at night, and although the common toad is widespread, it can more easily be found in March on warm, wet evenings, as it migrates to its spawning ponds. Here they can gather in large numbers. But be wary of picking one up – toad skin exudes a rather distasteful secretion. Just watch a dog lick one! While frogs tend to prefer shallow, even temporary pools, toads pre-

Grass snake in water

Reed bunting at nest with young   *Mallard on nest*

fer to spawn in deeper, more permanent ponds. Both frogs and toads can be surprisingly vocal during their breeding seasons, and listening is often the best way to find them. There are several places in the county where road signs warn of toads crossing during their breeding season in March. They generally move at night.

NEWTS All three species of newt, the **Common**, **Palmate** and the **Great-crested newt**, can be found in Devon. The Great-crested is the largest, and the male is by far the most spectacular, with its dark wavy dorsal crest and bright yellow underparts; it is best seen in spring. But be careful – not because they are harmful, but the great-crested newt is rare and you need a licence to handle one in Britain. More widespread, the common and palmate newts may even be seen in moorland pools. The males sport yellow or orange underparts during the breeding season.

SNAKES All snakes can swim, but the one most likely to be encountered in a pond is the **Grass Snake**. They can grow up to two metres in length but are harmless to people. They are surprisingly aquatic, even hunting underwater for frogs, fish and newts. The female lays up to 40 eggs in June or early July, usually seeking a warm compost heap or pile of rotting vegetation. The young grass snakes generally hatch in August, and being just pencil-size, they will hunt tadpoles and tiny froglets for the first few years of their life.

POND BIRDS

Ponds play a vital part in the lives of many birds: some depend on ponds for food, others as a place to nest, and a few seem to spend their entire lives on a pond. Only the largest lakes are suitable for **Mute Swans**, as they need a long runway to take off. The same is also true for the **Great-crested Grebe**, and even **Coots** prefer bigger ponds. But **Moorhens** can be found on some of the smallest. They only need a plentiful supply of emergent and aquatic vegetation which makes up nearly three-quarters of their diet – the rest consists of insects, worms and small aquatic snails.

The **Water Rail** is much less obvious, skulking around in reeds and wading through pond side vegetation. Although they breed in a few places in Devon, they are more likely to be seen as winter visitors or passage migrants in spring.

The best place to look for them is from a bird hide or bridge overlooking a pond.

Little Grebe, or **Dabchick** as it is also known, will sometimes nest in deep water ponds with a good supply of small fish, shrimps and other aquatic insects. Ungainly on land, they are able swimmers, diving frequently to find food.

The **Mallard** duck will often nest close to the edge of a pond, but her drab brown colouring can make her almost impossible to see. Once the ducklings all hatch, they leave the nest site to follow their mother, dabbling for tiny insects and crustaceans in the water.

The **Kingfisher** normally nests in a river or streamside bank, but will take advantage of any water with fish. They always swallow fish head first, but will sometimes turn one the other way round, before flying off to present it to their mate or feed a hungry brood. Listen for a high-pitched whistle and then a flash of orange and electric blue as they hurtle past – kingfishers always seem in a hurry.

Ponds are wonderful places to watch wildlife, but some are better than others. One of the most thrilling spectacles to see in Devon is a rare bird of prey hunting low over water. The fast flying **Hobby** migrates south at the end of each summer, and sometimes they visit a forestry pond on Haldon Hill in south Devon, where they may spend a few days catching dragonflies on the wing.

Reservoirs

Devon relies on reservoirs for much of its domestic water needs. Their construction is always controversial, as important wildlife habitat is often sacrificed for less interesting deep water. Often built on high ground, their natural value is always going to be limited. On the Devon and Cornwall border, the relatively new Roadford Reservoir and Tamar Lake attract a number of breeding and migrant wildfowl, and where the margins are shallow enough to allow abundant aquatic plants to grow, the nature is much richer.

Where trout fishing is encouraged, I have even heard of the local foxes benefitting – a friend once lost his catch to a bold young cub investigating the bag he left on the bank!

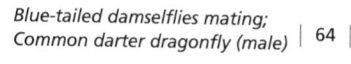

Blue-tailed damselflies mating; Common darter dragonfly (male) | 64 |

Large red damselfly female at rest   *Four-spotted chaser dragonfly, newly emerged*

Rivers and Streams

Thirteen rivers wind their way over 400 miles of Devon, and some 60 miles of those are tidal. Five major rivers – the Teign, Taw, Tavy, Okement and the Dart – all begin their lives on the heights of Dartmoor, and four smaller ones – the Plym, Yealm, Erme and Avon – seep from its southern slopes. In the east of the county, three more rivers rise just over the border in Somerset and head south-west into Devon. The Culm is a major branch of the much larger Exe, while the Otter and Axe separately empty into Lyme Bay. The East and West Dart rivers become one before leaving the moor, and the Bovey flows into the Teign.

But the two largest and longest rivers in Devon both rise elsewhere, near the north coast: the Exe in the east and the Tamar in the west separately travel the length of the county from north to south, before flowing into the English Channel.

On the north coast, most streams lead short but spectacular lives. The exceptions are the Taw and Torridge, which combine to form the biggest river system in north Devon. They rise over half the county apart, yet meet to discharge through a common channel. While the Taw flows due north from Dartmoor to Barnstaple, the Torridge follows a more convoluted course. It rises on the coastal heights of Hartland, initially flowing south-east towards the heart of Devon, before doing a U-turn and heading back north to Bideford. But here the Taw and Torridge are in a league of their own. Along most of the north coast the watershed seldom stretches more than a few miles inland, and many smaller streams find their way rapidly down to the sea; some near Hartland Quay even form impressive cliff waterfalls during periods of heavy rain.

RIVER AND STREAM PLANTS

Fast-flowing moorland streams, fed by low scudding clouds, emerge as a trickle from great green carpets of Sphagnum bog. Lower down, they can quickly turn to raging torrents after heavy rain, but on high ground, flood water seldom stays long. The streams soon scour their beds of silt, and only gravel and bare rock remain. Here there are few opportunities for plants to get a foothold, but more primitive life can cope with the conditions. **Diatoms** cover the rocks with a slippery olive-green film, and an aquatic black trailing moss clings to the downstream side of boulders. After filtering through clumps of sedge, rushes and coarse grass, tiny streams unite to form faster flows. Only the pools slow the headland pursuit. Here the race slackens before careering on down, squeezing between great granite boulders and pouring over smaller stones. Spray dampens the air, and mosses, ferns and liverworts thrive in the shade. Lower down, streams grow into young rivers, and again the flow eases as the terrain flattens where ancient seas once cut near-level benches into the hillsides. Here higher plants take root in the silt and stones of the river bed – the white flowers of **Water Crowfoot** and **Water Milfoil** are common. Winding its way across rough moorland pasture, the young river cuts through dry stone walls, and where bracken dominates, the overhanging fronds tickle its surface.

Now its pace quickens again. The clear moorland water begins to writhe and foam, plunging into the enchanted setting of a wooded valley, or 'combe' as they are known in Devon. Here the flow is deeper, the surroundings darker. In summer only shafts of sunlight can pierce the shade cast by the leafy canopy arching above. These woodlands consist mainly of oak, beech, alder and willow. In places **Wild Daffodils** and **Primroses** line the banks in spring, and **Bluebells** may flank its course in early summer. As rainwater pours off the moor, swollen by tributaries, all coloured by Devon's fertile soil, the flow widens and slows in its middle reaches. Now the river winds through valley pastures, past arable fields, and the amphibious plant life becomes richer. Willow and alder scrub grow vigorously with their roots in water. Islands of vegetation with **Purple Loosestrife**, **Hemp Agrimony**, **Greater Willow Herb**, **Water Dropwort** and **Common Skullcap** colour its course. But it is not long before the effects of the sea begin to taint its freshness; in Devon the tidal influence stretches far inland up through drowned river valleys.

RIVER AND STREAM INSECTS

Fast-running moorland streams and lazy peaty pools on Dartmoor abound with aquatic insects. **Caddis Fly**, **Mayfly**, **Stonefly**, **Dragonfly** and **Damselfly** lar-

Wild daffodils

Perch with roach behind

Roach

vae are common, along with **Water Beetle**, **Small Chironomid Fly** larvae and **Water Skaters**.

RIVER AND STREAM MUSSELS AND SHRIMPS

Hordes of tiny, slowly sliding flatworms and leeches abound in most moorland streams. In pools and slower flowing water, **Freshwater Shrimps**, other tiny crustaceans and **Freshwater Mussels** can thrive. Perhaps the most interesting mollusc of deeper moorland streams is the **Freshwater Pearl Mussel**. However, the pearls which can occasionally be found within their fleshy mantle are small and irregular in shape.

RIVER AND STREAM FISH

In terms of its nature, a river can be broadly divided into three parts according to its flow. Starting from its source, there are fast, medium and slow waters, with two intermediate zones, making five in all. Nature, however, is never simple, and not all zones are present in every river. So what follows is a broad guide only to the zones and fish life of rivers and streams.

In the upper reaches of a Devon river the fastest water is known as the torrent or trout zone. This has very clear, well oxygenated water flowing over a rocky or pebbly bottom. Here **Trout** and **Salmon** can commonly be found. Sometimes also **Minnow**, **Bullhead** and **Stone Loach**, but these mainly frequent the intermediate area which is also known as the **Grayling** or **Minnow** zone. **Grayling** can also be found in the medium waters along with **Barbell**, **Chub**, **Dace**, **Gudgeon** and **Bleak**. Here too **Roach**, **Rudd** and **Perch** can live, along with the **Common Eel**, which will inhabit any unpolluted water.

   Continuing downstream, the lower intermediate zone between medium and slow water is the home of **Bream**. Here the gradient is slight, the current gentle. **Pike**, **Perch**, **Rudd** and **Roach**, **Bream**, **Carp**, **Tench** and **Three-spined Sticklebacks** can all be found.

   The fifth zone is known as the flounder or mullet zone. The river bed here has little or no gradient, and the flow can be either up or down stream, as it is

Dipper with food in beak

North American Mink

tidal and the water is brackish – this is the realm of the estuary.

Over 50 different species of freshwater fish live in Britain, but not all can be found in the south-west of England. One of the most widespread is also one of the most important game fish. Watch any pool on the upper reaches of a Devon river for just a few minutes on a warm day, and you may well see a ring of ripples or a sudden splash – the mark of a feeding trout.

A plentiful supply of insect larvae underwater and winged adults fluttering or floating on the surface are a tempting meal for a trout. Sleek and powerful swimmers, they are beautifully adapted to life in fast-flowing rivers or streams. But not all trout are the same. Broadly, two forms of native trout can be found in Devon, as elsewhere in the UK. The first is known as the **Lake**, **River** or **Brown Trout**, spending its entire life in freshwater. The other is the **Sea Trout**, which migrates between river and ocean.

The brown trout found in rivers feed mainly on insects. Here they can grow up to 20 cm in length and weigh up to 1.5 kg. But compared with their lake-living kin they are small. The brown trout found in lakes also feed on other fish, even their own kind, and can grow up to 50 cm long.

Sea trout are much bigger again, and more impressive. When fully grown they can reach 80–100cm in length and weigh anything from 10–15 kg. In appearance and habitat they are very similar to salmon. Like salmon, sea trout migrate between salt water and fresh. Breeding in rivers, they live a large part of their lives in the sea, but while some salmon will return to the river of their birth only once when fully mature, sea trout may return several times to breed. The upper reaches of the Teign is especially famed for the size of its sea trout. Young sea trout, known as *school peal*, can be seen moving up the rivers on Exmoor in July.

Atlantic Salmon, the largest European fish of their kind, grow up to 150cm in length and weigh over 36 kg. Remarkably, it seems that each river appears to have its own unique race of salmon. After leaving fresh water and spending time at sea, they will only return to the stream of their birth to breed, and it seems that different races will return to their river of origin at different seasons. Some salmon move upstream in late autumn to spawn in November and

December far upstream on the gravel beds. Others arrive in the spring; they will rest in the river all summer until late autumn, when they will move further upstream to spawn.

In terms of their salmon, rivers can broadly be divided in two – spring or autumn runs. The river Plym has its run of salmon in December and January, while the Dart has a spring and early summer run. But the Teign and Taw/Torridge are not so clear cut. In the past, foreign salmon stocks were introduced into these rivers from elsewhere, so here the salmon run appears to be twice a year – one for the native race, the other for the introductions.

On Exmoor, mature salmon can be found from March onwards throughout the spring and summer. Here the largest runs take place in late summer into early autumn; it is then that the best views of these magnificent creatures may be had as they jump the weirs or bask in the deeper pools beneath bridges. Yet strangely, while there is plenty of insect food available in the rivers, adult salmon returning to spawn do not feed; but much to the delight of fishermen they will occasionally take an artificial fly.

Throughout history, so important has the salmon become to people that each stage of a salmon's life has been given a name. Young salmon are known as *alevins* when they hatch. But once the yolk-sac is absorbed they become *parr*, with their characteristic markings on each flank – 8 to10 finger marks, each separated by a single red spot. They also develop the trait of all their kind – a small grey green 'adipose' fin halfway between the big back dorsal fin and their powerful tail. After about two years most *parr* become *smolt*. Now they turn a silvery colour and head for the sea. Some *smolt* may travel thousands of miles, even reaching the coast of Greenland. After a year or more, mature and much bigger, they return to the river of their birth as a silvery *grilse*. As the time for spawning approaches, the males become more red coloured and the females darker. Both eventually develop a spotty, more mottled appearance with black, red and orange colours. The lower jaw of the male grows longer and more hooked. After spawning, their energy spent, sometimes battered and marked by their long struggle upstream, they become *kelts* and make their way back down river and into the sea. For some this will be their final journey as they now die, while others will return to breed again.

RIVER & STREAM BIRDS

The majority of birds in Britain need to visit fresh water if only to drink and bathe. But some spend their entire lives in, on and near it. While the richest part of a stream for fish life is where it flows fast through a wooded valley, the same is also true for its birds. One of the most intriguing is a plump little black bird with a white throat and chest – the **Dipper**. Flitting from mossy boulder to spray-splashed stone, bobbing constantly, dippers appear never to stand still, and they have a remarkable talent – they can walk underwater. Searching among the gravel and stones on the stream bed they find a rich source of caddis fly larvae and other aquatic insects.

Another wonderfully descriptive name for a stream-side bird is the **Grey Wagtail**, which also has the most beautiful eye-catching yellow chest and

Water forget-me-not

Kingfisher female

underside. They feed above water, darting after emerging caddis and mayflies, tails wagging furiously. The colours of the **Kingfisher** are even more dazzling. A tell-tale whistle and flash of blue and orange gold are the mark of these stunning little birds. They feed almost entirely on small fish, which they catch by spectacularly plunging into the water from a perch. Kingfishers are common in Devon, and may be seen on any stream, river, pool or coast – indeed wherever there is a plentiful supply of finger-sized fish.

RIVER AND STREAM MAMMALS

Bank Voles and **Shrews** can commonly be heard rustling in lush stream-side vegetation, but few mammals actually live in the water. The water vole, once common, is now rare if not absent from Devon. They need gentle flowing streams, not prone to large fluctuations in level, since this could flood their bankside homes. The River Clyst in East Devon used to be a stronghold, but most of Devon's streams are subject to winter spates and their flows are really too fast for water voles. So if any water voles still survive in the county they may be in canals and slow-running leats.

The **Water Shrew** is much more widespread, though also difficult to see. The only shrew in Britain to swim in water, it has a slate black back and pale grey underside. Wherever a stream flows through a water cress bed it is always worth watching carefully, as these attractive little creatures can be active at any time, day or night.

Devon has the dubious distinction of being the first county in Britain to record **Mink** living in the wild. If ever a county was ideal for the fast and effective spread of such an alien, water-loving predator, it was Devon. The speed of colonisation was impressive. When the first North American Mink first escaped from fur farms in the 1950s, some must have headed upstream. Reaching the headwaters on the top of Dartmoor, they soon found the sources for four other rivers – and the rest is history.

Devon has always been a stronghold for the **Otter**. Immortalised in the writings of Henry Williamson, *Tarka the Otter* was set in north and central Devon. While the creature's existence in England was seriously threatened during the 1960s and 70s, largely due to pesticide poisoning and the pressure of continued hunting, it is now fully protected and appears to have recolonised most of its former haunts. Sightings of otter crossing roads, even in towns and villages (wherever there is a river with fish of a suitable size), are becoming increasingly common. But the best evidence of their comeback is the frequency of their territorial markings, the fishy spraints they leave under bridges and on stream-side branches and stones.

Leats and Weirs

People, as much as wildlife, need freshwater. Wherever a stream flows, particularly since medieval times, we have attempted to harness its power or divert its course for domestic water supply. Over the centuries a network of stone-walled leats and hand-hewn channels have been constructed across the country, sometimes for tens of miles. Sluice gates control the flow of water, and weirs allow for changes of level. In time many leats have become forgotten, overgrown and lost, while others are now just neglected. Some leats, however, have become so naturalized that their man-made origin is no longer obvious. Only the stream's course, cut into the contours of the landscape, hugging the hills high above the valley bottom, give a clue to their unnatural history.

LEAT AND WEIR PLANTS

A weir is simply an artificial rapid and waterfall. Built across a natural stream bed or as part of a leat, a weir creates a deep pool on the upstream side. Here the flow is more gentle, allowing silt to be deposited before spilling over the downstream edge. Then, cascading down a smooth slope or splashing between boulders, it forms a miniature rapid before finally dropping a short distance in a white waterfall. Below, small islands of vegetation may form, allowing tall spikes of **Purple Loosestrife**, **Skullcap**, **Greater Willowherb** and **Hemp Agrimony** to grow in summer. Here, too, spectacular displays of **Hemlock Water Dropwort** sprout, their little umbrella-like clusters of small white flowers shading the stream as it pushes between its tough stems. But these islands are temporary havens created by the last winter flood, and most will be swept away by the first spate at summer's end.

In Devon, many leats were dug to provide power for stamp machinery, used to crush tin ore before smelting. On Dartmoor, the build-up of silt in a neglected leat can form an interesting marshy wetland. In summer it may be

| 71 |

Marsh marigold; Ragged robin

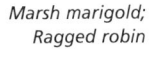

bright with a carpet of **Water Crowfoot, Pondweed, Water Blinks** and **Starwort.** Where the flow is reduced to a trickle, the pools can also be colonised by frogs and newts.

LEAT AND WEIR FISH

On larger streams and rivers, weirs can be spectacular places after heavy rain. The force of a flood hurtling headlong down a slope is daunting enough to watch, let alone attempt to swim. Yet after a long dry spell, that is exactly what **Salmon** and **Sea Trout** have been waiting for downstream. Few spectacles in nature can rival the breathtaking beauty of a large salmon leaping clear of the torrent and powering its way up river.

Marsh

Slow-draining soil and a good supply of rain can create a marsh in water-logged ground, and they can form anywhere. It may be a small area of poorly drained pasture, around a pond edge, alongside a stream or in a roadside ditch. But when is a marsh not a marsh? When it is more of a bog. Temporary pools often form on heathland during winter, but their waterlogged soils tend to form acidic wet heath, rather than more neutral marshland.

MARSH PLANTS

Marsh plants are not so much aquatic as damp-loving for much of the year. Unlike a bog, marsh soil is rich in dissolved mineral salts, but is still oxygen deficient, so the vegetation is lush with large-leaved plants.

The splendid golden yellow flowers of **Marsh Marigold** bloom early in many parts of Devon. By March, when winter has killed much of the countryside's colour, marigolds glow in dank places such as wet woodlands and along flooded stream sides. By April, the heart shaped leaves of **Butterbur** and delicate **Lady's Smock**, with their pale lilac or white flowers, paint patches in damp pastures. The tiny white flowers of **Blinks** are also common along with the wonderfully prehistoric-looking **Marsh Horsetail**. But that primeval feel is best where giant **Tussock Sedge** impressively reach above head height. Nothing however, is more colourful than a marshy meadow in the early summer sun, sparkling with dew. Here yellow **Flag Iris** fly their colours, great purple spikes of **Southern Marsh Orchid** rise from the grass, and tiny blue creeping **Water Forget-me-nots** and pink **Ragged Robins** form large clumps of colour.

By June, **Marsh Pennywort** with their characteristic round leaves can be commonly seen along with **Purple Loosestrife, Marsh Thistle** and a variety of pink **Willow Herbs**. As if this cacophony of colour were not sufficient, yellow mounds of **Greater Birdsfoot Trefoil** and paler **Lesser Spearwort** add to the spectacle. Tufts of **Soft** and **Compact Rush**, and **Cornish Moneywort**, which is just as plentiful in parts of Devon, are all features of marshlands in the county.

July is also good for marsh colour. **Hemp Agrimony, Meadowsweet,**

Marsh orchids

which can often be seen covering roadside ditches, as well as **Wild Angelica,** **Greater Willow Herb** and the daisy-like flowers of **Common Fleabane**. A closer look may reveal **Water Pepper** and **Water Mint** almost anywhere it is damp, as well as **Wavy St John's Wort.** Here, too, the **Yellow Loosestrife** can sometimes be found with **Sneezewort** and **Marsh Woundwort.**

Reed beds develop around many larger pools, but the biggest and best areas tend to grow alongside estuaries.

Canals

Compared with elsewhere in England, few canals were constructed in Devon, but those that remain still have some navigable lengths. The best is located in its heartlands. The Grand Western Canal is a designated Country Park. Running between Tiverton and Holcombe Regis in north-east Devon, it is over 11 miles long, with an accessible and level towpath along its entire length. It has many historical features to excite the industrial archaeologists – twenty-four bridges, two old lime kilns and nine milestones – yet strangely, no locks. This is because it was constructed to follow the contours of the landscape. The canal meanders through picturesque farmland with pockets of woodland, and offers spectacular views of the surrounding countryside.

CANAL PLANTS

Situated amongst beautiful Devon countryside, the Grand Western Canal provides a habitat for many wild plants and animals. Amongst the most attractive flowers, **Early Purple Orchid** and **Common Spotted Orchid** grow on the bank sides, while in some places, elegant wild water lilies bloom. The leaves of the **Arrowhead** give good reason to its name as they stand above the surface on long stalks. But the plant also has other leaves. In spring it first produces submerged translucent, grass-like leaves. Next come the more oval floating form, and finally the arrow-shaped foliage. It is not common in Devon, being confined mainly to the Tiverton and Exeter canals.

CANAL INSECTS

The waterway teems with freshwater creatures such as water boatmen and dragonfly larvae, living on a variety of oxygenating and emergent vegetation. In spring, summer and early autumn, many butterflies are common.

CANAL BIRDS

The canal also attracts a wide variety of birds. **Kingfishers** are a regular sight anywhere along its length, and waterfowl can be found on most stretches, with **Moorhens**, **Mute Swans** and **Mallards** being a common sight. The hedgerows and bank-side vegetation provide further food, shelter and a safe corridor for birds, including **Grey Wagtail** and **Long-tailed Tit.**

Moorhen

CANAL MAMMALS

Small mammals such as bank voles and shrews are frequently seen, but more often heard. One creature used to be quite common in Devon: Ratty, from *Wind in the Willows* fame, is actually a **Water Vole**. Now they are sadly rare, perhaps due to the fact they feature large on the menu of **Mink**. Even where they can still be found they are not easy to see. The tell-tale 'plop' of one diving under-water is probably the best giveaway of their presence. The Grand Western Canal was one of their last strongholds in Devon, and even here they may now be extinct – if you see one, please notify the Devon Wildlife Trust. But the news is not all bad. It appears that mink may be on the decline, and the otter is mak-ing a comeback in the area.

Heathland

When is a moor not a moor? The answer is when it is a heath. It may look like moor, and even have many plants and animals in common, but heath can form at much lower altitude. There are two types of heath found in different places – one on the coast, the other inland. Both may contain similar plants and animals, as well as some distinct differences.

Most lowland heaths are man-made by accident. They have formed in places once covered by deciduous wood, where the soil is acidic. After trees are felled and the land has lost most of its valuable mineral salts through weathering, the soil is no longer able to support its original woodland cover. Heathland develops – but it does not always need people to create it.

Coastal heath

If you want to see a real primeval landscape, you can travel back in time. Take a stroll along the top of a sea cliff, especially in the north and west of Devon. Here, between the cliff and countryside inland, is a narrow coastal strip devoid of trees. It was thought this was once wooded, and over the centuries grazing animals reduced it to open heath. But now we know that this ribbon of wild land, often no more than a few hundred metres wide, was perhaps never shaded by trees. Remarkably, this heathland may be the original prehistoric vegetation. Swept by Atlantic winds, it once divided the cliff edge from the great deciduous forest that could only grow inland, away from salt laden spray. At its most severe, where wind blasting lays the stems of heather bare, the plants grow away from the prevailing breeze and flower in the lee. In effect it creates a rolling sea of heather – a wave heathland.

Today, many of these coastal heathlands bear more than a passing resemblance to those found much further south in Europe. Here, plants that are rarely found or are absent elsewhere in Britain seem to flourish, forming an intriguing, so-called Lusitanian flora. The **Dwarf Western Gorse** adds brilliant patches of yellow to the pinks and purple of heather and ling in late summer.

Inland heath

Inland, away from coastal winds, the heaths are sheltered, and many more interesting plants and animals are found. Some of the

Emperor moth

Hobby at nest

finest lowland dry heaths, rich in wildlife, can be found in south-east Devon. This area has an extraordinary history reaching back to the age of the dinosaurs, and these heathlands have developed on ancient Triassic pebblebeds. During that period it was a vast desert stretching into France, with colossal rivers depositing layer upon layer of pebbles. As the millennia passed it became ice age tundra, then as the climate finally warmed, thick forest. Iron Age people arrived around 2500 years ago and built a great hill fort on one of its most prominent hills. Eventually all the trees were cleared, and heath began to develop. Today Woodbury Castle overlooks some of the most important places for wildlife in the county. Over time the heathland has become fragmented, but Woodbury remains the largest, an area which consists of both wet and dry heath, lowland bog, pine and alder scrub with patches of deciduous woodland, all teeming with life.

HEATHLAND PLANTS

The heaths contain all three species of heather – **Ling**, **Bell Heather** and in the wetter areas, **Cross-leaved Heath**. **Western Gorse** is common with some patches of the larger **Common Gorse.** The wet heath and boggy areas are of particular interest to botanists, with a range of unusual plants such as **Pale Butterwort**, **Bog Pimpernel**, **Sundews**, **Lesser Butterfly Orchid** and **Saw-wort**, with many species of **Sphagnum moss**.

HEATHLAND INSECTS

During the summer more than 30 species of butterfly are recorded each year. **Silver-washed Fritillary**, **Brimstone**, **Grayling**, **Silver-studded Blue** and **Purple Hairstreak** can all be found, as well as the **Emperor** and **Fox Moths**. **Dragonflies** are also common, including the **Southern Damselfly**, a rare species in Britain that is confined to just a few parts of the south-west.

Stonechat with food in beak

Nightjar, well camouflaged

HEATHLAND BIRDS

Beneath the ramparts of the Iron Age hill fort, the heathlands attract a wide variety of birds. **Stonechat, Yellowhammer, Curlew, Tree Pipit** and even a few **Woodlark** can all be found. The woodlands provide nesting for **Buzzard, Kestrel, Raven** and **Green Woodpecker**. Even the **Hobby** can be seen passing through on migration, and may remain during the summer, attracted by the wealth of dragonflies. To watch this fast-flying falcon catch and consume a dragonfly while still on the wing, is a thrilling sight. So too is the winter view of a **Hen Harrier** or **Great Grey Shrike**.

The East Devon Commons are particularly famed for their population of **Dartford Warbler**. This was one of their original strongholds in Britain and they are still doing well.

Nothing can compare to a calm summer's evening when the busy birdlife of day gives way to the quiet of dusk. As the sun dips below the distant moor, a distant churring sound carries across the silent heath, followed by a wing clap or two – a **Nightjar** has risen. Its buoyant, floating flight, hovering and wheeling against the afterglow of a setting sun, is a moment never forgotten. The white wing patches of the male flash as he cartwheels over the heath on falcon-like wings. Gradually his soft churring call descends into a slow bubbling. Then he disappears from sight into a tree. The nightjar is unique among British birds; it does not sit across a branch like all others, it sits along it, and its camouflage is among the best on earth. Indeed it is so good that a nightjar crouching on the ground, eyes closed, surrounded by dead bracken and broken twigs, is almost impossible to distinguish, even from just a pace away.

HEATHLAND REPTILES AND MAMMALS

The heathlands of east Devon are also good places to see reptiles and mammals. **Adders** live in the dry parts, while **Grass Snakes** often frequent the wetter places as they hunt for frogs. **Common Lizards** bask on the banks, warm stones and logs in spring and summer. The heath also supports a thriving population of **Roe Deer**.

Limestone and Chalk

A warm summer breeze and fine country or coastal views, the song of skylark above and buzz of busy bees below – what could be better? As grasshoppers leap from your path and blue butterflies dance across a sea of grass flecked with wild flowers, there is only one place in the world you can be – calcareous grassland.

Grass is often taken for granted, trampled and torn by tyre marks, played on, ploughed or fed to farm animals. Yet there is far more to grass than just a green sward. Calcium rich soils produce a wonderfully distinct grassland all of their own.

There are two forms of limestone – hard and soft. In Devon, limestone-rich soils are relatively scarce. A few patches of hard limestone rock can be found around Plymouth and Torbay, with smaller outcrops at Chudleigh, Buckfastleigh and Torbryan. More extensive softer chalks and limestone occur in East Devon. Both derive from sediments of calcium carbonate laid down in ancient warm tropical seas, formed from countless tiny shells of marine creatures, larger trilobites, brachiopods and ammonites and the skeletons of corals over millions of years.

Limestone Caves

Most of the hard limestone outcrops in Devon are found near the coast, yet there is one inland which hides an extraordinary secret world. At Buckfastleigh and Ashburton, where Victorian workmen quarried for marble, a complex labyrinth of caves was discovered. Created by rivers and streams following natural fractures and fissures in the rock, a series of passageways and chambers were dissolved and eroded over vast periods of time. Before the last ice age the wildlife of the area was very different. During this interglacial period, hippo wallowed where the River Dart now flows, lion preyed on herds of elephant and hyena scavenged from kills. The collapse of a cave roof over 80,000 years ago opened up a new den in which predators could hide and devour their meals. As time passed, the chamber gradually filled with mud and bones, until it was finally sealed by the rising mound – a natural tomb.

In 1939 some enthusiastic young cavers began exploring tunnels previously exposed by workmen at Higher Kiln Quarry. Over the ensuing years the mud and bone pile, known as a Talus mound, was partially excavated – it was a revelation. Today the remains form the richest collection of mammal bones ever discovered in a British cave. It includes the tooth of a baby elephant with the bones of rhinoceros, wolf and giant deer from an age we can only try to imagine.

Near Plymouth, the working of limestone quarries to build the breakwater in Plymouth Sound was the first recorded excavation of a cave in the British Isles. The year was 1816. Remarkably, it appears that numerous animal bones were unearthed, along with some human remains. In those days it was thought that ancient creatures never lived alongside modern humans. So the importance of the find was never realised, and the human bones were just tipped over the cliff!

Thankfully not all such important evidence of early people met such an ignominious end. In Torquay, an impressive system of caves was spared from the quarryman. Kents Cavern has a special claim to fame. Privately owned but open to the public, it is the oldest scheduled ancient monument in Britain. What it revealed astonished the experts of the day, and the latest scientific techniques have confirmed the earliest dates. It contains the most extraordinary evidence of archaic human habitation in the entire country, and one of the oldest such finds in Europe. As if the remains of ancient fires and stone hand axes made 450,000 years ago were not enough, the discovery of a 31,000-year-old modern human jawbone at Kents Cavern is the oldest of its kind in Britain.

Caves can hold other natural treasures. If we could travel through time, aeons in the blink of an eye, we might witness the creation of some of nature's more fabulous sculptures. Water, that original architectural agent of caves, continues to furnish a cave's interior. Seeping through cracks in the limestone, it appears as a droplet hanging from the roof deep underground. Carbon dioxide dissolved in water is released into the blackness of the cave atmosphere, leaving a tiny ring of calcite around the water drop. Eventually the drip falls to the cavern floor and is replaced by another on the ceiling. The process is repeated time after time, century after century, and millennia pass. Slowly the calcite deposit grows. The best cave formations occur when the climate is warm and plant growth outside on the surface is producing sufficient carbon dioxide to dissolve the limestone. During the cold of the ice ages, calcite formation is limited. Eventually a straw hangs from the ceiling and begins to grow into a thicker stalactite. Depending on the rate of dripping, their shape and form can vary from a simple cone to a curtain or something more weird and wonderful. Fluctuating water levels flooding the cave, combined with a barely discernible movement of air, can create the most fantastic irregular shape called a helictite.

The same process also happens when a drop of water hits the floor of a cave. Here a stalagmite is formed. Sometimes stalactites and stalagmites will join and create a column. Water seeping down the side walls of the cave can also leave a calcite deposit known as flowstone, that looks more like a waterfall frozen in time. And crystal pools grow where lime-saturated water is trapped in small basins. Colours can be spectacular. While pure calcite is white, staining from other dissolved minerals in the water can produce dramatic streaks and washes of unearthly hues. Iron stains red, copper green, while manganese is black. But the process is slow. Depending on the cave, it can take over a thousand years for a calcite formation to grow barely two centimetres.

Limestone cave, Buckfast

CAVE LIFE

Inside a cavern beyond the threshold of light, you enter a world of complete and utter darkness where only dripping water breaks the silence. Here, sun-loving plants can no longer survive. Even shade tolerant ferns and mosses struggle and eventually give way to bare rock. Yet the blackest of caves can support a variety of life. With only a limited ability needed to detect light, and skin colour serving no useful purpose, permanent cave-dwelling creatures tend to be devoid of pigment and virtually blind.

Some cave pools support a tiny community of **Freshwater Shrimps** and lively little copepod relations. Nearer the entrance in the twilight zone, pink and white **Woodlice** forage the floor, along with small beetles and tiny **Springtails**.

CAVE INSECTS AND SPIDERS

The **Cave Spider** is the only British species to be found exclusively in holes and caverns. Since adults are rarely if ever found outside, it must be young spiderlings which colonise new caves.

Autumn and winter brings new life in from the cold. Compared with the air outside in summer, caves are cool, yet in mid-winter they can be relatively warm. The **Herald Moth** is the most spectacular insect to hibernate in a cavern, hanging in a state of suspended animation from the damp cave walls. But seldom can more than a few be found. Other creatures seem to prefer a crowd.

CAVE MAMMALS

Bats are the biggest cave dwellers to spend the entire winter underground. As little or no insect food is available from October to April, they must hibernate in order to survive. Cold will not kill them, but starvation surely will. Eight species of British bat inhabit caves, but only two can be found together in large numbers – **Lesser** and **Greater Horseshoe Bats**. Although these two species were more common in the past, now up to 500 may still share a single roost.

Cave spider on egg case

Greater horseshoe bat

Sand martin at nest

Bats are intelligent, social creatures with a relatively long life, some living up to 30 years. During late summer and early autumn they must gorge on insects to build up sufficient fat to see them through the coldest months. Once warmer spring days arrive they usually leave their winter roost to find their summer breeding place, often an old building.

Quarries

For thousands of years people have cut and carved stone, and excavated sand and gravel from the ground. What remains is a new place waiting to be exploited by wild animals and plants.

QUARRY BIRDS

To a bird the towering rock face of a worked-out quarry must seem just like a natural cliff. In Devon stone and gravel are extracted from granite and sand quarries as well as some limestone ones. Most birds that nest in such places only require a suitable ledge. The exception is the **Sand Martin**, which will dig its own tunnel into a low cliff face of soft sand and gravel. They form a colony, mining their individual nests close to each other in the same seam.

A sheltered ledge high on the face of a deserted hard limestone quarry is a popular place with other birds. The earliest to nest is the **Raven.** Once a common scavenger, seen in every city in Tudor times, its range today is limited to the north and west of Britain. Here there is usually a pair or two wherever sheep are found. As scavengers they make a quick meal of natural fatalities and clean up any after birth. Their cronking call carries a long way in the skies over Dartmoor and surrounding lands.

In contrast the **Kestrel** prefers smaller holes in a quarry wall. It preys on small mammals – mainly mice and voles – but sometimes even large insects, smaller birds and bats are taken. The strategy for which they are best renowned is their masterful ability to hover; easy in a breeze, but when the wind dies their tail is fanned and wings must beat extra hard. They drop in steps, closer to the ground and their victim is taken more by surprise than speed. Although a fast flyer, the kestrel is outclassed by a bigger bird of prey that will also nest in the quarry – the peregrine.

The tactic of the **Peregrine** is finely tuned. Soaring high above its hunting territory, it will seem too remote to be menacing. Its principal prey is often a stray pigeon. Diving with wings held next to its body, travelling at speeds of 180 miles an hour, it closes on its chosen victim in seconds. The velocity at which the birds collide is literally stunning. The peregrine's outstretched feet take the full force, delivery a devastating blow that can break a pigeon's neck.

Limestone cliff grassland

Forts and flowers are a great combination for anyone interested in human history and wildlife. Berry Head in south Devon must be the most impressive outcrop of Devonian limestone in the county. As a promontory, it forms the southern edge of Torbay, standing over 65 metres tall. The headland drops sheer into the sea and shelters the bay from the prevailing south-west winds. For centuries it has been a landmark for mariners and local people, forming the bay's first defence against both the weather and hostile invaders. It is an important heritage site, designated and protected because of its wildlife and archaeological remains. More details of its famous seabird colony can be found in the *Sea Cliffs* chapter.

Having survived 400 million years, its limestone is obviously hard and highly resistant to erosion. Any surrounding softer rocks have long since come and gone – only the sea has left its mark. The rock forms the headland itself, cliffs provide safe haven for seabirds, and the thin overlying soils support a highly specialised and unusual community of plants. Caves in the rock are home to rare and endangered bats, and the stone itself was used to build massive fortifications that still stand today.

While there is evidence that Berry Head was used in the Iron Age, it was during the Napoleonic Wars that the most imposing fortresses were built. They now rank among the best preserved in Britain, and as such are protected as an Ancient Monument.

BERRY HEAD

BERRY HEAD PLANTS

The combination of limestone, its extreme southerly position, and the hordes of nibbling rabbits, also explain its extraordinary community of wild flowers. Berry Head is renowned for its floral displays, with some 500 species of plants identified on the cliffs and grasslands. Many are nationally scarce, with nine being classed as rare. Thin soil and exposure to wind and salt spray also means that many of these plants are tiny. The **Small Hare's Ear** is only found here and at

Beachy Head in Sussex. It stands just 3 centimetres tall. Others are more common further south on the continent, but only have a toehold here in Britain. The attractive **White Rock Rose** with fluttering petals has a long flowering period from April to July, which means visitors get a good opportunity to enjoy its blooms. Others worth looking out for include the **Small Rest Harrow** and the autumn-flowering **Goldilocks Aster**, found here among the rocks along the coast path just south of the Old Redoubt. Between August and September bright patches of its yellow flowers may be seen around Durl Head.

The common plants also found on limestone soils are equally showy. The blue **Viper's Bugloss**, sturdy stems of pink **Tree Mallow**, **Thrift** and **Red Valerian** all stand out against the deep blue of the sea beyond.

Orchids never fail to impress. At Berry Head each season has its own highlight, and eight species of orchid provide colour from April through to September. Spring finds **Early Purple Orchids** flowering along scrub margins, and even on the ramparts of the north fort. Then **Green-winged Orchid** flower in just a few places from May to June. As summer arrives in the woodland, so the **Twayblade** appears. On more open areas of grassland, beautiful **Bee Orchids** bloom in June and July; they are perhaps best seen in the North Fort opposite the café. A few **Common Spotted Orchids** flower about the same time, while the North Fort and quarry are good places to find **Pyramidal Orchids** into August. **Autumn Lady's Tresses** are the final orchids of the season in August and September, around the South Fort.

The clean air and humid conditions of Berry Head also suit many rare mosses and lichens. One rare moss is only known at four other sites in the British Isles. More information on the nature of Berry Head can be found in the chapter on *Sea Cliffs*.

Calcareous Grassland

Parts of the landscape in south-east Devon owes its origins to a great age of dinosaurs, particularly the Cretaceous. The soils that its rocks produce are special. Chalk and limestone is highly porous, their soils thin and dry. Calcium levels are high, but they lack other nutrients essential for lush plant growth, so their soils are relatively impoverished. Yet that is their strength. Grasses grow well in such conditions, as do other small plants. Despite their simple leaves, grasses are not primitive plants but

Green-winged orchid; Small restharrow; Harebell

highly evolved ones, and their flowers are easily overlooked. Growing out in the open, exposed to maximum light with a constant breeze, they have no need for showy petals to attract insects. Tall stems lift their pollen high and they are spread by wind. Grasses can tolerate the extremes of drought and fire, regular cutting or tearing by teeth: they are tough. Yet surprisingly, they only evolved long after the time reptiles dominated life on earth – some 25 million years ago – and our native grasslands are much more recent than that. These areas are often simply known as Downs.

CALCAREOUS GRASSLAND PLANTS

The clearance of the original wildwood just a few thousand years ago by the first farmers brought about a revolution in the British landscape. Cut and cleared, the only way grasslands can flourish is by regular grazing. Otherwise they revert to scrub, then back to wood. People need grass, and grass needs people. Yet few other places in the world can boast grasslands as rich and green as ours. Where calcareous land has remained unploughed for centuries, the turf can be astonishingly rich in wild flowers, insects and snails. In fact, calcareous grassland is one of the richest habitats in the country. A single square metre can contain over 30 different plant species.

The presence of numerous anthills is a good indication of ancient pasture, and well worth a closer look – getting down on hand and knees is the only way. Grasses survive nibbling rabbits and sheep by growing from the base. Other plants have different tactics. The **Rough Hawkbit** has its growing point in the centre of a flat rosette of leaves. The **Bird's Foot Trefoil** spreads vegetatively and can withstand trampling.

Many wild flowers in Devon can only grow on calcium-rich soils. **Bulbous Buttercups**, **Old Man's Beard**, **Wild Basil**, **Marjoram**, **Cowslip** and **Hedge Bedstraw** are all typically found on calcareous grasslands. Others such as **Red Clover**, **Lady's Bedstraw**, **Selfheal**, **Salad Burnet**, **Kidney Vetch** and the **Harebell**, which is rare in Devon, do best in alkaline soils but can also be found elsewhere. Some flowers also have local forms where they grow on isolated outcrops of calcareous rock: the widespread white **Bladder Campion** has a red form on Plymouth's limestone.

Some flowers need an even closer relationship with grasses to grow well. **Yellow Hayrattle** and **Eyebright** are semi-parasitic plants. Although capable of living independently, they will also tap into the roots of grasses to boost their own growth. But a special type of orchid, **Broomrape**, can only survive where attached to its specific host plant, and that includes grasses.

Orchids are one of the best-studied plants in the world. That is not surprising, considering their amazing diversity and beauty. Calcareous grasslands are rich in a wide variety of these spectacular plants. Some are common, others extremely rare. The **Common Spotted**, **Green-winged**, **Bee**, **Pyramidal** and rare **Fragrant Orchid** can all be found in Devon.

Glow worm flightless female
attracting a mate

CALCAREOUS GRASSLAND INSECTS AND SNAILS

The diversity of plant life is one reason why so many insects and other invertebrate creatures live here. The other is the variety of climatic conditions. South-facing slopes are hot and dry, while northerly aspects may be moist. Deep combes provide shelter, ideal for butterflies and other more delicate insects. Steep slopes on chalk may favour those creatures that only need sparse plant growth. Rabbits also influence insect numbers. They disturb the ground with their diggings, and fresh droppings attract dung flies and downland butterflies.

Snails need calcium to produce their shells. So it will be no surprise to learn these grasslands are grazed by hoards of these molluscs in a variety of shapes and sizes. Round, ribbed and spired, plain and fancy striped shells, some big and many more small, the wealth of these little lumbering grazers is remarkable. They also provide a source of food for one of our most enchanting creatures. As darkness falls on a warm summer's night, some grasslands begin to glow with tiny green lights. The **Glow Worm** is a strange creature, sadly misnamed, as it is a beetle not a worm. The adults seldom feed; that is left to the larvae. Following a snail trail, the grub easily overtakes its prey. Injecting an enzyme into the shell soon reduces the contents to soup.

The adult female glow worm is flightless, and appears to have a deeply segmented body – hence the confusion with a worm. The light is cold and chemically made, and from egg to adult all produce a glow, though at some stages more than at others. The female has the brightest light, hidden beneath her tail. Climbing a grass stem, she slowly waggles her abdomen in the hope of attracting a mate. He looks more like a beetle and flies above the grasslands. When they mate, they even turn out the lights.

But there are distractions to his mission. Sadly, the indiscriminate use of lighting in the countryside and brighter city lights are luring male glow worms away. (Unfortunately, energy-efficient bulbs seem to attract the most). No wonder they are becoming so rare. The best places to find glow worms today is where there is little or no artificial illumination.

While snails are common, ants are everywhere, especially on old calcareous grasslands. Although one of the smallest creatures, they create some of the most prominent features: small mounds. The home of the **Yellow Field Ant** is built by worker ants to provide a warm place for

Pyramidal orchid; Speckled bush cricket, female; Bee orchid

their brood chambers. They move their eggs to which ever side the sun is on. Up to twenty thousand ants may inhabit a single nest, and their grubs form an essential food for the **Green Woodpecker**.

Butterflies are by far the most conspicuous insects of calcareous grasslands during spring and summer. Not all can be easily seen, but the following have all been recorded in Devon: **Brown Argus**, **Common Blue**, **Small Copper**, **Marbled White**, **Dark Green Fritillary**, **Small Skipper**, **Large Skipper**, **Dingy Skipper**, **Meadow Brown**, **Green Hairstreak**, **Small Heath** and lastly the **Wall Butterfly**, which appears to be becoming more scarce. All their caterpillars feed on grasses or the small flowering plants that prefer limestone or chalky soil.

Grassland moths include species that fly by day and at night. The **Six-spot Burnet** is a conspicuous black and red day-flying moth. Night-flying moths tend to have more cryptic colouring so they can hide during daylight hours. However the **Small Elephant Hawk-moth**, with its red and gold colouring, is a spectacular exception.

Grasshoppers and **Crickets** are some of the largest and noisiest insects that may be found on calcareous grasslands. Twenty-nine different kinds live in Britain in a variety of habitats, although only ten are common. All are active only during summer and they are easy to tell apart, although getting close enough to see these agile jumpers in detail is not so easy. Grasshoppers in particular use their long legs to propel themselves into the air, then their wings enable them to fly some distance. Grasshoppers have short antennae, while those of crickets are often longer than their bodies. The adults of both, usually males, draw attention to themselves by 'singing'. Male crickets produce their 'song' by rubbing the bases of their front wings together, while male grasshoppers rub their hind legs against their wings. Whatever the method employed, the calls of these creatures on a warm summer's day bring the grasslands to life. While grasshoppers usually call only in sunshine, crickets tend to take over in the evening.

Marbled white butterfly

Lundy

Brooding on the distant seaward horizon, a tantalising dark shape can be seen from the cliffs of North Devon. An island lies where the North Atlantic meets the Bristol Channel, 12 miles north of Hartland Point, 30 miles south of Wales. Lundy beckons. It takes an hour and forty minutes to reach by boat from Ifracombe, just 25 miles away. In summer, straggling lines of Gannets cross your bow as you head into the long low swell. Fulmar fly close, checking for any fishy offerings thrown overboard. At first there is sea. Then there is cliff. Only as you near the island, approaching the landing bay, does its true awe-inspiring scale become apparent. Rising sheer over 100 metres high, the natural granite bastion of Lundy towers above the waves. Nothing but ocean lies between it and America. Three and a half miles long and half a mile wide, it is an island apart from the rest of Britain, a remote, peaceful and unspoilt wild haven.

There are 6,289 islands around the coast of Britain, but this one is special in many ways. Lundy was once the haunt of pirates and privateers, royalists and refugees from justice. Scattered across the island there are still many reminders of its more colourful and tragic past. Even from the last century, the rusting engines of a crashed German bomber are in vivid contrast to an owner who set himself up as a self-styled king, issuing his own coins and stamps. Yet evidence of people on the island stretches back much further in time, to the Stone Age. Remains of ancient settlements and fortifications litter the wind-blasted tops and more sheltered valleys, from the Bronze Age through Roman occupation to modern times. Although there is little historic proof for any Viking habitation, the name Lundy is Norse, meaning 'puffin island'.

Lundy is mostly granite, and recent research suggests that it may be the remnants of an extinct volcano. Many of the minerals associated with such a fiery formation can be found: the deserted quarries along the east coast are a good place to look. Lundy is also strategically located on the migration routes for countless numbers of birds. Over the years several unusual species have made their first European landfall on the island. It is also home to an unusual range of plants including a special flower – the Lundy Cabbage.

LUNDY PLANTS

Living in such an exposed place, wind is a major influence on island life, for people as well as nature. Bracken covers much of the island in summer. The contrast between east and west sides is great: the east is more sheltered. The cliffs here are not as sheer

Lundy east cliffs

Lundy Cabbage

Sika deer

as those on the west coast, being more lush and green with seasonal displays of **Bluebells** and **Foxgloves**. The south-eastern cliffs are home to a plant species that occurs nowhere else in the world. The **Lundy Cabbage** is unique and can easily be seen as you walk up the main path from the landing beach. Another rare plant, the **Balm-leaved Figwort**, was more recently discovered on this south-eastern side. The only other place this figwort can really be seen is around the Kingsbridge estuary in South Devon.

The central top part of the island is a gentle plateau, with heathland towards the north. On the western edge the heath takes on a special form. Exposed to the prevailing wind it has created a Wave Heathland, protected by European law. The area is rich is in lichens, including the rare **Golden Hair Lichen**. Elsewhere bracken dominates, and the grass between is kept short across the central areas of grassland and heath by grazing rabbits and Soay sheep, a rare breed that copes admirably in such harsh conditions. Some boggy areas allow wetland plants to grow. Here the carnivorous **Sundew** may be common. Most of the southern end of the plateau is farmed.

The west side of Lundy is very exposed, open to the full force of the Atlantic, blasted by wind, waves and salt spray. Yet, incredibly, life still thrives here. Pink carpets of **Sea Thrift** cover the cliff tops in spring and early summer.

LUNDY INSECTS AND SPIDERS

There are two special insects to be found feeding on the Lundy Cabbage, the **Lundy Cabbage Flea Beetle** and the **Lundy Cabbage Weevil.** Both are unique to the island.

Another interesting insect lives mainly on the western side of the island. Caterpillars of the **Thrift Clearwing Moth** feed on the pink plants that give it its name. Another unusual creature, the **Purseweb Spider**, is Britain's only member of the bird-eating spider family. But don't worry – it is not that big here. The spider is small, and lives in a silk-lined burrow on the cliffs waiting to prey on beetles and other tiny creatures.

Lundy 'earthquake'

LUNDY BIRDS

Where the rock is sheer and bare, and ledges provide suitable sites, colonies of seabirds including **Guillemots**, **Razorbills**, **Shags** and **Kittiwakes** breed. Lundy is nationally recognised for its variety of wildlife, especially for the importance of its breeding **Manx Shearwater**. These birds nest like the puffin, deep underground in a burrow. Over 90 percent of the world population of Manx Shearwater breed on islands around the UK and Ireland. Based on a survey in 2001, estimates suggest there are now no more than 166 pairs on Lundy. In 1940 the population was thought to be over 1000 pairs and perhaps many more.

Sadly, the seabird that gave the island its name is now in a similar position. Historically the **Puffin** is a very important part of the island's wildlife. In 1939 some 3,500 pairs bred on Lundy, but surveys over the last 60 years show it has declined almost to the point of extinction. Less than 10 breeding pairs were present on the island in 2000. The culprits are thought to be rats. They eat the eggs and chicks of many seabirds. The fight to bring puffins and Manx shearwaters back to their former level on Lundy has already begun. The rodents are now being controlled, so only time will tell.

The few puffins that nest on the island arrive in mid-March. They burrow underground and lay a single egg. After hatching, young puffin remain hidden in their nest. Adults and young leave Lundy in late July or early August, and spend their non-breeding season feeding across the north Atlantic.

The **Oystercatcher** is a common breeding bird on Lundy, its piping call echoing off the surrounding cliffs. Here they tend to breed on ledges, just out of reach of the waves.

Gannets no longer breed on Lundy – the last recorded egg was in 1903 – but they can often be seen offshore. The nearest nesting colony is at Grassholm, just off the Pembrokeshire coast nearly fifty miles away.

The bird observatory on Lundy has a long and illustrious history of records. Accounts in the past of seabirds and numerous rare and exotic migrants rank the island among the best bird migration watching points in Britain. While the observatory is no longer operational all year round, the variety of birds has not diminished. While **Skylark** and **Meadow Pipit** are common summer residents, but it is the number of warblers and other migrants, as well as much rarer birds, that make Lundy a great spring and autumn destination for watchers. **Hoopoe**, **Dotterel**, **Golden Plover** and even **Montague Harrier** and **Merlin** are seen most years.

LUNDY MAMMALS

The **Pygmy Shrew** is Lundy's only native terrestrial mammal. All other land mammals, such as mice, rabbit, rat, deer, goat and sheep, were introduced by man. The pygmy shrew is tiny, with a very long snout. It makes a network of runways in vegetation on top of the ground, where it feeds on insects, spiders, snails and woodlice. Listen for their high-pitched calls as they hunt through the matted grass.

While **Feral Goats** browse the west and northern cliffs, songbirds and herds of surprisingly large **Sika Deer** shelter amongst shrubby vegetation on the eastern slopes. Early morning is the best time to catch the deer feeding in the steep valleys. But one thing has always fascinated me. Just how can a deer with such large antlers simply vanish into seemingly impenetrable **Rhododendron** scrub? The fact is that a network of small tracks and trails weave their way through tunnels in the tangled vegetation on the edge of the cliff, but the trick is none the less impressive.

LUNDY SEA LIFE

The waters around Lundy are rich and clear, with so many rare species that it was designated as Britain's first Marine Nature Reserve in 1986.

Up to 70 **Grey Atlantic Seals** live all year around Lundy. Most are found around the eastern and northern sides of the island. **Basking Shark** can also be seen anywhere off the coast, and Lundy is one of the best places in the country to see these magnificent creatures.

Lundy Marine Highlights

Baked Bean Sea Squirt – relatively small members of their family about 1.5cm across. They live in dense communities on rocky seabeds, boulders, wrecks and can even be found on the landing beach jetty.

Ballan Wrasse – the largest of their kind found in British waters. They can reach up to 60cm in length and live to be several years old.

Brown Crab – one of the most common crabs found around Lundy. They have black-tipped pincers and a distinctive pink-brown colour with a 'pie-crust' edge to the shell.

Common Brittlestar – delicate creatures, close relatives of the starfish.

Common Hermit Crabs – commonly found in rock pools on the shore as well as underwater.

Common Prawns – closely related to lobsters and crabs. Usually found in rock-pools, they keep to the base of kelps or hide in cracks and crevices in a rocky seabed.

Common Sunstar – this distinctive animal is found on hard seabeds at depths below 10 metres. It is closely related to starfish.

Common Urchins – members of the starfish family. They are found down to depths of 20m, usually on boulders in kelp forests.

Puffin, which gave the island its name

Corkwing Wrasse – commonly found around rock- and boulder-strewn areas.

Cotton Spinners – members of the sea cucumber family and related to starfish.

Crawfish – relatives of lobsters and prawns.

Cuckoo Wrasse – a fish of deeper water than Ballan wrasse, usually from 10 metres downwards to 30m. The males can be very colourful.

Devonshire Coral Cup – like the sunset cup-coral, it is a solitary coral.

Elephants Hide Sponge – live down to a depth of about 20m in and around the kelp forests.

Featherstars – look like plants, but are actually animals.

Jewel Anemones – very small but beautiful creatures about 1 cm across, but can grow in massive numbers on a rock face.

Kelp – brown seaweeds, found from the bottom of the shore down to a depth of 20 metres.

Lesser Spotted Dogfish – belong to the same group of fish as sharks, rays and skates.

Long-clawed Squat Lobster – small relatives of lobsters and prawns, their body reaches only 3cm long.

Pink Sea Fan – colonies of individual animals.

Plumose Anemones – very tall, usually ghost–white anemones that are very common around Lundy.

Pollock – belong to the same fish family as cod. Similar in appearance, they lack the barbel on the chin.

Red Band Fish – rather mysterious ribbon-shaped fish, most often found in deep water such as Scottish sea lochs.

Red Sea Finger – actually colonial soft corals related to the 'hard' corals of the tropics.

Ross Coral – a colonial animal, not actually a coral but a type of sea mat.

Spiny Spider Crabs – large scary-looking creatures with long spider-like legs that can gather together in big numbers at certain times of the year.

Sponges – common, several different species live around Lundy. Branching Sponges are very basic animals which have numerous different growth forms.

Sunset Cup Coral – easy to recognise due to their bright yellow colour.

Trumpet Anemone – live up to their name.

Yellow Anemones – very delicate, and grow in large numbers.

Many of these creatures can be found elsewhere around the shores of Devon, but seldom all together.

Moorland

DARTMOOR

Devon contains two high areas of true moorland. Dartmoor is the biggest and highest moor in the county towering over South Devon. Reaching over 620 metres high and covering nearly a thousand square kilometres, it is England's largest true wilderness and was designated a National Park in 1951.

Spring arrives early in the south-west, even up on the moors. By March, along the upper reaches of the river Teign, colourful drifts of wild daffodils bloom in the Dunsford reserve near Steps Bridge. Here the fresh green shoots of bracken are already peeking from beneath their rusty veil of last year's fronds. Soon the valley woods and scrubby copse erupt in a patchwork of bright translucent greens, yellows, oranges and reds, as their leaves unfurl in the soft spring light. Ravens cronk and buzzards mew as the rushing peat-brown streams of spring gradually calm to a glassy sheen. Then, as a leafy canopy begins to shade the woodland floor, the bright green foliage of oak and bracken darkens. Summer warmth is sweeping across the moor.

Now up on the drier parts, the pale waxy lanterns of the whortleberry flowers appear, while yellow bog asphodel spangles the soggy mires where white flags of cotton grass dance in the breeze. Wheatear flit between the boulders, disturbed by grazing ponies, lapwings cry, and the songs of skylark and meadow pipit fill the sky. Suddenly great swathes of the moor begin to bloom – first the deep purple of bell heather, and then the paler pink of true heather, Ling. But all too soon the vivid songs and colours of summer begin to fade. Days shorten and a damp coolness pervades the air. The first autumn mists swirl around the granite tors. Fronds and leaves turn to gold as black, red and purple berries swell. When the last tourist coaches leave, black-faced sheep once again have the narrow roads to themselves. The bustle of summer has gone. Dry stone walls winding up onto the open moor now stand proud, and snow flurries soon build on the stones. Dartmoor is different from the surrounding Devon countryside – wild, high and remote.

Dartmoor is made up of two high moorland plateaux, along with conifer plantations, oak woods, rivers, streams, pools and farmland with fields, walls and hedgerows. It also has several picturesque villages that are popular with visitors. The influence of people on the moor is not new. Most of Dartmoor was once wooded up to some 600 metres, and above that it was probably

Dartmoor: Foxtor mine and leat | 101 |

treeless. But climate change and the activities of people had a big impact on the nature of the moor. There is good evidence that large areas of moorland were once farmed, and ancient settlements lie scattered across the moor, most from the Bronze Age over 3000 years ago. Now Dartmoor has a rich and varied mix of habitats, but some are much larger than others. Huge areas of peat formations, known as blanket bog, cover the two main summits. They contain both wet and dry places, unlike the valley bogs. Most of these wet areas are shallow, but some mires can be dangerous, reaching a depth of nearly 4 metres – deep enough to engulf a horse – so it pays to be wary. Despite popular myth, none are bottomless. Compared to the open moor, bogs are rich in wild plants and animals. Moorland plants can broadly be divided into wet and dry.

Wet Bog

WET BOG PLANTS

Cotton, **Deer** and **Purple Moor Grass** can all be found in bogs with bright green squelchy carpets of sphagnum moss. **Cross-leaved Heath** and rushes are common here, yet even in the wettest places occasional dryer islands of **Heather**, **Bent** and **Sheep's Fescue** grass can be found, sometimes thick with bracken.

Bogs are poor places for plants to survive, especially on the higher moors. Even in the valley bogs, the ground contains few nutrients and the wet condi-

Sundew

tions leach away what little goodness remains. But some plants have found a solution – they feed on animals. **Sundews** are well named; glistening in the sun, their sticky, tentacled pads trap and digest flies and other hapless insects. The **Butterwort** is another carnivorous plant employing a similar strategy, but this time the entire strap-like leaf rolls slowly inwards to consume its prey.

WET BOG REPTILES AND AMPHIBIANS

Difficult to reach and seldom disturbed by grazing animals, the drier islands of heather are a favoured place for **Adders**, our only venomous snake. Basking in the morning sun, their cryptic camouflage makes them difficult to see, even when close. But they are shy, sensitive creatures, usually detecting our presence by vibrations through the ground, slipping away long before we catch a glimpse of them. They prey on the **Common Lizard**, which is plentiful in the drier parts, and on small mammals. The **Grass Snake** also frequents the valley bogs, where it may hunt for **Frogs** and **Palmate Newts**.

Dry Moor

MOORLAND PLANTS

On the drier parts, away from the bogs, bell heather, ling and grasses dominate the growth. Where bracken and gorse grow, few other plants can compete, but in patches between the taller vegetation, smaller plants can flower profusely. Down on hands and knees is the best way to appreciate the beauty of **Tormentil**, **Milkwort** and tiny **Heath Bedstraw** flowers.

In late summer the real glory of the moors comes into its own. This is when **Heather** and **Western Gorse** bloom.

MOORLAND INSECTS

Heather moor is not rich in insect life. The **Fox Moth** is probably the most commonly seen insect. Its silky-haired, fawn-coloured caterpillars can be very conspicuous on grassy tussocks between July and September. The **Emperor Moth** is bigger and more spectacularly marked, though less common. The adults emerge during April and May, and can be seen flying fast and low over the heather. Its caterpillars are coloured, a striking bright green with black hoops, and can be found hidden among the heather in summer. The only other moth to be easily seen on the moor, the **Plume Moth**, is small and delicate in appearance and is normally found amongst bracken.

Meadow Brown is the most frequently seen butterfly on the moor, often found in the same sort of places as the **Gatekeeper** and **Small Heath**, whose caterpillars all feed on grasses. **Common Blue** and **Small Copper** are only locally common, while the **Grayling** keeps to the drier slopes. The **Large Blue** was once declared extinct and although still rare, it has recently been reintro-

Silver-washed fritillary butterfly

Keeled skimmer dragonfly, female

duced. Of all our butterflies it leads one of the most complicated lives, feeding on wild thyme as a caterpillar and relying on a particular species of myrmica ant to carry it down inside its nest. Here it survives the winter, pupates and then emerges as an adult.

During the warmest months, near bracken or woodland, you may also see **Silver-washed**, **High Brown** and **Pearl-bordered Fritillary** butterflies. **Purple** and **Brown Hairstreak** butterflies are restricted to where they can find their food plants, blackthorn and oak leaves. In contrast the beautiful little **Green Hairstreak** butterfly is much more widespread, especially where whortleberries flourish.

Beetles are common, but rarely seen as most keep close to the ground. The exception is the spectacular green-coloured, rose-spotted **Common Tiger Beetle**. These active little hunters can be seen racing and flying over the heather in early summer searching for food – they eat other insects.

The only bee which is commonly active on the high moor throughout the warmer months is the handsome **Bilberry Bumble Bee**.

On fine summer days both **Damselfly** and **Dragonfly** can be encountered around the valley bogs. Their aquatic larvae prey on other creatures in shallow boggy pools before emerging as adults. Elsewhere, on blanket bog and higher valley pools, it is only the more powerful, fast-flying dragonflies that are likely to be found in mid-summer.

Dartmoor granite wall

MOORLAND BIRDS

Soaring high above or perched on a granite tor, the **Buzzard** is a common sight in any season. So too is the hovering **Kestrel**. But the tiny **Merlin** and fast flying **Hobby** may only fleetingly be spotted during summer, which is also when the rare **Montagu's Harrier** may occasionally be seen. **Short-eared Owl** and **Hen Harriers** also hunt out over the grassy plains and heather moor in spring and autumn, and sometimes over winter. At any time of the year, the cronking call of the **Raven** can be heard and is the easiest way to distinguish this large moorland scavenger from any passing rook or crow.

The moor really comes to life in summer. This is when with the song of **Skylark** and **Meadow Pipit** comes pouring out of the blue. Listen too for the **Cuckoo**, which can be heard anywhere on the moor looking for pipit nests from April to early June. On the high tops a few nesting **Red Grouse**, **Dunlin** and even **Golden Plover** may still be found.

Where gorse and bracken dominate, **Stonechat** and **Whinchat** can be seen flying between the bushes, and up and down to the ground. Amongst the granite clitter-strewn slopes and alongside stone walls, the flashing white rump of the **Wheatear** is an easy way to identify this striking bird. It has its English stronghold on Dartmoor.

Above an altitude of 400 metres, be sure to check out any **Blackbirds**. They may occasionally be found here, but so too can the rarer **Ring Ouzel** with its characteristic white bib. A summer visitor, the ring ouzel can be found near quarries and abandoned buildings. Their favourite place however, is among old tin workings, especially where mounds of mining spoil have created a chaotic landscape of miniature gorges and mountains, such as around the Warren House Inn in the middle of the moor.

In the wettest places with grassy tussocks, a few **Curlew** and **Lapwing** may still breed during the early summer months, but both these birds are becoming nationally scarce. More commonly, **Snipe** may also nest in these places. Alongside fast flowing moorland streams and rivers, the aptly named **Dipper** and **Grey Wagtail** do what their names imply – they are both active birds, seldom standing still.

Dense conifer plantations provide a home to only a few, but interesting, birds: **Crossbill**, **Nightjar** and **Redpoll** are not otherwise found commonly on

Dartmoor ponies in winter

the moor. In some of the native oak woods around the moorland margins, the spectacular **Pied Flycatcher** and **Redstart** breed regularly. Even the **Dartford Warbler**, once a real rarity, is now becoming more widespread wherever there is a good covering of gorse. It is again returning to Trendlebeer Down near Yarner Wood, after a devastating moorland fire.

MOORLAND MAMMALS

Apart from the obvious Dartmoor ponies, cattle and sheep, **Rabbits** must be the most commonly seen mammal on the moor. Dartmoor is probably one of the earliest places where rabbits were introduced to Britain as food in the 12th century. Place names that contain the word 'warren' are a reminder of their economic importance in the past.

Mink and **Otter** are both widespread on the rivers in the south-west of England, and evidence of both can be found on the moors. But the otter is less likely to be seen by day, as it tends to be a highly nocturnal creature, like the badger. The fox is much more commonly encountered.

The **Dartmoor Fox** is said to be paler than its lowland relatives. But this is probably because as there are fewer trees they spend more time out in the open, under the sun. While lowland foxes feed extensively on earthworms, in the acid, calcium deficient soils of the moors, worms are absent and snails rare. Only unappetising large black slugs are commonly encountered. So moorland foxes feed mainly on **Short-tailed Field Voles**, which are common. Foxes are opportunist scavengers, taking any carrion they find. Despite plenty of anecdotal evidence to the contrary, they seldom kill sheep or lambs.

Stoat prey principally on rabbit, and **Weasel** hunt for even smaller mammals: **Woodmice** and voles. The high-pitched shrieks of the tiny **Common Shrew** can be heard as they hunt for their insect prey amongst the heather and rough grass.

Dartmoor Tors

The highest rocky peaks on the moors in Devon are known as tors. This is where the granite core of Dartmoor is exposed. Blasted by wind and drenched in rain, frozen over winter and baked dry in summer, thousands of years have sculpted them into fantastic shapes. Only in the deepest cracks can life survive the rigours of such extremes. Here tiny liverworts, mosses and ferns cling to a fragile existence. **Black Spleenwort**, a few stunted **Whortleberries** and **Heather** may be found growing between the bare, broken, weathered boulders. Ponies, cattle and sheep all take shelter in the lee of these tors, and their nibbling keeps down any growth. But the tops provide a grand bird's eye view of the surroundings, and all the biggest birds use them as a perch.

Haytor rock from quarry

Moorland Woods

After the last ice age had ended some six thousand years ago, when freezing arctic winds had given way to warm temperate weather, a vast forest covered most of lowland Britain. In the south-west of England it was dominated in parts by great oak woods. Over time, people gradually cleared the land, and only in the most isolated parts did some remnant of that original wildwood survive. High on Dartmoor a few vestiges of **Oak** wood still cling to the hillsides today. They are remote and spooky places in the mist, with gnarled twisted trunks bedecked with thick growths of moss, lichens and ferns.

Three ancient patches of wood are recognised on Dartmoor: Black Tor Beare, Pile's Copse, and the most weird, wonderful and famous of all – Wistman's Wood. This is a place where fantasies and legends are born. The wood consists mainly of the common **Pedunculate Oak** with some **Rowan**, often known as Mountain Ash. What makes this place so remarkable is not the species of tree, although they are growing close to their maximum altitude – it is their incredible stature. Many of the trees are between 300 and 500 years old yet no more than 6 metres high. Most are nearer half that height but twice as wide. Their growth is extremely stunted and severely twisted, and they are rooted amongst a jumble of gigantic mossy boulders. The result is an extraordinary tangle of rock and bough entwined in a writhing mass, seemingly frozen in time. Whatever the cause – nibbling sheep or harsh moorland weather – Wistman's Wood is an eerie place, more suited to the realms of some magical, fantasy land. Today few trees grow on the moor apart from recently planted conifer forests. Perhaps the most remarkable fact about Wistman's Wood is that it survives at all.

MOORLAND WOOD PLANTS

Ferns flourish, actually growing on the trees, lodged in forks and along suitable branches. **Common Polypody** and the **Broad Buckler** fern are typical plants of this arboreal habit – known as epiphytes. And they are not alone. **Whortleberry** is commonly seen sprouting from the trees, and amazingly, another tree even grows on the oaks – Rowan. Down between the rocks several other plants may be found: **Ivy, Honeysuckle** and the occasional **Sallow**. Beneath the trees a community of other plants also grows: **Great** and **Hair Woodrush, Narrow Buckler Fern, Common Male Fern** and **Bracken**, which dominates the rock clitter beyond the woods. The yellow flowered **Tormentil** and charming little **Wood Sorrel** are also both common.

EXMOOR

Designated a National Park in 1954, only some 77 square miles of the moor's 265 square mile area is contained within the county boundary of Devon. Most of Exmoor lies in Somerset, and the central upland plateau of The Chains forms its heart. This is a vast blanket bog containing the largest area of **Deer Grass** in southern England. Here the rainfall is highest, and the bog a giant sponge.

Streams quietly trickle from its sodden ground, as on Dartmoor. Only rarely has its natural efficiency been tested, most notably the deluge that swept through Lynmouth in 1952 – a national disaster.

Much of Exmoor's uplands lies between 200–300 metres, but Dunkery Beacon rises to nearly 600 metres at its highest point. The high ground is divided by fast-flowing streams dashing through deep, densely wooded valleys. Most of the streams emanate from the northern edge of the moor, where wooded slopes give way to coastal heathland. Here impressive cliffs fall steeply into the Bristol Channel.

The influence of the sea is far greater on Exmoor than on Dartmoor. Exmoor summers are relatively warm, and winter temperatures less severe. Yet despite the fact that over one and half metres of rain falls, more days of mist occur and more snow falls here than elsewhere in the south-west, and really hard frosts are rare.

The wildlife of Exmoor is very similar to other moors in the south-west. But Exmoor is renowned for its large numbers of the biggest native wild animal in Britain – **Red Deer**. These magnificent creatures have probably survived here since the end of the last Ice Age. The best time to watch them is during the rut, when the stags fight for possession of their harem of hinds. Beginning in mid-October after the first frosts, it reaches its peak in the third week, before ending in mid-November.

Vixen suckling cubs in den

Sand Dunes

In mid-summer, the grey light of dawn greets the rolling surf and laughter of gulls. The rising sun casts your shadow over the sandy shore, and the warmth of a new day is tempered by the coolness of waves swirling gently around your feet. Sinking into the softness, your footprints leave a temporary trail until the turn of the tide. Fine sand is the essential ingredient for a good beach. If you pick up a handful, the mixture of shell fragments and finely ground grains of rock that run through your fingers have a quality quite different from other beaches nearby. Although carried by the same currents and deposited by waves, sand has a composition and character unique to every coast. Underwater it may have travelled many miles, and that movement is continued onshore by the breeze. As the tide ebbs from the beach, more sand is exposed. Sun and wind rapidly dry the surface layers. Gusts then gather up the finest grains, driving them into great piles, and a dune is born. They can eventually reach over 30 metres high, yet strong winds will continue to move them. The process is intriguing to watch; it occurs wherever there is fine sand, from the driest desert to the shores of Devon. Sand particles blown up the gentle windward slope pour over its crest. Then, in a series of miniature landslips, the sand grains slide down the steeper face. Blasted and battered by gales, with new supplies of sand reinforcing the front, ranks of dunes slowly advance inland. In this way dunes move relentlessly forward.

Rising sea levels at the ending of the last Ice Age caused massive dunes to drown coastal forests in a sea of sand. Occasionally the evidence for such dramatic events comes to light when winter storms scour away a beach. At Thurlestone in south Devon, a gale revealed the remains of a peat bed embedded with wood for just a few short weeks. It was a remarkable glimpse into another era. Twisted roots and trunks of trees lay where they had fallen over six thousand years ago.

Dune formation is a process that seems to have accelerated during historical time. The discovery of old buildings inundated by sand provides proof of their massive movement. North Devon is famed for the scale of these natural ramparts made of sand. The vastness of Braunton Burrows is one of the largest and most famous in Britain, while Dawlish Warren in the south is smaller, though no less important. Both are fine examples of extensive sand dune systems.

When sand is on the move, it seems as if nothing on earth can stop it. But plants can – almost. By trapping and binding the grains, they can at least slow the movement to a trickle. The pro-

Dawlish Warren dunes with marram grass

Sea holly

Evening primrose – common on Dawlish Warren

cess of consolidation begins down on the shore. Where waves deposit a strandline of rotting seaweed, nutrients leach into the sand. Few plants can survive the harshness of the conditions here between land and sea. There is no soil or humus, and the only minerals come from the remains of shells. At high noon on a cloudless day, the sun bakes the beach. Temperatures can soar to 60°C, while at night they plummet. Drying winds bring more salt-laden sand, and the returning tide threatens to drown the top of the shore. So only during summer when this area is beyond the tide's reach, can a few special plants take root.

DUNE PLANTS

The flora of Braunton Burrows is particularly well studied. Although there is a military firing range at the northern end, some of the most interesting marked trails allow access when permitted. Watching for red flags and reading firing notices is a sensible precaution. Dunes can be unstable enough at the best of times, and much movement has already taken place at Braunton over the years, not all of it natural – some is caused by human disturbance. The biggest threat to dunes is from people trampling and lighting fires, from litter, cars and even building. For all their enormous scale, sand dunes are fragile. If the protecting plants are destroyed, the dunes can easily be blown away.

The dunes at Braunton Burrows are basically arranged in two parallel uneven ridges. On the seaward side, **Sea Rocket**, **Saltwort**, **Orache** and creeping **Sea Convolvulus** may be among the first pioneers to germinate every year. Both **Sea Spurge** and **Sea Stock** can grow at the top of the shore, while **Sea Holly** actually needs the tide to disperse its seeds. But these plants cannot cope with too much sand rising around them. Others can: **Sea Couch Grass** has the ability to grow with a rising dune, at least for a while, although half a metre is its limit. Above this height a stronger, more vigorous plant takes over: **Marram Grass**, which is the best builder of dunes. As sand is trapped between its growing stems and roots, it slows the processes of wind erosion and the dunes grow taller. Braunton boasts some of the biggest dunes in the British Isles.

Marram grass also helps other less tolerant plants to survive by consolidating the first line of sand mountains on any dune – these are the so-called Yellow Dunes. They seldom exceed more than 15 metres, and are often very mobile. Yellow Dunes have no soil and marram is the dominant growth, but between

Sand crocus, with common daisy for scale

Bird's-foot trefoil

its growth some **Sea Holly, Sea Spurge, Red Fescue Grass, Sand Sedge** and **Cat's Ear** may also be found. **Prickly Saltwort** and the upright green spikes of **Portland Spurge** are especially characteristic of western dunes.

Beyond the Yellow Dunes lies a small valley, known as a dune slack. The next line of dunes can grow bigger, perhaps as high as a ten-storey building. Yet, incredibly, even these monstrous mountains can move. From their sandy tops, looking down through the wind-jostled leaves of marram grass, you can see more sheltered, older dune slack, often with some permanent pools of water, known locally as pans. These support a more interesting community of plants and animals. The water is often a rich reddish brown in colour, caused by an oxide of iron. When compared with the rest of Devon, rainfall here is low, but at night, even in summer, temperatures can plummet. The heavy dew that results helps many plants to survive the driest months.

The next ridge of so-called Fixed Dune is much lower and relatively static. Further inland a scattering of sand hills then merges into sandy pasture. Many different types of mosses grow on the dunes, but the older, Grey Dunes have the best growths. In the pans where the water table is close to the surface, a swamp can develop. Here a variety of **Creeping Willow** grows which is only common in the south-west, and in France and Belgium.

Away from the permanent pools **White Bent Grass** is abundant, while the damp ground is ideal for **Sea Pearlwort** and a special orchid. The **Marsh Hellerborine** is distinct among British orchids, for its purple-brown and white flowers produced in July and August.

Lichen commonly carpet the ground in the damper parts of the dune, as well as two species of filamentous green algae. **Sea Rush** flourishes in the wettest parts of the dune slacks, with **Dwarf Yellow Sedge** growing wherever willow trees seem to do best. Rushes are not the most charismatic of plants, and while the **Clustered Club Rush** is common, a scarce **Club Rush** only does well at Braunton. But the species that plant enthusiasts seem to get most excited about is a rather sprawling, pale purple flower – **Water Germander** – which is rare elsewhere in Britain.

Among the most attractive little flowers to be found on the Burrows are two violets: the rare yellow **Seaside Pansy** and the more common blue **Hairy Violet**. Both are a delight to find in early summer. Even common plants such as

Fleabane, Horehound and **Woodsage** can look different here – they are more hairy in appearance. This is an adaptation to the drying winds of summer and an effort to retain moisture.

Bracken is highly invasive, and not a beneficial plant as it suppresses the growth of other more interesting vegetation nearby. Parts of Braunton Burrows have been invaded despite efforts to control it. But where rabbits have nibbled the grass and produced a fine turf, some surprisingly tall **Centaury** plants grow. More interesting are the pale pink flowers of **Sea Storksbill**. This is an Atlantic speciality confined to the west coast, with rather sticky, undivided leaves. It is smaller than its common cousin that also grows here. Another flower frequently found only in the south-west of England during summer, is the yellow **Lesser Hawkbit**. Other rarities found at Braunton Burrows include **Shore Dock, Sea Knotgrass** and **Shore Weed**.

For real floral excitement nothing can beat a crawl around Dawlish Warren. The tiny **Sand Crocus** is so rare that it is found nowhere else on mainland Britain. This exquisite little pale lilac-blue flower hugs the turf so tight that you need to get close just to see it. Add this to the fact that it only opens in spring sunshine around midday, and you have a flower that is difficult to find. Yet, extraordinary as it may seem, this tiny beauty not only occurs on the nature reserve, but also on the adjacent golf course. Here, despite the spiked shoes of the players and regular mowing, it seems to thrive on the fairway.

The wetter areas of Dawlish Warren also put on a fine floral display of spectacular **Marsh Orchids** every year. Sometimes thousands of one of our most beautiful wild orchids can be seen here in May and early June.

DUNE INSECTS AND SNAILS

High summer is the best time for insects on the dunes, especially when hot in July and August. **Painted Lady, Peacock, Small Tortoiseshell, Common Blue, Small Copper, Red Admiral** and **Fritillary Butterflies** can all be seen during the summer season.

Some butterflies are migratory and large numbers of **Painted Lady, Red Admiral** and **Large** and **Small White Butterflies** cross the Channel every year. At Dawlish Warren on the south coast, these bright winged migrants are a common sight as they stop to refuel from nectar rich flowers. Mass migrations are not so frequent, but when they do occur the results can be spectacular. Once in a while hosts of **Clouded Yellow Butterflies** appear all along the south coast.

At dusk, **Common** and **Smoky Wainscot Moths** can be seen flying among the Marram. By morning they hide again. Many moths are not strong flyers, and easily attract the attention of hungry birds during the hours of light. In contrast, some day-flying moths are positively eye-catching. So how do they survive? The **Six-Spot Burnet** and **Cinnabar** are common moths in dunes. The black and yellow football-striped caterpillars of the cinnabar moth feed on the highly noxious leaves of ragwort. Indeed, so dangerous is this weed it can kill a horse if accidentally consumed with hay. Cinnabar caterpillars seem to chew its leaves unharmed, concentrating the plant's poisons in their bodies. But there is method in this madness. The caterpillar stripes serve as a warning to birds that

Garden tiger moth, 'Woolly bear' caterpillar

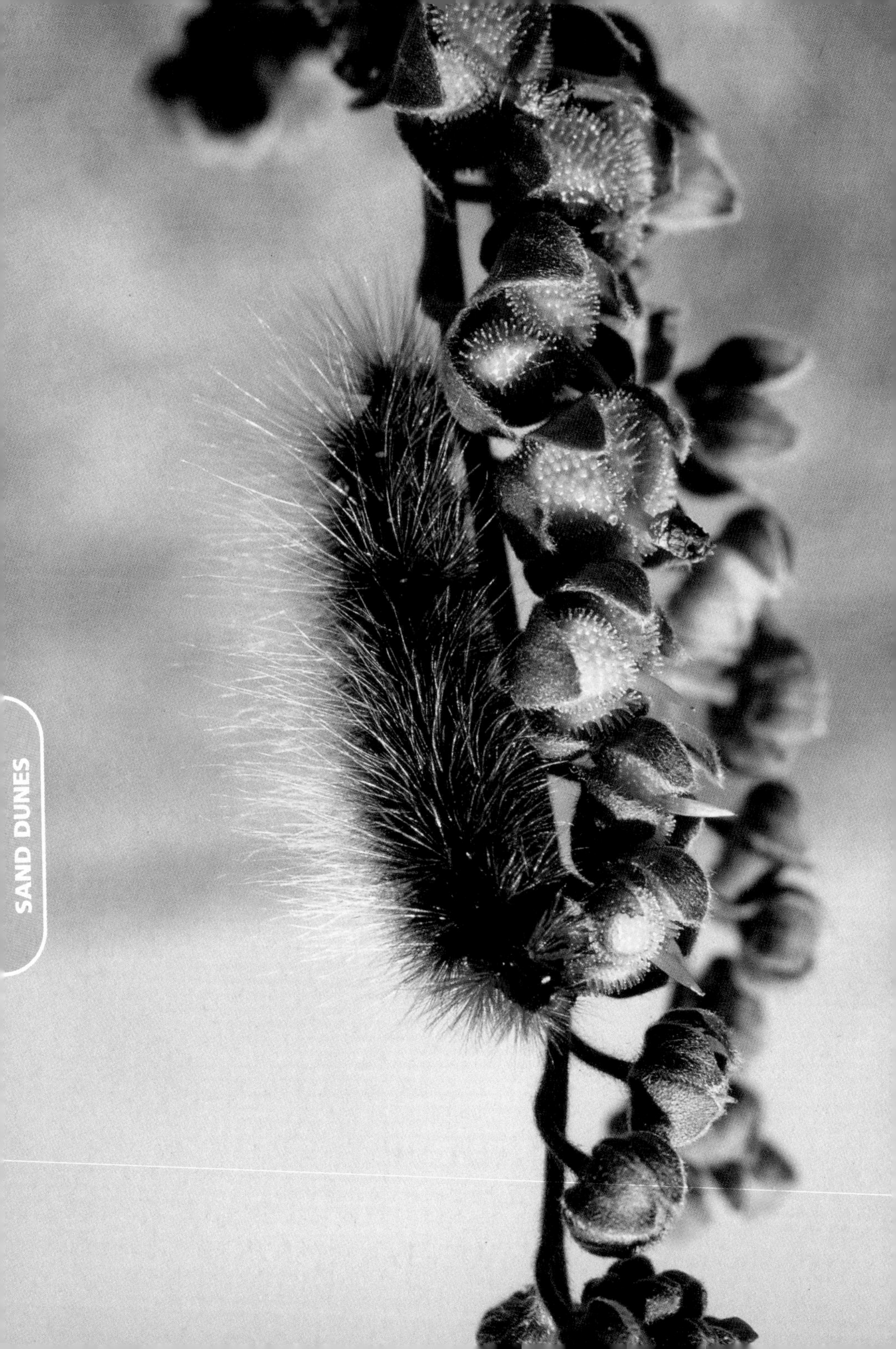

they are highly toxic if eaten. These powerful alkaloids then persist in the adult moth. The old adage of once bitten, twice shy is certainly true for birds. They seem to remember the horrid taste and leave the cinnabar well alone.

In some years large numbers of large hairy caterpillars may be found marching across the dunes. These are the caterpillar of the **Garden Tiger Moth** searching for a suitable place to pupate.

Other insect life is more often heard than seen – grasshoppers and crickets especially. Sand dunes support many of these agile creatures. The **Great Green Bush Cricket, Common Ground Hopper, Mottled Grasshopper, Meadow Grasshopper** and **Common Field Grass Hopper** can all be found in sand dunes.

Swamps and pools in the dune slacks attract many dragonflies, especially the fabulous large **Golden Ringed** and smaller **Ruddy Sympetrum**. They can be seen flying during the warmest months, from June onwards. Early in the morning, often before sunrise, the mature dragonfly nymph climbs out of the water, where it may have spent several seasons. Hanging on some vegetation, its back then splits open to reveal the soft crumpled wings of an adult. The emergence from its old nymphal case can take an hour or more, and it takes the same amount of time again before its wings and body harden sufficiently to fly. Perhaps even more amazing, is that its emergence has remained virtually unchanged since before dinosaurs ruled the earth. So if you want to witness a primeval scene, before breakfast is the best time to find these amazing creatures hanging around a pond.

Pulverised sea shells produce high levels of calcium, and that is good for building more shells. **Snails** are abundant: **Banded, Pointed** and **Common Garden** all occur in great numbers. But the hot sand is a limiting factor for any creature living in the dunes. Their survival strategy is simple: during summer, as the day gets going, so do the snails. Although the temperature at the surface of the sand may reach 60°C, just off the ground it can be bearable. Upwardly mobile molluscs climb the vegetation during the worst heat of the day. Here they wait for the cool of night to begin feeding.

Other snails head the opposite way. Even when sand is searing, just a finger's depth below the surface it can be cool and moist. The **Sandhill Snail** will bury itself if the weather gets too hot. This is a tactic also employed by some solitary wasps. One of the most active of these **Digger Wasps** is the **Spider Hunting Wasp**. Harmless to humans, the female first finds a spider in the dunes before paralysing it with her sting. She then carries the spider to a suitable site and furiously begins excavating a tiny burrow. Inside she lays a single egg on the spider before she reseals the chamber. Other wasps in the dunes provision their nests with an assortment of caterpillars and other larvae. When the wasp grub hatches it finds a ready-made meal.

DUNE BIRDS

In winter **Merlin, Harriers**, even the occasional **Short-eared Owl** all visit sand dunes from time to time. Summer finds several ground-nesting birds taking up residence. **Shelduck** and **Wheatear** will breed in old rabbit holes, while **Skylark** and **Meadow Pipit** seek out the quietest parts of the dune slacks.

DUNE REPTILES AND AMPHIBIANS

Lizards are commonly found in dunes, but snakes are rare. Frogs and toads may also occasionally frequent some of the ponds.

DUNE MAMMALS

Rabbit, **Fox**, **Woodmouse**, **Field Vole** and **Shrews** are the most frequently encountered creatures, particularly on the scrubby landward side of dunes. Even if you do not actually see them, their diggings as well as tracks and trails criss-crossing the dunes show up clearly in the early light of the morning sun.

Painted Lady butterfly

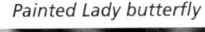

Sea Cliffs

Few experiences in life rival the fascination and fear of standing on a cliff edge in the teeth of a howling Atlantic gale. The taste of salt on your lips, wind tearing at your clothes and the scream in your ears is like nothing else on earth. Far out in the Atlantic Ocean, a storm is racing towards the north Devon coast. Far below, the sea swell produced by the depression arrives ahead of the rain, rolling relentlessly towards the cliffs. Rank upon rank of huge waves rear their heads before toppling forward as their crests tear open, revealing a wall of white water hurling itself at the rocks beneath your feet. The tremor from each gigantic explosion sends a judder through your body as the energy of a thousand miles or more is unleashed on the sea cliff.

The history of the earth's formation is held within its rocks. There are few places where these can be more clearly read than in the sheer face of a towering coastal cliff. No matter whether the rock originally came from the fiery furnaces of past volcanic activity, ancient reefs, deposits of lime-rich shells or flood-borne silt many millennia ago, they now lie exposed and are gradually being worn away. The destructive energy of wind and wave is powerful. But cliffs have other forces at work on them, which, although more subtle, can move mountains bit by bit.

Most rocks acquire fractures and faults as a result of titanic pressures and strains. Winter rain seeping into these cracks can freeze overnight and expand. The resulting forces shatter the surface, prising off slabs of rock and growing hairline cracks into yawning fissures. Year after year the relentless cycle of freezing and thawing eats into the coast. Down below, at the foot of the cliff, the mechanical action of waves scours away softer rocks and gnaws away at its base. The resulting overhang eventually becomes unstable and falls into the waves. Slowly but surely the sea gains at the expense of dry land.

The cliffs of Devon offer breathtaking scenery, sumptuous sea views and a feast of wild flowers. Nesting sea birds add another dimension, filling the invigoratingly pure air with their cries. As a vantage point for watching their nesting behaviour, aerial antics and migratory movements, cliff tops are unsurpassed. The county has two very different coastlines, totalling over 160 miles in length. Access is good, with a famed coastal footpath running almost the entire distance.

East Devon contains the oldest part of the Jurassic Coast, a World Heritage Site. Beer Head is the most westerly exposure of chalk in England, and the coastline here is shaped by the sea into many dramatic arches and stacks. Between Beer and Branscombe,

*Cormorant nest colony
on Mewstone*

the Hooken Landslide also has some spectacular pinnacles of chalk. Today, a path runs from Branscombe Mouth through a landslip that took place in 1789, and offers some of the best views along that part of the coast. But when compared with other south-west cliffs, those in North Devon reach new heights – Great Hangman and Holdstone Barrows rise to over 300 metres.

Devon has several headlands well known for the number of migrating birds seen every year. Though few have the facilities or convenience of Berry Head in Torbay, others can be less busy and offer even more spectacular scenery. Prawle Point and Start Point on the southernmost tip of Devon provide an interesting coastal walk, with a chance of seeing **Grey Atlantic Seal** as well as **Basking Shark**. Prawle in particular is renowned for its wide variety of migrant birds.

The majestic undulating cliffs of both coasts are not continuous, but broken by numerous rocky inlets, enticing sandy coves and estuaries. While the dramatic northern cliffs offer a home to more seabirds, the south has a softer landscape, rich in many wild flowers. Some places, however, can offer the best of both worlds.

BERRY HEAD

BERRY HEAD PLANTS

Situated on the south coast of Torbay, near Brixham, the imposing limestone outcrop of Berry Head is famed for its seabird colony as well as its unusual wild flowers. The tops of the garrison walls are a good place to see **Wild Thyme** growing in profusion. (More details of other plants can be found in *Limestone & Chalk* chapter.)

BERRY HEAD INSECTS

Although Berry Head is perhaps best known for its birds, many other creatures can also be found here. The headland is a great place to watch migrating butterflies, moths and even dragonflies pass through in spring and autumn.

BERRY HEAD SHARKS AND SNAKES

For real excitement, watch the water. On warm summer days when barely a ripple disturbs the sea below, it is always worth looking for a large dark shape with a triangular fin and tail cutting the surface. **Basking Shark** will feed lazily along plankton-rich tide lines close inshore. As a toothless filter feeder, they pose no danger to people, unlike another creature found on the cliff tops – the **Adder**, Britain's only venomous snake. Considering how common they are along cliff tops, it is surprising how few people encounter them. Despite their reputation, these snakes are not aggressive, and being very sensitive to the vibration of approaching footsteps, they soon slither out of harm's way. Depending on your attitude to these fascinating creatures, you will actually be lucky to see one.

Adder at Berry Head in defence posture, ready to strike

Fulmar

BERRY HEAD BIRDS

On the sheer cliffs below the Old Redoubt fortress, a series of narrow ledges become the home for the biggest gathering of **Guillemots** on the South coast of England. Up to a thousand birds breed here every year. Even before winter has ended, the first Guillemots appear on the cliffs. Guillemots are gregarious in the breeding season, crowding the ledges in raucous groups; they make no nest, just relying on the extreme conical shape of their egg to prevent them rolling over the edge.

Fulmar, **Kittiwake**, **Herring Gull**, **Shag** and **Jackdaw** all use the cliffs at Berry Head for breeding, but the most exciting seasonal resident is the **Peregrine**. Sometimes a fulmar will try, with occasional success, to oust a sitting peregrine from her sheltered nest. Fulmar are so called tube-nosed seabirds, related to albatross but smaller. Although graceful-looking birds with tremendous soaring skills in the fierce updraughts of the cliff, they can be a formidable foe. Their name comes from their foul habit of disgorging the evil-smelling contents of their stomach at their enemy. Birds of prey and predatory gulls tend to keep well clear of a fulmar on its nest.

Berry Head is important as a migration point for birds, as well as a breeding site. Over 200 different species have been recorded on and around the headland. During the spring and autumn, migrating birds treat the reserve more like an avian airport. Feathered travellers turn the site into a transit lounge. Many of the birds breed in other parts of Britain or elsewhere in the world and are just passing through. Because it is such a prominent site, Berry Head is an obvious landfall when seen from far out to sea. Strong winds at migration time can also push sea birds on passage close inshore. The glimpse of a **Great Shearwater**, **Black Tern** or **Pomarine Skua**, even through rain, can be an exciting distraction to a cliff top walk. On the top of the headland, the scrub can hide **Redstarts**, **Willow Warblers** and **Sedge Warblers**, whilst more open grassy areas occasionally provide a welcome stopover for **Wagtails**, **Wheatears** and **Pipits**, especially early morning before many people arrive.

Compared to the warmer months, winter can be quiet. **Grebes** and other water birds may be spotted out to sea more easily on an overcast day. Cliff headlands tend to be exposed, windy sites, but sunshine and unseasonal warmth can produce a **Stonecha**t or two, and even the occasional **Dartford Warbler**.

BERRY HEAD MAMMALS

Apart from rabbits and the occasional early morning fox, the most interesting mammals to be seen occasionally from Berry Head are **Grey Seal** and **Dolphin**.

HARTLAND POINT

HARTLAND POINT BIRDS

Hartland Point, on the north Devon coast, is a rugged towering cliff. On a clear day it offers far-reaching views out over the Atlantic and the island of Lundy. The powerful lighthouse also acts as an attractant for birds that migrate at night. **Wheatears** and **Warblers** are common passage visitors around the small coves, scrub and rocky promontories. One of the most exciting scenes in summer is to watch long, low strings of **Manx Shearwater**, flashing black and white as they bank and skim over the waves. Several thousand have been counted in a single day, and the record is over 15,000 early one morning. Feeding parties of **Gannets**, **Kittiwakes** and **Auks** may all be seen during summer.

THE GREAT UNDERCLIFF

Cliffs are dangerous places at the best of times, where the unrelenting forces of weathering and coastal erosion dismantle or wear away the hardest of rock. But where coasts consist of softer material, the effects can be even more dramatic.

On Christmas night 1839, on the east Devon cliffs near Axmouth, the coastguards on duty witnessed a terrifying event. In the darkness they heard a horrible sound 'resembling the rending of cloth'. The ground shook, great cracks opened beneath their feet and out to sea they saw a great dark shape rise from the water. But this was no seismic tremor from deep within the bowels of the earth; it was the shock waves produced by a vast section of cliff collapsing. The

Peregrine feeding chick in eyrie

catastrophic event was precipitated by an unusually wet autumn and heavy rain leading up to Christmas. Daylight revealed the extent of the disaster. A gigantic landslip of some six hectares of farmland, complete with hedgerows, trees and even a field sown with wheat, had slumped towards the sea. Separated by a gaping ravine over half a mile long and the height of a 40-storey building, the subsidence had thrown up a new reef offshore. But the new island did not last for long: consisting of soft calcareous rock, it was soon worn away by the waves.

By February, more earth movements extended the rift, as a series of smaller landslips crept alarmingly along the cliff. But it was the first big Christmas landslip that drew the Victorian crowds. They must have gazed in wonder, not only at the scale of the disaster but the wheat that continued to grow and ripen in its new slumped location. On the 25th August 1840 we can only try to imagine the scene as six thousand people gathered to watch the harvest from the cliffs above. A team of reapers, armed with sickles tied with blue ribbons and accompanied by maidens, complete with brass band, crossed the newly named Great Chasm to the stranded section of cliff – now called Goat Island.

Although complex, we now know the reasons for the unstable conditions at the Undercliff. The rocks that make up the coastline here are composed of ancient chalk beds, sandstone and a type of shale, which is more like a crumbling slate, along with impermeable clays. Many of these layers were laid down during the age of dinosaurs, and now form part of the famous Jurassic Coast, a World Heritage Site. As rain percolates through the rocks, it causes the waterlogged shales to slide over slippery clays, leading to the occasional landslip.

Today, nearly four and a half miles of coastline between Axmouth and Lyme Regis is a rugged and dangerous place, still prone to subsidence. This is the Great Undercliff. Here, the largest naturally regenerated ash forest in Britain dominates the dense, almost impenetrable scrub and hidden crevasses. For some people it is a nightmarish place, where you stray from the path at your peril. For others it is wild and dramatically beautiful wilderness, teeming with life. But visitors should be careful: every year unwary walkers are lured from the well-worn path and rescue services are called out to find the lost or injured.

The importance of the Undercliff can be seen from the fact it was designated a National Nature Reserve in 1955 and is maintained by English Nature. It must be the only reserve in the country where large parts keep moving away. However, the subsidence is usually gradual, measured in months rather than minutes, which is why the cataclysmic slump in Victorian times became such an historic event.

UNDERCLIFF PLANTS

The Undercliff has the closest feel to a 'rainforest' anywhere in Britain. The place is a botanist's dream, with many rare and endangered plants and a wealth of orchids found here: **Bee, Marsh, Greater Butterfly, Early Purple, Pyramidal** and **Fragrant Orchid**, along with **Marsh Helleborine** and **Twayblade**, and even one of the strangest of its kind, the solitary, shade-dwelling **Bird's Nest Orchid.**

The surrounding grasslands are calcareous in nature. For more information of the life of such places please refer to the chapter on *Limestone & Chalk*.

UNDERCLIFF INSECTS

The Undercliff is also rich in insect life: butterflies, moths and glow worms during the warmest months.

UNDERCLIFF BIRDS

The bird life of the ravines is as good if not richer than any Westcountry woodland. It is also good for warblers during the spring and autumn migration. The Undercliff with its sea breezes and updraughts is also an excellent place to watch **Buzzards**. They nest in the inaccessible woods or on ledges, and can usually be seen hunting along the cliff tops. **Kestrel** are also resident here, hovering in the sea breeze.

TYPICAL BIRDS SEEN FROM A SOUTH DEVON SEA CLIFF
(based on surveys from Prawle Point)

Resident birds – **Raven, Buzzard, Kestrel, Cirl Bunting** and **Yellowhammer**.

Autumn passage migrants – peak time is the first two weeks of September. Early morning is best:

Waders – the best conditions for waders are an easterly wind followed by calm weather. **Bar-tailed Godwit, Curlew, Common Sandpiper, Dunlin, Grey Plover, Knot, Oystercatcher, Redshank, Turnstone, Spotted Redshank** and **Whimbrel**.

Sea birds – After a gale can be an especially good time for seeing less common sea birds. **Arctic Skua** and **Great Skua, Arctic, Common** and **Sandwich Tern, Black-headed Gull, Common Gull, Gannet, Guillemot, Herring Gull, Kittiwake, Lesser Black-backed Gull, Manx Shearwater, Razorbill** and **Shag**.

Land birds – **Chiffchaff, Willow Warbler, Whitethroat, Garden Warbler, Grasshopper Warbler, Blackcap, Pied Flycatcher, Tree Pipit, Wheatear, Whinchat, Wagtails** and **Swallow**.

Bird's-nest orchid; Butterfly orchid

UNDERCLIFF MAMMALS

Roe deer are common, as are signs of **Badgers** – their trails and latrines. **Dormice** seem to thrive in the understorey of hazel, where an abundance of honeysuckle grows. They strip its stems for nest material, and visit its flowers for nectar. **Pygmy Shrew**, our smallest insectivorous mammal, is also common. The rich insect life of the area combined with plenty of old hollow trees also provide ideal conditions for **Bats**.

Roe deer

Sea Shore

To watch a child peer into another world for the first time is to relive your own first experience. Rock pools are full of weird and wonderful forms of life from an environment that is alien to most of us – the sea. As a hunting ground for inquisitive minds, they are second to none. Beneath their mirror-smooth surface, trapped by the outgoing tide, is a fantastic collection of marine life. Here prawns prance, crabs creep and squat lobsters skulk. Rock pooling must surely be one of the simplest and most satisfying pleasures for children and big kids alike. But what makes our sea shore so rich?

The vast expanse of the Atlantic Ocean bathes British shores in its relentless eastward drift and warm prevailing winds. The ocean movement owes its origin mainly to the mighty Gulf Stream, which starts in the Caribbean Sea. It is a warm flow, some 80 kilometres wide and 500 metres deep, driven by the rotation of the earth and unfailing south-west winds. Crossing the ocean into the colder waters of the western Atlantic, its spreads into four currents and slows. Turbulence brings up nutrients from the sea floor to feed a rich supply of microscopic marine life. Now it is more accurately known as the North Atlantic Drift. While the main flow passes up the west coast towards Scotland, another enters the English Channel. And so the Gulf Stream gives rise to the incredible fertility of the seas around our coast.

Jutting out into the ocean, the south-west peninsula divides the drift in two. The coastlines of Devon are very different. While the north is pounded by foaming Atlantic waves, the south is washed by the usually calmer waters of the English Channel. And this is reflected in the character and nature of the shores.

Most estuaries have sand spits across their mouths. Sandy beaches are common, but shingle ones also occur, especially on the north coast. Except for where sand dunes build, beaches are backed by high, often spectacular cliffs. These stony faces usually rise above a wave-cut shelf, where a veritable marine zoo is revealed at low tide.

ROCKY SHORES

Twice daily, a vast area of seabed is exposed to the air, and twice it is drowned. Unlike a sandy shore, where animals can burrow for safety, on rock there is often no place to hide. Even captured in countless rock pools at low tide, thousands of creatures must survive the rigours of the elements and terrestrial predators until the sea returns. Sunlight is essential for seaweed growth, but heat

Dawlish Warren sands: sunrise with cormorant on groin

they can do without. Warm water can reduce the levels of life-giving oxygen, as well as threatening to cook the inhabitants; rain dilutes its salinity, and gulls and crows will feed on anything they can reach. Then, in summer other scavengers arrive, often hunting in packs. A combination of curiosity and excitement brings an army of groping fingers and sweeping nets, and the harvest is a haul of hapless creatures plucked from their temporary homes and placed in plastic buckets. Even among young children the hunting instinct is strong. But creatures replaced within a few minutes generally survive unharmed. If upturned stones are also put back the urge is satisfied and life in the pool can continue undisturbed, at least until the next ebb tide.

Rocky shores are rich foraging grounds, and not just for children. Different rocks weather and erode at different rates and in different ways, so some shores have better rock pools than others. However, the life of shores is more heavily influenced by their exposure to wind and wave than pure geology. In terms of their wildlife they can be divided into exposed, semi-exposed and sheltered shores.

Exposed shores are open to the full force of the Atlantic, hammered by exploding waves and scoured by strong currents. This applies to much of the north Devon coast, although headlands in the south also take a battering. Only a special sort of life can survive here. Mussels and barnacles dominate these rocks, living in their own bomb shelters.

Semi-exposed shores suffer less violent conditions, often protected by headlands or rocky islets offshore. These are the most common shores in the south-west, and are usually dominated by forests of wrack – brown seaweeds.

Sheltered shores are mainly found along the south coast of Devon, especially inside estuaries and creeks.

The life of a rocky shore is not randomly scattered. The highest part of the shore has the most limited marine life because it is exposed to the air for longest. Here life must also withstand being heated by the sun and drenched in fresh water when it rains. Further down the shore, these hazards become less of a problem. The result is that different parts from top to bottom are dominated by different forms of life best able to cope with the conditions. The banding this produces can sometimes be quite striking. So the life of a rocky shore between high and low water marks, can be broadly divided into zones – the **Upper, Middle** and **Lower Shore**. On a shallow sloping site, these zones may be wide, while on a steep face they will be narrow.

Teign estuary sunset

Lesser black-back gull

Common tern with chick

Sea spray can affect the growth of other plants on rocky shores way above the level of the highest tides. But marine plant life is special. Although the pounding of waves can be severe, the sea is relatively warm. Light is gradually filtered as it passes through water so most weed growth occurs in shallow seas. In the clearest water it may reach 50m of usable light; in a turbid estuary, perhaps just waist-deep. Conditions are very different to those on dry land.

At low tide, swathes of seaweeds hang limp. They are more correctly known as marine algae. Dry on top, they remain moist underneath, covering the rocks in a slippery shaggy rug. As the sea returns, they are transformed. Their drab fronds lift and sway with the waves. But in the sea, the biggest problem is staying put. At the base of each plant is a tangle of root-like limbs called a holdfast, which clings onto the surface of the rock. The holdfast of algal weeds has no other function than to hold on. Seawater supports the plant, so a rigid stem is unnecessary as long as the fronds can float. But the plant must be strong enough to withstand the battering action of waves and exposure to fresh air. Over 700 different types of marine algae live on British shores. Some are more dominant than others, and it is these algae, along with the animal life, that best distinguish the different zones.

Working our way down from the top of the shore, the highest part – beyond the reach of even the biggest tide – is known as the splash zone. Here, few plants can survive on bare rock, being baked in the sun or drenched in salt spray. Yet colourful orange and grey **Lichens** seem to thrive. Lichens are extraordinary. They are made up of two different plants living together – an algae and a fungus. Both gain from the relationship, surviving in places where each would perish alone. Below the splash zone lies a band of black lichen right on the high water line, where they are only briefly immersed in the sea.

Upper Shore

UPPER SHORE PLANT LIFE

The upper shore starts at the high water mark. Here, the first band of algal growth festooning the rocks is a small brown sea weed appropriately known as **Channel Wrack**. It can withstand long periods out of water, but eventually merges and gives way to **Spiral Wrack** further down the shore. Here **Purple Laver** weed also grows. Where freshwater flows over the rocks, it seems to inhibit brown weed, but allows long green strands of soft tubular **Gutweed** to fill the space.

UPPER SHORE ANIMAL LIFE

High tide brings out the **Black Periwinkle** to graze the lichen zones. Tiny scavengers roam these finely nibbled lichen lawns. **Sea Slater** look like large woodlice, and along with marine **Bristletails**, feed mainly at night. Life here in rough weather can be tough. The **Acorn Barnacle** probably has the best bomb shelter of all; cemented to the rock, it grows where no other life can survive. At high water it snatches at passing plankton, using hairy legs as filters, and at low tide it battens down the hatches.

Different periwinkles live at different levels on the shore. **Rough Periwinkle** can wedge themselves into cracks and crevasses if waves threaten to dislodge them. Their rough shells appear to give them a better grip than smooth-sided ones. Even if they do get washed down the shore, like all periwinkles, they seem to know their place and simply migrate back again.

Middle Shore

MIDDLE SHORE PLANT LIFE

Bladder Wrack is often the most dominant sea weed of the middle shore, especially if exposed. On sheltered shores the **Knotted Wrack**, which is the longest lived but least adaptable of the algae, is often more common. The air bladders of both seaweeds help them to float, so avoiding being beaten by waves on the rocks.

Shore crab and serrated wrack

Limpets at low tide

The most abundant green algae here is likely to be bunches of finely branched, feathery green **Cladophora**, which can only grow where protected by tougher brown wracks. The green **Sea Lettuce** also grows well where sheltered.

MIDDLE SHORE ANIMAL LIFE

What a whopper! The joy of finding a large crab on the shore is always evident from the squeals of delight from adults and older children. Young children seem to have an innate wariness of anything that has large claws. But even the biggest crab is only about four years old. The **Edible Crab** is migratory, living and spawning offshore. A female crab can carry over 800,000 eggs underneath her body. Hatching releases the tiny larvae to take their chance in the current. They become part of the plankton, the free floating soup of miniature life that forms the smallest link in the food chain of the sea. The larvae settle as young crabs on the shore, and as they mature they move into deeper water. Keeping young and old apart is one way to reduce competition. **Shore Crabs** cope better with the vagaries of living between the tides, remaining low down on the shore, even as large adults.

Two types of periwinkle are common on the middle shore. The **Flat Periwinkle** lives and feeds on the Bladder Wrack. The **Edible Periwinkle** grazes the rocks, and is the most widespread of its kind found on all shores.

Sea anemones are solitary, sedentary animals. They feed on tiny particles trapped by their tentacles. Unlike the **Snakelock Anemone**, which is confined to pools at low tide, the **Beadlet Anemone** can survive out of water by withdrawing its feeding tentacles inside its soft body. They can often be found above pools, clinging to overhangs and shady rock walls.

The shape and strength of a **Limpet** shell might lead you to suppose that this is a creature evolved to survive big waves and big beaks, and you are right. The limpet is not restricted to any one zone on the shore. Their large muscular foot clamps down hard, creating a 'vacuum' to prevent them from drying out or being easily dislodged. They also vary in shape. Flatter ones live in the most sheltered places, and tall domed ones wherever there are more waves, usually higher on the shore.

The **Common Mussel** attaches itself to the rocks by threads. Large numbers often huddle together. They are filter feeders, drawing water between their shells through a siphon. Despite their thick shells, they are preyed upon by many creatures: **Starfish**, **Dog Whelk**, **Oystercatchers** and **Eider Duck** all feed on mussels. Given half a chance, if a shell is gaping, even crabs will have a go.

Lower Shore

LOWER SHORE PLANT LIFE

Serrated Wrack, with a saw-tooth edge to its fronds, is the most common seaweed of the lower shore. Tufts of calcareous **Red Algae** and **Pepper Dulse** are also the start of the red seaweeds, highly shade-tolerant algae, capable of living in much deeper water than brown wracks. Red algae are also prone to bleaching in the sun, so may not always be bright red.

LOWER SHORE ANIMAL LIFE

Bread Crumb Sponges tend to grow encrusting the rocks in the humid shelter of brown seaweeds. Other animals actually live on the fronds of these algae. Several different types of **Hydroids**, tiny colonial living creatures, grow on stalks attached to the seaweed, where they feed like miniature anemones, catching particles of food on their tiny tentacles.

Topshells superficially resemble periwinkles, but can easily be distinguished by the presence of a little depression in the centre of the underside of their shell. Their tops are also often worn, revealing a glistening underlayer of mother-of-pearl. **Purple**, **Grey** and **Thick Topshells** can all be found, but the biggest and most beautiful is the **Painted Topshell.**

Sea Slugs, **Scale Worms** and **Tube Worms** can all be discovered on the lower shore. They are all vulnerable to drying out and can only survive out of water for a short time. Even the most common fish of the lower shore, the **Blenny**, can tolerate being out of water, as long as it remains moist.

Some animal life of the lower shore can also live further up. They survive in rock pools, but life here can be precarious, especially for any fish left stranded by the tide. Wading in the shallows gives a bird a distinct advantage over shorter legged competition. While **Herons** often search shorelines, the most exotic-looking bird to be seen hunting here was once a real rarity. The last decade has witnessed a dramatic increase in the brilliant white **Little Egret**. Taking up residence in some of the country's most sought-after seaside locations, they are now almost a common sight on some of Devon's shores. Stalking the shallows, they hunt for small fish.

Laminaria Zone

Beyond the lower shore lies deeper water, seldom ever exposed by even the lowest spring tide. This is where the Kelp beds begin. **Kelp**, or Laminaria as it is more properly known, is a tough plant. It needs to be, as wave action here can be powerful. Light levels are low, and competition for space is intense as conditions are less stressful than further up the shore. Five different types of kelp can be found around British shores. The longest, the **Sea Belt**, can grow up to four metres long and its holdfast can be bigger than a man's hand. Marine life is abundant in the Laminaria zone. One small mollusc, the **Blue-rayed Limpet**, actually lives on the Laminaria. In the most sheltered places here, small fish,

Rocklings and **Shanny** are common, and **Goldsinny Wrasse**, **Butterfish**, **Cornish Lumpsucker**, **Long-spined Sea Scorpion** and **Lesser Sand Eels** can all be caught in a small net. Even the young of large, deeper water fish take shelter in the Laminaria zone – **Pollack**, **Mullet** and **Whiting**.

Sandy Shores

SANDY SHORE ANIMAL LIFE

Devon has a wealth of fine sandy beaches on its north and south coasts: some shingle, and a few more pebbly in nature. But some of the most enchanting are the so-called Shell Beaches. Many sandy coves have parts where different sea shells seem to accumulate. Occasionally, where wind and tides combine in some exceptional way, vast quantities of exquisitely formed empty shells are regularly washed ashore. North Devon has some of the best known shell beaches, where tiny **Cowrie Shells** are some of the rarest and most beautiful to find.

The constant movement of sand means that plants cannot get a grip, and the few animals that manage to live here must survive by digging. The burrowing **Sea Urchin** and **Sand Eel** can both be found on the south coast. Another inhabitant of these undersea deserts is the notorious **Weaver Fish**. They bury themselves in the sand, leaving just the tip of their dorsal fin exposed. If disturbed, this is raised – it carries a painful poison. Injected into the bare foot of an unwary bather, the result can be excruciatingly painful, although not life-threatening.

Every tide brings a potential harvest for the beachcomber. Strandlines fascinate people, and deliver a twice-daily food service for scavenging birds. Several days of strong prevailing winds from the west can bring the best haul. Then the tides leave real evidence of the Gulf Stream's exotic origins. The seeds of tropical trees, big Macuna and Entada beans from the Caribbean and South America are not uncommon treasures. Another castaway from the south Atlantic is the **Goose Barnacle**. Attached to floating wood, they sometimes end up on our shores.

Violet sea snail and by-the-wind sailor

Goose barnacles washed on shore

Wind is used as a form of propulsion by some warm sea creatures. The **Violet Sea Snail** floats beneath a raft of bubbles in search of its favourite prey – vast swarms of **By-the-wind Sailors.** At first glance they appear to be a small jellyfish, but they actually belong to another group of complex colonial marine animals. The closely related infamous **Portuguese Man-of-war** also uses the wind as a means of propulsion. They, too, have a float, albeit bigger and gas-filled, which catches the breeze. Thankfully, while the By-the-wind Sailor are often found on our shores, its bigger, more dangerous relative is rare in British waters.

There is one creature however, that relishes the almost transparent, long trailing tentacles of the Portuguese man-of-war. The **Leatherback Turtle** is seemingly immune to its agonising stings. The largest of five turtles occasion-ally found around south-west costs, the Leatherback is also the most frequent to be washed ashore. Sadly they seldom are found alive, but in summer can sometimes be encountered at sea.

The remains of fish, egg cases, and crabs litter the strandline, but by far the greatest quantity of flotsam and jetsam is made up of seaweed. If you disturb a piece, a hopping hoard of tiny creatures leaps into action – **Sandhoppers**. Related to shrimps, they appear to be curled up and sideways compressed, a shape that may help them burrow in the sand. The power of their hop is impres-sive, as some can jump over two metres. They are scavengers, feeding on the decaying life of the strandline, and can occur in large numbers. Up to 25,000 have been counted on a single square metre of sand. Along with kelp flies, they can be more of a nuisance than any menace, but after dark they do seem attracted to light. Beach barbeques glowing strongly at night seem particularly inviting to these nocturnal hoppers. As some species can also bite, they can really get the party going elsewhere.

Off Shore

OFF SHORE ANIMAL LIFE

Basking Shark are big but harmless plankton feeders, common around south-west coasts in summer. They are fair weather summer visitors that sometimes occur in large numbers. Any coastal headland – such as on Lundy and Berry Head – is a good place to watch, but they can also come quite close inshore at places like Slapton Sands.

Grey Atlantic Seals are resident around Lundy, and can occasionally be seen off any headland. Their pups are born in late summer, and during the Autumn young pups are often washed on to north coast beaches.

Porpoise and **Common Dolphin** can sometimes be seen in good numbers, but more usually keep to small family groups. While their movements are unpredictable, they are regularly encountered in Lyme Bay and off Plymouth Sound.

Slapton Ley

Slapton is special. Situated between Dartmouth and Start Point, a massive beach of shingle and sand over 3.5 kilometres long has created a large natural lake by the sea – a freshwater lagoon. It is the biggest lake in the south-west, and the largest area of freshwater to be found along the coast of the English Channel. It contains some 82 hectares (200 acres) of open water. So important is the Ley for wildlife that it is designated a National Nature Reserve and Site of Special Scientific Interest. Owned by the Whitley Wildlife Conservation Trust, which also owns Paignton Zoo and the Living Coasts in Torbay, it is managed by the Field Studies Council, which runs many excellent environmental courses each year.

The Ley is divided into two parts: the dense, reed-covered higher Ley to the north, which has strictly controlled access for people; and to the south, the larger open-water lower Ley. Here the nature trail, which winds its way around the reserve and has access to two large bird hides, makes it a popular place for students and casual visitors alike.

SLAPTON PLANTS

The shingle ridge that protects the freshwater Ley from winter surf contains fascinating plants. The **Yellow Horned Poppy** with its papery yellow flowers is easy to find during summer. **Sea Radish**, **Sea Spurge**, and the white-flowered **Sea Campion** are all common, along with the more colourful **Sea Pink** or **Thrift**, **Sea Mayweed** and rarer **Sea Holly**. Perhaps the most striking plant, standing tall, is the **Viper's Bugloss**. However, it is the water plants that most visitors find so attractive. Throughout the spring and summer a succession of flowers colours the reed beds fringing the Ley, as well as the marshy margins and the shallows. Among the most spectacular are tall spikes of **Purple Loosestrife** and **Great Willow Herb**, and the golden discs of **Fleabane**. In the water, beds of **Water Crowfoot** and **Water Forget-me-not** form blue and white mats across the surface. One of the rarest plants, the tiny-flowered **Strapwort**, is perhaps the easiest to overlook – it is found nowhere else in mainland Britain.

SLAPTON INSECTS

Throughout the spring and summer many different butterflies can commonly be seen while walking the nature trails that encircle the Ley.

Slapton Ley in spring, with swans, mallard and reed growing

Closer to the water, in sheltered spots away from the wind, hundreds of dainty **Common Blue Damselflies** can also be found decorating the reeds. Try looking along the Ley shore near Slapton Bridge on a warm summer's day in May and June. Emerging in the early hours from their aquatic larval stage, the delicate lace-like wings of the damselflies sparkle in the sun. Many **Dragonflies** can also be seen during summer. Slapton Ley is one of the best places in Britain to watch these harmless insects as they feed on smaller prey. Indeed, 17 of the 41 species recorded in the UK have been discovered on the reserve.

More insects can be found underwater – joining a pond dipping group from the Field Study Centre is the best way to learn more about the Ley. Among the most obvious insects, the **Water Boatmen** can easily be seen rowing away on the surface. There are two types but you have to get close – the **Greater Water Boatman** swims on its back, and the **Lesser Boatman** swims on its front.

SLAPTON FISH

Amongst anglers, Slapton Ley is famed for its fish, particularly the weight of its **Pike**. These can grow to a formidable size, being quite capable of grabbing a duckling, but more frequently feeding on smaller **Rudd** or **Roach** and even the occasional frog. In some years, during warm summers, great shoals of young fish can be found in the tepid shallows. This is when shadowy glimpses of large pike may be seen lurking just beyond the shoals, quite close to the shore. Slapton Bridge and opposite Torcross car park can be good places to look.

At Torcross, the most southerly end of the Ley, a culvert carries any overflow from the lower Ley under the road and out to sea. In spring this is also a way in for some extraordinary little creature – **Elvers**. They are tiny, almost transparent young eels that have just completed one of nature's most epic journeys. After crossing the Atlantic Ocean, from their birth place in the abysmal depths of the Sargasso Sea, they sense the freshwater outflow from the Ley. At the height of the spring tide they work their way upstream under the cover of dark and, in a wriggling horde, pass through the wet shingle, along the culvert, and up and over the weir. Eventually they enter the freshwater Ley. Incredible as it may seem, their parents and hundreds of thousands of their kind, left European waters the previous year as large, fully mature adults all heading for their spawning grounds.

Water forget-me-not, water crowfoot and yellow horned Poppy

Coot with young

Pike

Now some of their offspring returning to the English Channel have found the freshwater flow from the Ley. But they have one last trial to survive. As a new day dawns, after swimming and struggling across three thousand miles of ocean, some tiny elvers will meet a wretched end – greeted by a reception party of hungry herons and kingfishers.

SLAPTON BIRDS

The bird life of Slapton Ley reflects the rest of its natural wealth. One of the most common birds is the **Coot.** There may be 50 pairs or more nesting around its margins in the warmest months, while in winter up to 3,000 have been counted. Several pairs of **Mute Swans** breed at Slapton, but most overwinter on estuaries like the Teign just to the north. It is during the coldest months that wildfowl seem to take over the Ley – Slapton is a great place to watch large numbers of ducks. Usually there are a few **Goldeneye** and many more **Tufted Ducks**, **Teal** and **Wigeon**. Winter is also the best time to keep a look out for the **Bittern** skulking among the reeds. All year round, one of the biggest attractions here is the **Great Crested Grebe.** Up to five pairs of great crested grebe breed every year at Slapton, and in spring their courting antics can easily be seen from the hides that overlook the lower Ley. Whilst not uncommon over the rest of the country, these handsome birds reach the westernmost limit of their range at Slapton.

Reed beds really come to life in summer. They provide important cover, feeding and nesting places for many birds, including the **Reed Warbler**, **Sedge Warbler** and even the occasional **Grasshopper Warbler**, and, the most interesting by far, the rare **Cetti's Warbler**. More commonly found in southern Europe, this was first recorded at Slapton in 1974, and now up to 15 pairs breed regularly. It seldom ventures out of the vegetation; its call is explosive – a sudden and surprisingly loud burst – but its song can best be heard in spring when it is claiming its patch of reed bed. Cetti's warbler lay some of the most unusual and spectacularly coloured eggs of all British birds – a rich deep red.

One of the most exciting spectacles at Slapton is the annual migration of **Swallows**. In late August and early September, thousands of these beautiful birds collect in vast swooping and chattering flocks to roost in the reed beds overnight. But they may only be present for a few days at a time. Once refuelled, feasting on the abundant insect life of the reserve, and with the weather conditions just right, they leave on their long journey south to Africa. And they are not the only ones: **House** and **Sand Martins** do the same in smaller numbers, but tend to leave our shores earlier than swallows, while **Starlings** and even flocks of **Wagtails** may be seen roosting amongst the reeds throughout the winter months.

SLAPTON MAMMALS

The most famous resident of the Slapton reserve is unfortunately the most shy and nocturnal. The **Otter** is seldom seen during daylight, but its fishy droppings, or spraints as they are known, are easier to find. Deposited on prominent tree stumps, tussocks of grass or lake-side stones, they can be commonly encountered on a walk around the Ley.

The **Mink**, however, is much more likely to be seen by day. Easily mistaken for an otter at a distance, it can be surprisingly bold. Related to the European otter but originating from North America, mink were accidentally introduced after escaping from fur farms in the 1950s. Since then they have taken to the British countryside with a vengeance. Their success is probably due to their diet. They thrive on a much more varied feast than our native otter, which mainly eats fish, especially eels. Mink can be encountered almost anywhere on the reserve, but can most often be seen around the boats at Slapton Bridge.

Little grebe on floating nest

Otter

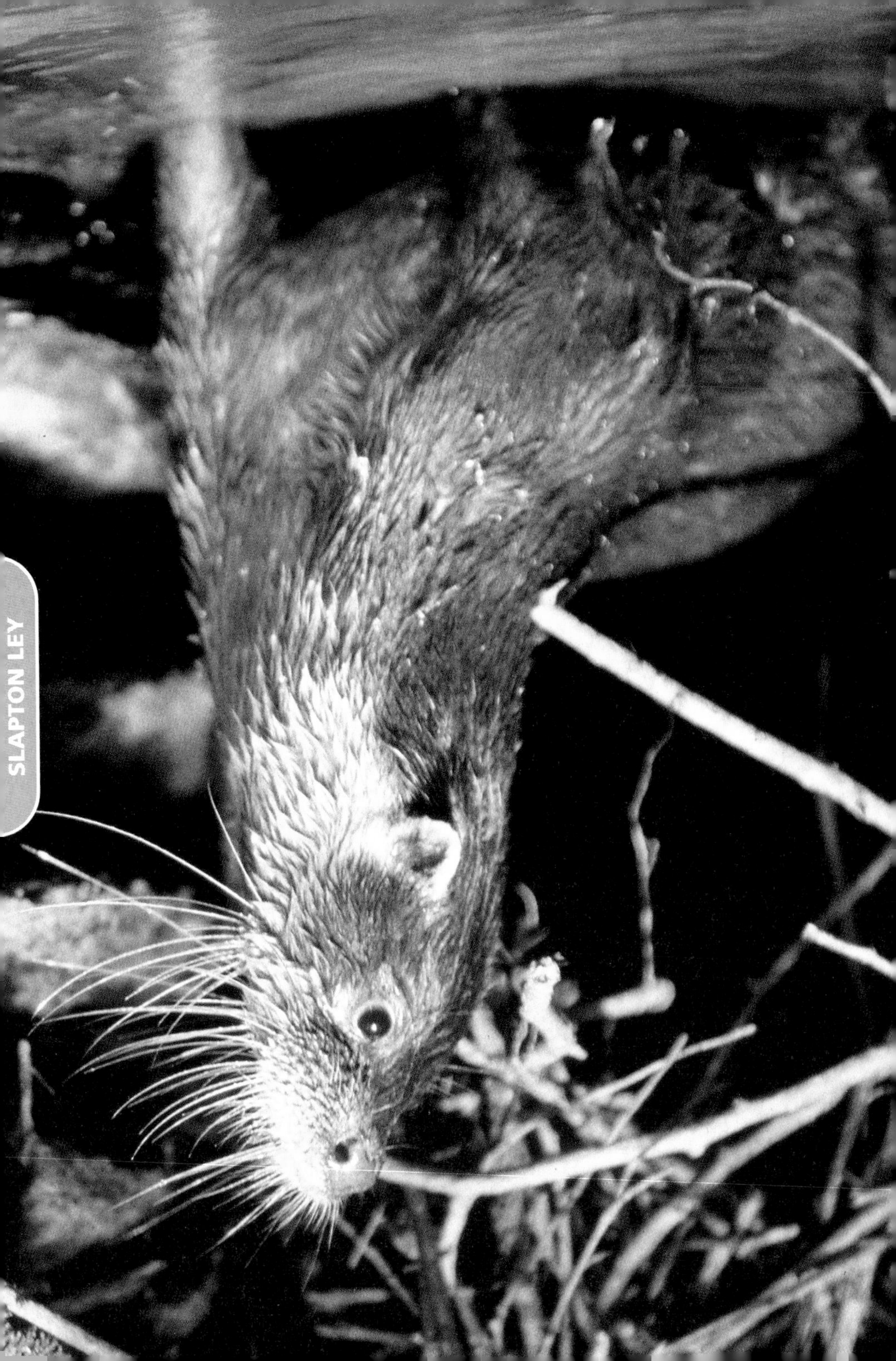

Wood Pasture and Parkland

The traditional park of grassland scattered with large old trees is nothing new. From prehistoric times to the present day people and wildlife have enjoyed their wide open spaces and welcome summer shade. Many plants and animals have developed an intricate relationship with ancient trees. In more recent centuries wood pasture and parkland was created mainly for two reasons - landscaping around a grand house or a deer park to enhance the view and provide a handy supply of venison.

DEER PARK

As the warmth of September fades and the golden hues of Autumn spread through the trees, the year of the fallow deer begins with the rut. It is the middle of October when the bucks fight each other for the prize of fathering the next generation, and this is the best time to watch them. The females, called does, are gathered in harems where they are defended by a dominant male – the buck. It is noisy and spectacular time as buck fallow deer work themselves into a frenzy. The females just feed and watch from the sidelines.

When antlers are fully regrown and ready, the fallow deer rut begins soon after the first frosty spell. Bellowing and thrashing at vegetation is just a prelude to the main event – the clash of antlers. It is a sound which carries far in the stillness of a frosted dawn. The biggest bucks start by sizing each other up, walking side by side, antlers held high so the full expanse of their weaponry may intimidate their rival. The challenge can also end at this point if one buck decides he is not up to the fight, turns and runs away. Or he may not. Suddenly heads drop, the bucks swing round and charge at each other. Their entire body weight is hurled into battle. The force of impact sends a ripple down their flanks. Drenched in sweat, often smeared with blood, a contest can continue for several minutes, sometimes hours and, sporadically, over days. For a month mature bucks and younger hopefuls enter the fray. Then all goes quite again, at least for another year.

The biggest fallow bucks have the finest antlers. A dominant male may have a dozen or more does in his harem, so he is kept very busy during the rutting season. Younger males can be seen in bachelor groups, keeping an eye open for any sign of weakness from the dominant bucks herding their harems. All cast their

Heron with young

Fallow fawn

antlers in April or May, but by August they have regrown in time for the start of the next rutting season.

Were it not for a passion and a fashion, we might have been deprived of some of England's most enduring picturesque and graceful landscapes – wood pasture and deer park. Their creation was both practical and appealing. The Norman passion for hunting deer and wild boar was served by protected Royal Forests. Deer parks enabled a good supply of mature hard wood and fine meat to be kept in view rather than lost to poachers. It was also a fashion to improve the setting of a grand house. But the origin of wood pasture is far older.

There is no doubt that Stone Age people cleared some forest, but tackling giant hardwood oaks must have been quite daunting with a flint axe. Hunting in dense forest is difficult and dangerous. Well spaced mature trees allow grass to grow well, which attracts grazing animals. Perhaps dozing in the branches of a mature oak with a bow and arrow, while waiting for your roast lunch to arrive, was more attractive than chasing it through the wildwood. Stone Age people were no different from us – they just had less technology to hand. So open wood pasture created and controlled by slashing and burning is nothing new.

The Romans are thought to have reintroduced the Fallow Deer to Britain. Although there is good evidence of native Fallow Deer from before the last Ice Age, there is no sign of their survival into historic times. But they were well known in Roman Britain, and deer parks were popular with the Normans. By the early 17th century some 700 parks were recorded in England, but the Civil War resulted in many being lost. The popularity of the deer park was then revived by the Georgians, and by the end of their reign some 400 parks contained an estimated 71,000 deer. The legacy it left us today is a wealth of ancient trees, mainly oak. Old trees are important for wildlife. They have more holes, nooks and crannies in which creatures can hide and breed. They also appear to be an English speciality, as they are rare on the European continent and very few are found in North America.

The hollow trunk and dead boughs of so called 'stag head' oaks are not so much the symptoms of a dying tree as a strategy to survive old age. Some of the best examples of these ancient trees can be found in surviving deer parks. The medieval castle at Powderham alongside the Exe estuary is just one fine example of several old large estates containing deer parks. Autumn is a beautiful time in Devon, but it can on occasions be noisy. At daybreak the castle sometimes seems to float on a sea of mist, and the golden colours of the season are everywhere. Beneath the battlements, a Fallow buck throws back its fine antlered head and roars. The rut has started. For centuries the sound of deer in the rutting season has echoed through these trees. Good views of the Powderham deer park on the edge of the Exe estuary can be gained from the Starcross road, or from the train on the main line between Dawlish and Exeter.

Escapes from parks were inevitable, and parts of Britain now have many feral herds living in the wild. **Fallow Deer** are graceful creatures, smaller than the native **Red** but larger than the native **Roe**. All other deer – the Japanese **Sika**, **Muntjac** and **Chinese Water Deer** – are introduced.

The wood pasture created by deer park also creates ideal conditions for many other creatures. Ancient oaks have many interesting and some rare lichens. **Mistle Thrush** and **Lesser Spotted Woodpecker** both frequent such places, and the tall trees in Powderham are home to the biggest nesting colony of **Herons** in the county. But at high tide on the adjacent Exe estuary, Powderham also serves as a roost for hundreds of wading birds. **Redshank**, **Spotted Redshank**, and flocks of up to 200 **Greenshank** can sometimes be seen during spring. During the coldest months it is also a good place to see **Teal** and **Tufted Duck**.

Powderham creek

Woodland

When Britain finally became an island after the ending of the last ice age over 6,000 years ago, virtually the entire land was covered in trees. Indeed, so dense was that original wildwood that it is said that a red squirrel could probably have leapt its way from Land's End to John O'Groats, without putting a paw on the ground. Apart from moorland bog and mountain tops, lakes and wetlands, a vast forest stretched as far as a buzzard's eye could see. Pine and birch wood primarily covered the far north and uplands, while the lowlands and further south were dominated by massive oak. It must have been an amazing and terrifying place. Beneath huge trees lay a jungle of colossal fallen trunks. While bluebells carpeted the glades, wolves and bears roamed widely. This was a realm where people feared to tread, a dappled world inhabited by giant wild cattle, lynx and wild boar. Then the first Stone Age hunters arrived. But it was not until the Iron Age that people made a real impact on the forest, as they cleared the land for farming on a larger scale and domesticated wild animals for stock. By the time the Romans set foot in England, the woodland cover was, in many places, not much more than what we see today, particularly in East Anglia and South-East of England.

When the results of the Domesday survey were written in 1086 barely 4 per cent of Devon was wooded, although many other counties contained considerably more woodland. Only Cornwall, Leicester, Lincoln and the Isle of Ely had less. In 1688, when William of Orange landed at Brixham in south Devon, the great forests of England were said to cover some four million acres of land. Yet half of Devon's 767 Domesday woods were small, covering less than 17 acres in size. This probably tells us more about the way people managed woodland than the tenacity of trees to survive. Without domesticated mowers, given half a chance, trees return with a vengeance. Cattle and sheep, along with millions of rodents and rabbits, destroy vast numbers of germinating tree seeds. If ever the countryside were deserted again, just as it was in times of war or plague, bramble and scrub would soon recolonise the fields, and oak and ash saplings then rise from their midst. Woodland is the natural plant cover for much of Britain.

Devon now appears to be well wooded, but that impression is partly due to the huge number of hedgerow trees and countless leafy lanes. Since Devon now has a network of some 8,000 miles of road, the longest of any county, and trees flank many routes, a ribbon of woodland laces the shire. At present, trees cover less than 8 per cent of Devon – a bit lower than the national average. But large tracts of woodland still exist in the county, especially in

Wood anemone

Oak cherry galls

the sheltered valleys of south Devon, where they extend almost down to sea level. The native wood here is deciduous oak and elm, although the latter has now been reduced to a sad scattering of young suckers, fighting the scourge of Dutch elm disease. During the 1970s this fungus wiped out most of our magnificent old elms. It seems that of all the varieties of elm in Britain, the southern variety of English Elm was most susceptible to the disease. But some still survive in hedgerows as vigorous young growth. So why are there so few mature elm trees? Try putting your hands together to form a circle, fingers and thumbs touching. It appears that most elm trees with a trunk much bigger than what you can hold, get cut down by the disease. Perhaps in time the mighty English Elm may one day return to Devon and grace our rolling landscape again.

Snow does not linger long in Devon, except over the moors, so you have to be quick to make the most of it. Walking through a winter wood can be a lonely affair. Bare branches reach for cloud-filled skies, and nothing seems to stir. But the snow tells a different story. Footprints of a badger cross the path of a fox; the hesitant prints of a rambling roe deer show where it paused for a moment; and the wing prints of a startled bird show up clearly on the ground. For a few hours, at first light, a secret world of nocturnal life is written deep in the snow.

A shaft of sunlight breaks the spell, and all too soon melting layers drip and slump from the trees. Although still cold, the end of February sees the first real stirrings of woodland life. Mixed flocks of blue, great and long-tailed tits party through the trees. Deep underground, the badgers already have young, and the first green leaves are poking bravely from the sodden ground. Spring comes surprisingly early in sheltered south-facing Devon valleys. Nestled in a warm glade, the first primroses bask in the sun. Then all around, the woodland floor seems to explode with shoots of green – wild garlic and bluebell leaves. A gentle breeze stirs the dangling tails of hazel catkins, and clouds of pollen waft free. Plant life is on the move, and everywhere birds are singing. Soon the woods burst into colour with a succession of wild flowers: pale yellow primrose, darker celandine, swathes of bluebells and then, beneath the trees, a strange sight. A new fall of snow seems to have appeared overnight – but this time it is wild garlic, and its aroma soon fills the air.

Then the leafy canopy above expands to shut out the sky. The floor is plunged into shadowy gloom, and most of the ground plants die. Their time has come and gone, and their seeds are shed for another year. Now the glory of a great tree in full leaf can be seen and admired. Some, like the old oak, have survived several human generations – five hundred years is not uncommon. Just think of the seasons it has seen, the history that has past and the multitude of creatures that have sheltered and bred in its branches. A great oak is humbling to humans.

Summer arrives, and the coolness of woodland on a hot day is eagerly sought by people and wild animals. Then, all too soon, leaves fade and fall. Autumn is a golden time in Devon. Looking across a valley wood, the foliage turns from green to gold and every shade of rust. In the damp conditions, fungi burst overnight from fallen boughs, rising through the leaf litter in a myriad of ephemeral forms and hues – ghostly white, pale yellow and brilliant splashes of red. The year of the wood is turning. A gilded carpet scrunches underfoot, and fallen leaves chase speeding cars down country lanes. Wild fruit is ripening. Half-eaten hazel nuts and acorns litter the ground, and the signature of the culprit is often written large on the remains. An experienced eye can distinguish the teeth marks left by a wood mouse or bank vole. Even the dormouse carves its own unique mark – a neat, smoothly nibbled hole. Woodpeckers can split open a nut in a couple of blows, and an experienced squirrel in just one bite. Yes, practice does make perfect. Young squirrels must to learn to get it right!

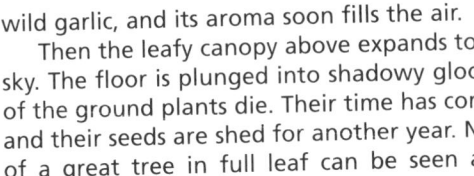

Deciduous Woodland

DECIDUOUS WOODLAND PLANTS

The original wildwood dominated by oak gradually declined as the numbers of people multiplied. Now only a few remnants of that ancient wildwood survive as isolated patches of stunted oak woods on the high moors. Wistman's Wood is the most famous. More about this extraordinary place may be found under *Moorland*.

All other deciduous woods have been modified in one way or another by people during historic times. Some woods changed more than others, but in many of Devon's oak woods, vestiges of that ancient wildwood

Primrose bank; Foxglove; Violet and lesser celandine

still remain, as can be seen from some of its plants. Although wolves and bears, along with that great bovine beast, the auroch, have long since gone, try walking through a neglected old wood and you can still imagine these creatures.

Coppice with scrub is the most modified woodland, practised extensively since medieval times and probably long before. The practice involves cutting down certain trees to provide a sustainable source of poles, harvested every 7 to 20 years depending on the species. Hazel grows quickly, and was used for fuel, hurdles and tool handles. Oak is slower, and was utilised for charcoal and fencing. If left for too long, woodland becomes scrub, an immensely rich cover for wildlife. Devon contains a vast area of scrub oak woods, typically found along the steeper river valleys.

Although called an oak wood, such places contain many different trees. Often dominated by **Pedunculate** and **Sessile Oak**, other trees such as **Holly**, **Ash**, **Birch** and **Rowan** can all thrive. Below the tallest trees **Hazel**, **Holly**, **Blackthorn** and **Honeysuckle** will grow, sometimes forming an impenetrable jungle with **Bramble** – nature's own barbed wire. For part of the year, when there are little or no leaves on the trees, oak wood is well lit and so many other plants can grow. Swathes of **Bluebell** can be a good indicator of ancient woodland, along with **Dog's Mercury** and the grass **Wood Melick**. **Primrose** and **Wood Anemone** are common, and on the hills **Ling** and **Whortleberry** are widespread in woodland. Spring and early summer is obviously the richest time for woodland plants, but winter will reveal a typical south-west scene – abundant growths of fern and even ivy covering the floor. In a few places, Beech appears to have replaced the original native oak.

As the weather warms **Snowdrops** appear, then later come **Wild Arum** or **Cuckoo Pint**, **Wood** and **Common Violet**, **Wood Avens**, **Green Hellebore**, **Woody Nightshade**, **Ground Ivy**, **Yellow Archangel** and small bushes of **Spurge Laurel**. Others are easier to see, and in numbers can put on an extravagant display. Devon is the **Primrose** capital of Britain. Some woodland floors can be dominated by **Wild Garlic**. But there is another flower for which a few Devon woods are renowned: Dunsford is a nature reserve in the beautiful Teign Valley, famed for its annual spectacle of thousands of **Wild Daffodils**.

Clearings in the woods or glades can be especially glorious in summer: rich in wild flowers and full of life. **Foxglove** thrives in good light, and can be very spectacular if found in large numbers. So too can orchids. Nearly half of the orchids found in Britain can also be found in woods. Most will grow in a variety of habitats, but some are very specific. The **Bird's Nest Orchid** is not common, although it may be found in some oak or more especially beech woods, growing in dimly lit places on bare calcareous, humus-rich soil. It is an extraordinary plant to chance upon.

A wood is not just plants. Leaves and timber, sap and soil all offer food or shelter to countless creatures. The relationship is sometimes simple, at other times complex. Some 15,000 invertebrates, often tiny creeping, crawling or flying creatures, depend on woodland plants for their survival.

Brimstone butterfly on heath lobelia

Wood white butterfly on thistle

DECIDUOUS WOODLAND INSECTS

A single oak tree may support some 423 species of insect alone. Not surprisingly, the oak has the richest insect life of any tree south of the Humber. Further north it is only beaten by Birch and Sallow, but here in the south, Devon is rich in oaks, all buzzing with life.

Butterflies are among the most splendid insects to be found in a summer wood. Many of the larger more spectacular species are confined to southern Britain, and the **Purple Emperor** is king. Never common in Devon, there are just a few woodlands, chiefly in the east of the county, where it was once recorded every year. The Purple Emperor is usually on the wing between July and August, at about the same time as another butterfly that belongs to the same family – the **White Admiral.** This smaller and less colourful inhabitant of larger woods is now rarely seen in a broad band across the centre of the county, as well as one or two places beyond. Devon is a stronghold for some other rare butterflies in Britain, but even here they are not common. The caterpillar of the **Heath Fritillary** feeds on cow-wheat, a plant of the woodland edge. A few areas in the county are now being actively managed to encourage them, with some success.

Other butterflies of deciduous woodland include the **Silver-Washed**, **High Brown** and **Pearl-Bordered Fritillaries**. The beautiful yellow **Brimstone Butterfly** may overwinter as an adult in thick clumps of ivy, so is often one of the earliest butterflies to be seen on the wing. The next generation can then be observed from July. The more common **Speckled Wood** is surprisingly territorial in clearings and rides. They are often encountered in aerial battles seeing off a rival male, spiralling upwards towards the light before returning to a favoured leaf. Smaller still are the **Hairstreak** butterflies – **Purple**, **Brown** and **Green**. The last one in particular ought to come with a health warning. In common with some other woodland butterflies they spend much of their lives high in the canopy, so a crick in the neck is a real hazard.

The **Wood White** is another rare butterfly of woodland clearings and wide tracks cut through forests, but they can be found in the Haldon Hills and east Devon. More common and widespread is the delightful **Holly Blue** butterfly. Its caterpillars feed on holly and ivy. They produce two broods a year, which means they can be seen flying in spring and again in late summer.

Hordes of other insects also depend on woodlands for survival. **Gall Flies** are responsible for the rash of golden brown spangled galls on the underside of oak leaves. These are caused by small **Neuroterus Wasps** which are abundant from late summer. Just as eye-catching are the so called soft 'oak apple' galls produced by larger **Cynipid Wasps**. These wasps are harmless to people, lacking the high powered sting of their bigger colony-living cousins. They also produce the more familiar, and harder, **Marble** or **Devonshire Gall**.

Stinging wasps can also be found in more open areas of trees, but the **Hornet** is a common woodland creature best avoided. It is formidable in size and temperament if its nest is disturbed, but will seldom attack unprovoked.

The **Oak Bush Cricket** and the **Speckled Bush Cricket** both live among trees. On warm summer nights these are the insects most likely to be heard rather than seen, although they will continue calling even in torchlight.

Whether sucking the sap, foraging through leaf litter or chewing their way through dead and decaying timber, the grubs and adults of bugs, beetles and flies all thrive in woods. And in summer the caterpillars of butterflies and moths as well as other larvae can reach astronomical numbers. It is reckoned that oak can support some 131 different butterfly and moth caterpillars, while hazel feeds just 35.

DECIDUOUS WOODLAND BIRDS

This munching multitude of insect life is one of the reasons why woods attract so many birds: the prospect of food. Yet woodlands can also provide birds with so much more. Hiding in holes in the trunks, nestled deep in ivy, or riding high on wind-tossed branches, trees provide birds with a wide choice of suitable nesting sites. In total some 92 species of birds nest in the woodlands of Britain, though not all in the same one! A large Devon wood is can probably support up to 55 different breeding birds.

One woodland bird, for which Devon is justly famed, frequently reaches the parts few others can attain. High above the trees in a clear blue sky, a tiny speck is betrayed by its familiar mewing call. The **Buzzard** is a big bird of prey. It usually nests in the tallest trees – often a large oak towering above the rest. These larger, more substantial trees can also attract nesting **Jays**, **Carrion Crows**, **Kestrels** and sometimes **Sparrowhawks**, although the latter will often choose one that is ivy-clad.

Many birds nest inside holes in trees. But there is only one that can hammer its own from solid wood – the **Woodpecker**. Where these birds boldly go, others then follow. The ability to chisel your own nest is a distinct advantage, and provides a ready made home for other birds. The **Nuthatch** needs a smaller entrance than the woodpecker, so plasters the hole with mud. **Tree Creepers** will sometimes use an uncompleted hole or a gap in the bark. Then, after several years, if a hollow enlarges enough through rot, bigger birds like owls can move in. Such places are popular with the **Tawny Owl**, the most common woodland owl.

The **Blue Tit**, **Great Tit** and **Coal Tit** will all seek out small nest holes in trees, but others are always on the lookout for the same. On the edge of Dartmoor the oak woods, here with hazel and birch, also play host to many summer migrants. At Yarner near Bovey Tracey, a national Nature Reserve, there is also a good population of **Redstart** and **Pied Flycatcher.**

Wood and **Willow Warblers**, as well as the **Chiffchaff**, are all summer visitors commonly heard or seen in Devon's deciduous woods.

DECIDUOUS WOODLAND MAMMALS

Most woodland mammals are more active after dark. The **Badger** is no exception. It is one of Britain's most ancient animals, living here long before people trod this land. Even as the last glaciers were melting further north, at the end of the last ice age over 10,000 years ago, badgers were digging into the woodlands that were spreading up from the south. They are highly social, mainly nocturnal creatures, often living in large family groups. Seldom encountered by people, they must be our most familiar yet least seen live large mammal. Unfortunately road casualties are common. Badgers are powerful creatures, and can they dig! Huge setts, excavated over hundreds of years, can be found in many parts of Devon.

The only squirrel now found in Devon, as elsewhere in much of England, is the introduced **North American Grey**. Although at times they can appear quite reddish-brown, the more attractive red squirrel has distinctive ear tufts. Although once native to Devon, the red squirrel has not been reported here since the middle of the last century.

The **Common Dormouse** was once widespread throughout England's woodland. It has declined dramatically over the last fifty years. Strictly nocturnal, it hibernates during the winter months and is mainly active from April to October. Stripped honeysuckle bark, which it uses for nest building – especially in spring and early summer – is a good sign of its presence, as are the discarded shells of its supper of hazel nuts. Despite being depicted in a classic tale as having a rather sleepy disposition, snoozing in a teapot, Dormice are sprightly climbers that can leap among the branches of trees – more squirrel-like than mouse-like.

The **Wood Mouse** is also an agile creature. With surprisingly long legs and an even longer tail, with large ears and blackcurrant-like eyes, the wood mouse is well adapted to life in the dark, and it can jump. But then, it needs to! Wood mice are a principal prey of the tawny owl. They spend much of their time up in the leaf canopy of the trees up to 10 metres above the ground, feeding on insects and seeds.

The **Bank Vole** is another woodland rodent, but is easily distinguished from mice by its snub nose and short tail. Although capable of climbing, it spends more time close to the woodland floor and forages along hedge banks looking for soft fruit and fresh leaves. Bramble is a favourite.

Common Shrews and **Hedgehogs** both frequent Devon's woods, feeding on a variety of insects living amongst the leaf litter, while bats make use of tree hollows. Both **Long-eared Bats** and the tiny, colonial-living, **Pipistrelle Bat**

Dormouse hibernating

Badger cubs playing in their sett

can commonly be found in Devon woods, particular in the south. Less common, but still more often found in holes in trees, is the largest British bat, the **Noctule**, and its smaller cousin, the **Leisler's Bat**. The **Bechstein's Bat**, one of our rarest, also roosts in tree holes.

Deer are the largest mammals to live in woodland. The native **Roe Deer** and reintroduced **Fallow Deer** are both widespread in the county. The larger red deer are more likely to be seen on the moors. It is thought the famous Exmoor herds are the direct descendants of deer that once roamed the area at the end of the last ice age.

Coniferous Woodland

Conifer trees grown in dark, dense plantations are poor places for wildlife. But where the saplings are thinned and management is more mindful of nature, the results can be nothing short of spectacular. Fewer plants survive beneath dense foliage. Some of the best woodland life interpretation centres are today found in former plantations of coniferous forest.

After the First World War there was a national shortage of trees, so the Forestry Commission was set up and charged with their growth. Mid-Devon became the site of Britain's first official forest, at Eggesford in 1919. The second was laid out on Haldon Hill, with magnificent views over South Devon. Planting began in the 1920s, with a variety of fast growing trees. Today some of the original conifers still stand tall. But the North American Douglas fir can reach over 20 metres, so even those on Haldon are still only part grown. Felling and thinning of mature trees has transformed many plantations into more wildlife- and people-friendly forest. Now, rather than replanting, after felling many areas are left to regenerate naturally.

CONIFEROUS WOODLAND INSECTS

The needle-strewn floor of a pine forest can appear devoid of animal life. Yet creatures that survive here can thrive. Warm, damp woodland is where an army of insects do best. The **Wood Ant** is the biggest of its kind in Britain. They live in massive colonies of over 100,000 workers. Since they hibernate during winter, one of the best times to see them is early in the year, when they first emerge. Their nests usually flank the sunlit rides through a forest. After the coolness of night, heat from the morning sun can cause an eruption. Like lava pouring from a miniature volcano they flood in a living stream from their old nest. Thousands of ants now warm themselves into action. Their first task is to build a home of fallen leaves and other woodland debris. These fortresses can reach nearly a metre high, and contain a labyrinth of tunnels and chambers. Throughout the warmest months, wood ants can be found in any suitable woodland, foraging for insect prey to feed their young or climbing a tree to milk herds of aphids. They are a formidable force in the forest. Most animals avoid getting too close to them, and that should also apply to us. Take care not to stand on one of their trails or touch the big soldier ants, as they are armed with powerful pincers; and keep a safe distance from the workers, as they have the ability to squirt formic acid. The industry of their activity is amazing to watch.

CONIFEROUS WOODLAND BIRDS

The **Jay** is one of the most raucous residents of the forest, and readily engages in some extraordinary behaviour – anting. It is thought the formic acid sprayed by wood ants helps reduce parasites on feathers. By controlling tiny mites and lice, a bird's plumage is kept in good condition. Whatever the reason, the apparent ecstasy of a jay squatting over an ant nest, wings splayed, feathers raised, is a sight to see. Sometimes they will even pick up a squirting ant and place it where it is needed.

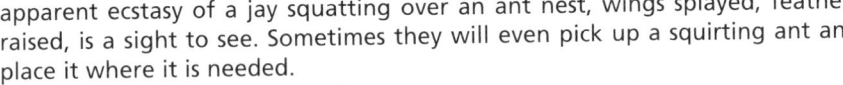

Wood ant nest

Wood ants on jay wing

Birds that live purely among conifers are few and far between, but those that do are intriguing. The **Goldcrest** is one of the smallest birds in Britain; it forages for small insect prey and makes a tiny nest of spider's web with moss, hidden carefully amongst pine needles.

The **Crossbill** is a more curious creature, highly adapted to feeding on the seeds of pine cones. Its distinctive crossed beak acts as a pair of fine forceps, to extract their protein-packed source of food.

Haldon Forest in south Devon is also home to one of the best raptor view-points in the country. From the top of the hill, looking down over the woodland below, it is often possible to spot several birds of prey in one day. **Buzzard**, **Kestrel** and **Sparrowhawk** are all resident, while migration time in spring and autumn can offer better opportunities. Sightings of **Honey Buzzard**, **Goshawk**, **Hobby** and even **Osprey** passing overhead have all been reported in the past.

CONIFEROUS WOODLAND REPTILES

The location of many forestry plantations in Devon on south-facing, well drained hills, provides reptiles with a great opportunity. **Adder**, **Slow Worm** and **Common Lizard** are all common in Devon's upland woods. Only the Adder is venomous, but it rarely strikes at humans and only then in defence. Leave well alone and it will do no harm. Considering how sensitive it is to disturbance, detecting the vibration of a footstep several paces away, consider yourself lucky if you see an adder at all.

Jay anting

CONIFEROUS WOODLAND MAMMALS

While Red, **Roe** and **Fallow Deer** will all inhabit coniferous forest, and it is thought these woodlands have also helped other deer to spread across the country. The introduced **Japanese Sika Deer**, an eastern relative of the native Red, is heading west and is now well established in east Devon and even as far as the Tamar. The smaller, large toothed, Chinese **Muntjac Deer** is also now extending its range into the county.

Young tawny owls

Plants

DEVON PLANTS NOT GENERALLY COMMON ELSEWHERE IN BRITAIN

Devon is a large county, around 80 miles square with a climate ranging from the sub-tropic to the sub-arctic. So you might imagine its plant life is rich – you are right! But it not evenly spread. Surveys over many years have revealed that the number of flowering plants present in a 2km square can vary from over 450 species at Braunton Burrows and Slapton, to as few as 20 on Dartmoor.

Some southern European plants reach their northernmost limit in the south-west of England, such as the wall pennywort. Others may reach their southernmost limit on the top of Dartmoor. Many introduced plants are now living wild, and the number of alien introduced plants around ports and harbours is high.

Along the western Atlantic seaboard from Spain to Ireland are plants that seem to enjoy dryer spring weather and moderately high summer temperatures. Many Atlantic plants seem to thrive in the damper Devon air. So here, typical woodland species such as bluebell and primrose flower freely in the open on banks, in hedges and fields. Also gorse, heather and foxglove do well. Other plants are much rarer, and a few may be confined to certain soils.

There are many more bacteria, algae, fungi and ferns than flowering plants in Britain, but their detail is beyond the scope of this book. In many parts of the British Isles, over 2000 well studied flowering plants and ferns can be found growing wild. Yet the *Flora of Devon* reveals the number of flowering plants in the county as being close to 2500. Many of these can also be found growing commonly elsewhere in Britain. So the list below provides a flavour of what makes Devon special in terms of its flowers and ferns.

Very special plants – an Atlantic and southern European distribution, some native others introduced, but all now living wild in Devon.

Torbay limestone – supports a remarkable and rare collection of plants.

Lusitanian plants are thought to be survivors from the last ice age.

Month* – An asterisk after the month indicates flowers that may last until first frost.

Plants are listed alphabetically by their common name.

PLANT NAME	WHEN IN FLOWER	Devon status and where found
Alexanders *Smyrnium olusatrum*	Apr – Jun	Cliff, hedge, wasteland
American Winter-cress *Arbarea verna*	Apr – Jun	Heath, cliff, hedge
Balm *Melissa officinalis*	Jul – Sept	Hedge, wasteland
Bastard Balm *Melittis melissophyllum*	May – June	Wood – locally frequent in woods and hedge banks, especially SW and between Exeter and Barnstaple.
Bell Heather *Erica cinerea*	May – Aug	Heath, hedge
Betony *Stachys officinalis*	June – Sept*	Heath, wasteland
Bilberry *Vaccinium myrtillus*	Apr – Jun	Heath, woodlands
Biting Stonecrop *Sedum acre*	June – Jul	Dune, cliff, wasteland
Black Bryony *Tamus communis*	May – Jul*	Woodland, hedge
Black Nightshade *Solanum nigrum*	June – Sept	Wasteland, farmland
Black Spleenwort *Asplenium adiantum-nigrum*	June – Aug*	Hedge
Blackthorn *Prunus spinosa*	Apr – May	Cliffs, woodland, hedge, wasteland
Bladder Campion *Silene vulgaris*	June – Aug	Wasteland, grassland, cliff
Bog Asphodel *Narthecium ossifragum*	Jul – Aug	Common damp heaths and moors
Bog Orchid *Hammarbya paludosa*	Aug – Sept	Dartmoor – locally common
Bog Pimpernel *Anagallis tenella*	June – Aug	Bog, wet cliff
Bristle Bent *Agrostis curtisii*	May – Jul	Heath
Bristle Club-rush *Isolepis setacea*	May – Jul	Marsh, freshwater
Broomrapes: Ivy *Orobanche hederae*	June – July	Parasitic on Ivy, infrequent on S. coast, scarce N. coast.
Wild Carrot *Orobanche maritima*	June – Sept	Parasitic on Wild Carrot, less common, S coast only
Buck's-horn Plantain *Plantago coronopus*	May – Jul	Cliff, salt marsh
Burnet Rose *Rosa pimpinellifolia*	May – Jul	Heath, dunes, cliffs, grassland
Chamomile *Chamaemelum nobile*	June – Aug	Heath, grassland – locally common
Chicory *Cichorium intybus*	June – Aug*	Wasteland, grassland
Columbine *Aquilegia vulgaris*	May – Jul	Widespread, frequent in hedge-banks
Common Bird's-foot-trefoil *Lotus corniculatus*	May – Aug*	Dune, cliffs, grassland
Common Calamint *Clinopodium ascendens*	Jul – Sept	Wasteland, grassland
Common Cottongrass *Eriophorum angustifolium*	Apr – May	Heath, bog

PLANTS

PLANT NAME	WHEN IN FLOWER	Devon status and where found
Common Cow-wheat *Melampyrum pratense*	May – Sept	Woodlands
Common Gromwell *Lithospermum officinale*	Jun – Jul	Dune, hedge
Common Milkwort *Polygala vulgaris*	May – Jun*	Grassland
Common Ramping-fumitory *Fumaria muralis subsp. boraei*	May – Jul*	Hedge, wasteland, farmland
Common Scurvy-grass *Cochlearia officinalis*	May – Aug	Locally frequent inland.
Common Valerian *Valeriana officinalis*	Jun – Aug	Hedge, wasteland, grassland
Corn Marigold *Chrysanthemum segetum*	Jun – Aug*	Wasteland, farmland
Cornish Elm *Ulmus minor subsp. angustifolia*	Feb – Apr	Woodlands, hedge, farmland
Cornish Heath *Erica vagans*	Aug – Sept	Naturalised at Lydford, Dartmoor.
Cornish Moneywort *Sibthorpia europaea*	July – Oct	Locally frequent by streams SW edge of Dartmoor.
Cowslip *Primula veris*	Apr – May	Heath, dune, hedge, grassland
Cross-leaved Heath *Erica tetralix*	Jun – Aug*	Heath, bog
Danish Scurvygrass *Cochlearia danica*	Feb – Sept	Dune, cliff, shore, hedge, salted roadside
Dodder *Cuscuta epithymum*	Jun – Sept	Heath, sand dunes
Dorset Heath *E. ciliaris*	July – Nov	Soussons Down, Dartmoor
Dyer's greenweed *Genista tinctoria subsp. littoralis*	Jul – Sept	Rough grassland – scarce
Early-purple Orchid *Orchis mascula*	Apr – Jun	Woodland, hedge, grassland, road verges
English Stonecrop *Sedum anglicum*	Jun – Aug	Freshwater, dune, cliff
Fennel I *Foeniculum vulgare*	Jul – Aug*	Hedge, wasteland, farmland
Fen Orchid *Liparis loeselii*	July	First discovered on Braunton Burrows in 1966.
Fern-grass *Catapodium rigidum*	May – Sept	Cliff
Feverfew I *Tanacetum parthenium*	Jul – Sept*	Hedge, wasteland, farmland
Field eryngo *Eryngium campestre*	July – Aug	Also known as Watling Street Thistle and related to Sea holly, grows on cliffs at Plymouth and elsewhere by the sea in S Devon.
Field Woundwort *Stachys arvensis*	Apr – May	Wasteland, farmland, grassland, hedge
Flax-leaved St. John's-wort *Hypericum linarifolium*	June – Aug	Rare, mainly on dry banks in the Teign valley.
Floating Club-rush *Eleogiton fluitans*	May – Sept	Freshwater
Foxglove *Digitalis purpurea*	Jun – Sept	Woodlands, hedge, wasteland

PLANT NAME	WHEN IN FLOWER	Devon status and where found
Glasswort *Salicornia agg.*	Aug – Sept	Shore, salt marsh
Goldenrod *Solidago virgaurea*	Jul – Sept	Heath, hedge
Goldilocks aster *Aster linosyris*	Aug – Sept	Not common at Berry Head
Gorse *Ulex europaeus*	Mar – Nov*	Heath, cliffs, hedge, wasteland, farmland, grassland
Greater Sea Stock *Mattiola sinuata*	June – Aug	Very rare, only site on the mainland of Britain on the cliffs at Saunton, N. Devon.
Great Wood-rush *Luzula sylvatica*	Jun – Jul	Woodlands
Greater Periwinkle *Vinca major*	Mar – Jul	Wasteland
Greater Tussock-sedge *Carex paniculata*	May – Jun	Marsh, woodlands, cliff
Green Alkanet *Pentaglottis sempervirens*	Apr – May	Hedge, wasteland
Hard-fern *Blechnum spicant*	Jun – Aug (spores)	Heath, woodlands
Hart's-tongue Fern *Phyllitis scolopendrium*	Jul – Aug (spores)	Common, luxuriant growth in woods and hedge banks.
Heath Lobelia *Lobelia urens*	Aug – Sept	Very rare, damp meadows S. Devon, see DWT reserves.
Heath Milkwort *Polygala serpyllifolia*	May – Aug*	Heath, grassland
Heath Spotted-orchid *Dactylorhiza maculata*	May – Jul	Heath, bog
Heath Wood-rush *Luzula multiflora*	May – Jun	Heath, woodlands
Heather *Calluna vulgaris*	Aug – Sept	Heath, cliff, hedge, woodland
Hemlock Water-dropwort *Oenanthe crocata*	Jul – Sept	Marsh, freshwater
Holm Oak *Quercus ilex*		Hedge
Honewort *Trinia glauca*	May – July	Locally frequent at Berry Head
Indian Balsam *Impatiens glandulifera*	Jun – Aug*	Marsh, freshwater, wasteland
Irish Lady's Tresses *Spiranthes romanzoffiana*	Aug – Sept	Very rare on Dartmoor
Irish Spurge *Euphorbia hyberna*	Apr – July	Locally common in Lyn valley, N. Devon.
Ivy-leaved Bellflower *Wahlenbergia hederacea*	July – Aug	Widespread in bogs on heath and moor.
Ivy-leaved Toadflax *Cymbalaria muralis*	Apr – Aug	Hedge
Japanese Knotweed *Fallopia japonica*	Sept – Oct	Hedge, wasteland

PLANT NAME	WHEN IN FLOWER	Devon status and where found
Kidney Vetch *Anthyllis vulneraria*	May – Aug*	Cliff, grassland
Lady-fern *Athyrium filix-femina*	Jul – Aug (spores)	Woodlands, hedge
Large-flowered Evening-primrose *Oenothera glazioviana*	Jun – Aug*	Dunes, hedge, wasteland
Lesser Periwinkle *Vinca minor*	Apr – Aug*	Hedge, wasteland
Lesser Skullcap *Scutellaria minor*	Jul – Aug*	Damp heath
Lesser Swine-cress *Coronopus didymus*	May – Sept	Hedge, wasteland, farmland
Little-Robin *Geranium purpureum*	May – Sept	Rock, hedge – scarce
Long-stalked Cranesbill *Geranium columbinum*	May – Aug*	Hedge, grassland
Lousewort *Pedicularis sylvatica*	May – Sept	Heath, bog, marsh
Lundy Cabbage *Rhychosinapis wrightii*	May – Aug	Confined to Lundy
Many-stalked Spike-rush *Eleocharis multicaulis*	Jul – Aug	Bog
Marsh Pennywort *Hydrocotyle vulgaris*	Jun – Aug	Heath, bog, marsh, dune, slack
Marsh St John's-wort *Hypericum elodes*	Jun – Sept	Bog, marsh, freshwater
Mat-grass *Nardus stricta*	Jun – Aug	Heath, bog
Mind-your-own-business *Soleirolia soleirolii*	May – Aug	Hedge, wasteland
Monkshood *Aconitum anglicum*	May – Jun	Local in damp shady spots under alder, near streams
Montbretia *Crocosmia x crocosmiiflora*	Jun – Aug	Cliff, hedge, wasteland
Narrow Hare's-ear *Bupleurum baldense*	Jun – July	Can be common at Berry Head
Navelwort *Umbilicus rupestris*	Jun – Aug	Hedge
Nottingham Catchfly *Silene nutans*	May – July	Only common on cliffs nr Seaton and Beer.
Opposite-leaved Golden-saxifrage *Chrysosplenium oppositifolium*	Mar – May	Marsh, woodlands, hedge
Pale Butterwort *Pinguicula lusitanica*	Jul – Sept	Widespread on damp heaths and moors
Pale Flax *Linum bienne*	May – Sept	Heath, wasteland, grassland

PLANT NAME	WHEN IN FLOWER	Devon status and where found
Pellitory-of-the-wall *Parietaria judaica*	Jun – Jul*	Hedge
Pencilled Crane's-bill *Geranium versicolor*	May – Jul	Well established garden escapee in waste places
Plymouth Pear *Pyrus cordata*	May	Scarce in hedgerows around Plymouth
Primrose *Primula vulgaris*	Mar – May	Woodland, hedge, grassland
Procumbent Yellow-sorrel *Oxalis corniculata*	May – Sept	Wasteland, farmland
Prostrate Broom *Cytisus scoparius subsp. maritimus*	May – Jun	Cliff – only Hartland and Lundy
Purple Gromwell *Lithospermum purpurocaeruleum*	May – July	Very local on calcareous soil
Purple Moor-grass *Molinia caerulea*	Jul – Sept	Heath, marsh
Purple-loosestrife *Lythrum salicaria*	Jul – Aug	Marsh, freshwater
Pyrenean Lily *Lilium pyrenaicum*	June – July	Naturalized, locally common N of county and hedge-banks around South Molton.
Red Valerian *Centranthus ruber*	May – Aug*	Cliff, hedge, wasteland
Rock Samphire *Crithmum maritimum*	Jun – Sept	Cliff
Rock Sea-spurrey *Spergularia rupicola*	Jun – Sept	Cliffs, hedge
Round-headed Club-rush *Scirpoides holoschoenus*	Jun – Jul	Dune slack – scarce
Round-leaved Crowfoot *Ranunculus omiophyllus*	Mar – Aug	Freshwater
Round-leaved Sundew *Drosera rotundifolia*	Jun – Aug	Heath, bog
Royal Fern *Osmunda regalis*	June – Aug	Not common, wet heaths and shady valley, SW Dartmoor. Much collected for gardens in past.
Sand Crocus *Romulea columnae*	Apr – May	Dawlish Warren – only British mainland site.
Sand Toadflax *Linaria arenaria*	May – Sept	Dune
Saw-wort *Serratula tinctoria*	Jul – Sept	Heath, cliff, grassland
Scaly Male-fern *Dryopteris affinis*	Jul – Aug (spores)	Woodlands, hedge
Sea Aster *Aster tripolium*	Jul – Sept*	Salt marsh
Sea Campion *Silene uniflora*	Jun – Aug	Dunes, cliffs, shore, hedge

PLANTS

PLANT NAME	WHEN IN FLOWER	Devon status and where found
Sea Carrot *Daucus carota subsp. gummifer*	Jun – Jul*	Cliff
Sea Couch *Elytrigia atherica*	Jun – Sept	Cliff; salt marsh
Sea Fern-grass *Catapodium marinum*	May – Jul	Cliff
Sea Mouse-ear *Cerastium diffusum*	Apr – Jul	Cliff, wasteland
Sea Pearlwort *Sagina maritima*	Jun – Sept	Heath, cliffs, grassland
Sea Plantain *Plantago maritima*	Jun – Aug	Cliffs, shore, salt marsh
Sea Spleenwort *Asplenium marinum*	Jun – Sept (spores)	Cliffs, old buildings
Sea Stork's-bill *Erodium maritimum*	May – Aug	Dunes, wasteland, grassland – locally common
Sharp-leaved Fluellen *Kickxia elatine*	Jul – Aug*	Hedge, wasteland, farmland
Sheep's-bit *Jasione montana*	Mar – May*	Heath, cliffs, grassland, hedge
Slender Club-rush *Isolepis cernua*	May – Jul	Heath, bog, cliff grassland
Slender Speedwell *Veronica filiformis*	Apr – Jun	Marsh, grassland
Slender Thistle *Carduus tenuiflorus*	May – Aug	Dunes, cliff, wasteland, grassland
Slender Trefoil *Trifolium micranthum*	May – Aug	Hedge, grassland
Small Hare's-ear *Bupleurum baldense*	Jun – Jul	Dry bank, limestone grassland – scarce
Small Rest-harrow *Ononis reclinata*	Jun – July	Numbers vary annually at Berry Head
Small-flowered Catchfly *Silene gallica*	Jun – Jul*	Wasteland, farmland locally common
Smith's Pepperwort *Lepidium heterophyllum*	May – Aug	Hedge, wasteland, farmland, grass-land
Sneezewort *Achillea ptarmica*	Jun – Aug	Heath, bog, marsh
Snowberry *Symphoricarpos albus*	Jun – Sept	Hedge
Snowdrop *Galanthus nivalis*	Jan – Mar	Widely naturalised from gardens but may be native alongside rivers and in damp woods.
Soapwort *Saponaria officinalis*	Jul – Sept	Hedge, wasteland
Soft Shield-fern *Polystichum setiferum*	Jul – Aug (spores)	Woodland, hedge
Southern Marsh-orchid *Dactylorhiza praetermissa*	Jun – Jul	Marsh, dunes

PLANT NAME	WHEN IN FLOWER	Devon status and where found
Spear-leaved Willowherb *Epilobium lanceolatum*	Jul – Aug*	Hedge, wasteland locally common
Spotted Medick *Medicago arabica*	Apr – Sept	Dunes, cliffs, wasteland, farmland
Square-stalked Willowherb *Epilobium tetragonum*	Jul – Aug	Marsh, woodlands
Squills *Scilla verna* – Spring S. *autumnalis* – Autumn	Apr – June July – Sept	Both locally common on S and N coastal cliffs of Devon
Stinking Iris *Iris foetidissima*	Jun	Dunes, cliffs, wasteland
Stone Bramble *Rubus saxatilis*	June – Aug	Southernmost site in Britain in N Devon
Strapwort *Corrigiola litoralis*	Jul – Aug	Only British site on the shores of Slapton Ley.
Tall Ramping Fumitory *Fumaria bastardii*	May – Jul*	Wasteland, farmland – locally common
Three-cornered Garlic *Allium triquetrum*	Apr – Jun	Dunes, hedge
Thrift *Armeria maritima*	May – Aug*	Marsh, cliff salt marsh
Tormentil *Potentilla erecta*	May – Jul*	Heath, cliff grassland
Trailing Tormentil *Potentilla anglica*	May – Jul*	Heath, grassland
Tree-mallow *Lavatera arborea*	Jul – Sept	Cliffs, hedge, wasteland – locally common
Triangular Club-rush *Schoenoplectus triqueter*	Aug – Sept	Rare speciality in the Tamar estuary
Tufted Hair-grass *Deschampsia cespitosa*	May – Jul	Heath, woodland, wasteland, farmland
Turkey Oak *Quercus cerris*	May	Woodland
Tutsan *Hypericum androsaemum*	Jun – Aug	Cliffs, woodlands, hedge
Twiggy Mullein *Verbascum virgatum*	June – Oct	Native and not uncommon west of the River Teign and nr Plymouth. Rare and perhaps introduced elsewhere
Vervain *Verbena officinalis*	Jun – Sept	Wasteland, grassland
Water Germander *Teucrium scordium*	Jul – Sept	Wet places, dune – rare
Wavy St John's-wort *Hypericum undulatum*	Aug – Sept	Local in wet places, NW Devon.

PLANT NAME	WHEN IN FLOWER	Devon status and where found
Welsh Poppy *Meconopsis cambrica*	June – Aug	Probably native on Exmoor and Dartmoor at Lydford Gorge, garden escapee elsewhere.
Western Gorse *Ulex gallii*	Jul – Sept	Heath, cliffs, wasteland
White Rock-rose *Helianthemum apenninum*	Apr – July	Scarce. Abundant on Torbay limestone cliffs
White Stonecrop *Sedum album*	June – Aug	Abundant, possibly native at Berry Head and Bolt Head, garden escape elsewhere
Whitebeam *Sorbus devoniensis*	May – Jun	Most common type, mainly NE Devon, others do occur.
Wild Carrot *Daucus carota subsp. carota*	Jun – Jul*	Dunes, cliff grassland
Wild Daffodil *Narcissus pseudonaracissus*	Mar – Apr	Wood, stream side – frequent especially Teign valley, see DWT reserves
Wild Madder *Rubia peregrina*	Jun – Aug	Heath, cliffs
Wild Thyme *Thymus polytrichus subsp. britannicus*	Jun – Aug	Heath, dunes, cliff, hedge, grassland
Winter Heliotrope *Petasites fragrans*	Jan – Dec	Hedge, wasteland
Wood Sage *Teucrium scorodonia*	Jun – Sept	Heath, dunes, hedge
Yellow Bartsia *Parentucellia viscosa*	Jun – Aug*	Wet grassland, dune, slacks – locally common
Zigzag Clover *Trifolium medium*	Jun – Aug	Heath, hedge, grassland

Rock rose

Bees, Wasps and Ants

These remarkable and industrious little creatures belong to a vast group of insects, made infamous by the fact that many can sting. Some are large, most small, but the majority are relatively harmless. As the sting itself is a modified egg-laying tool, only females have that ability. And only the biggest, social kinds of female wasps and bees readily do so in defence. Usually they are only aggressive if their home is disturbed.

The best known are social, living together in large colonies, but many more lead solitary lives. Britain has 7 social wasps, 19 solitary wasps, 40 solitary spider-hunting and 230 types of solitary digger wasps. There are also some 250 different bees, including 30 that are social. Only the honey bee will commonly sting if disturbed. All other bees are solitary. Last but not least, there are 36 different ants in Britain, all living socially. Unlike others of their kind, not all ants sting: some defend themselves by squirting formic acid. They also have tough jaws, and the biggest ants can deliver a painful bite. The most common or special to Devon are all listed below.

BEES, WASPS AND ANTS	Most active	Devon status and where found
SOCIAL BEE		
Honey bee *Apis mellifera*	Apr – Sept	Because of a parasitic mite, few colonies now survive long in wild, most in managed apiaries – farm, moor, heath, park, garden
SOLITARY BEE		
Early mining bee *Andrena albicans*	Mar – Sept	Common – farm, park, heath, garden
Patchwork leaf-cutter bee *Megachile centuncularis*	June – July	Common and widespread; cuts rose leaves – farm, park, garden
BUMBLE BEE		
Bilberry bumble bee *Bombus monticola*	May – Sept	Common moor
Brown-banded carder bee *Bombus humilis*	May – Sept	Scarce – coast, downs
Buff-tailed bumble bee *Bombus terrestris*	May – Sept	Widespread – farm, park, some all year
Red-tailed bumble bee *Bombus lapidarus*	mid May – Sept	Widespread – farm, park, heath
Common carder bee *Bombus parscuorum*	May – Sept	Common – farm, moor, heath
Hill cuckoo bee *Psithyrus rupestris*	May – Sept	Common, parasitizes red-tailed bumble bee nests – farm, park, heath

BEES, WASPS AND ANTS	Most active	Devon status and where found
SOLITARY WASP		
Big headed digger wasp *Ectemnius cavifrons*	Jun – Aug	Widespread
Hairy sand wasp *Podalomia viatica*	Apr – Aug	Widespread sandy places
Red banded sand wasp *Sphex sabulosa*	Apr – Aug	Common sandy places
Red banded spider wasp *Anoplius fuscus*	Apr – Aug	Common sandy places
Wall mason wasp *Odynerus parietum*	May – Aug	Common – farm, park, garden
SOLITARY WASP (continued)		
Giant wood wasp *Sirex gigas*		Uncommon – stingless, pine wood only
Oak Cherry wasp *Cynips quercusfolii*	May – June	Common – wood, farm, park, garden. Alternate generation female only emerges in Oct.
Robin's pin cushion *Rhodites rosae*	May – June	Common – hedge, wood edge, farm, park, garden
Ruby-tailed wasp *Chrysis ignita*	May – Aug	Common, parasitizes wall mason wasp – farm, park, garden
SOCIAL WASPS Nest usually underground or hollow tree		
Common wasp *Vespula vulgaris*	Apr – Oct	Common – farm, park, garden, wood
German wasp *Vespula germanica*	Apr – Oct	Common – farm, park, garden, wood
Hornet *Vespa crabro*	Apr – Oct	Widespread – wood, park, garden
Heath potter wasp *Eumenes coarctata*		Fairly common – heathland
SOCIAL TREE WASPS Nest usually hanging from branch in tree or bush		
Tree wasp *Dolichovespula sylvestris*	Apr – Oct	Common – wood, scrub
Median wasp *Dolicho media*	Apr – Oct	Second only to hornet in size. Spreading west – wood, scrub
ANTS		
Narrow-headed ant *Formica exsecta*	Apr – Sept	Rare – heath, S. Devon only
Red wood ant *Formica rufa*	Apr – Sept	Common – wood, heath
Jet ant *Lasius fuliginosus*	Apr – Sept	Uncommon – wood, farm, park
Red ant *Myrmica rubra*	Apr – Sept	Common – grassland
Small black ant *Lasius niger*	Apr – Sept	Very common under pavements – garden, farm, park, towns
Common yellow ant *Lasius flavus*	Apr – Sept	Very common – farm, park, grassland

Butterflies

These beautiful bright wings of summer are some of our most attractive and best known insects. There are currently 59 butterflies on the British list: many are widespread and common, others rare and seldom ever seen. A further 10 or so butterflies are scarce migrants that only occasionally reach our shores.

Considering the size of the county, ranging from moor to sea, it is hardly surprising that nearly two-thirds of British butterflies can be found in Devon, including the rare reintroduced large blue.

Status scale:
rare – scarce – uncommon – not common – locally common – fairly common – frequent – common – very common

Regular Devon butterflies *Caterpillar food plant*

BUTTERFLIES	WHEN FLYING	Devon status and where found adult and *caterpillar*
Whites & Yellows		
Green-veined white *Pieris napi*	Apr – Sept	Very common – wood, lane, damp meadow, garden *on garlic mustard and crucifers*
Large white *Pieris brassicae*	April – Oct	Very common – wood, farm, garden *on cabbage and nasturtium*
Small white *Pieris rapae*	Apr – Sept	Common everywhere *on cabbage and most crucifer*
Bath white *Pontia daplidice*	July – Aug	Very rare migrant S Devon – coast *on mignonette*
Brimstone *Gonepteryx rhamni*	Mar – Sept	Widespread, but not common – especially chalklands, wherever buckthorn grows
Clouded yellow *Colias crocea*	April – Oct	Migrant – usually S coast, *on clover, vetches and lucerne.*
Pale clouded yellow *Colias hyale*	May – Sept	Variable rare migrant – farm, clover fields, *on lucerne*
Orange tip *Anthocharis cardamines*	April – Jun	Locally common – lane, wood edge, *on garlic mustard and cuckoo flower*
Pale clouded yellow *Colias hyale*	May – Sept	Variable rare migrant – farm, clover fields, *on lucerne*
Wood white *Leptidea sinapis*	May – Aug	Very rare – wood edge, coast, *on tuberous pea*
Milkweed		
Monarch *Danaus plexippus*	July – Oct	N. America summer vagrant – anywhere, especially on south coast

BUTTERFLIES	WHEN FLYING	Devon status and where found adult and *caterpillar*

Admirals, Fritillaries & Vanessids

Comma *Polygonia c-album*	Apr – Oct	Not widespread, but common – wood, hedge, orchard, *on stinging nettle, elm, hop*
Painted lady *Vanessa cardui*	May – Oct	Migrant also breeds – *anywhere on thistle*
Peacock *Inachis io*	Apr – May July – Sept	Common – garden, farm, wood, park *on thistle, stinging nettle*
Purple emperor *Apatura iris*	July – Aug	Probably extinct – ancient oak wood, *on sallow*
Red admiral *Vanessa atalanta*	Apr – Nov	Common migrant also breeds – anywhere, *on stinging nettle*
Small tortoiseshell *Aglais urticae*	Mar – Oct	Very common – anywhere, *on stinging nettle*
White admiral *Limenitis camilla*	June – Aug	Rare – large deciduous wood, *on honeysuckle*
Dark-green fritillary *Argynnis aglaja*	June – Aug	Locally common – wood, scrub grass, moor, cliff, also coastal cliff, *on violet*
Heath fritillary *Mellicta athalia*	June – July	Very rare – wood clearings and edge, *on cow wheat, plantain*
High-brown fritillary *Fabriciana adippe*	July – Aug	Not common – bracken in wood edge, scrub, *on violet*
Marsh fritillary *Euphydryas athalia aurinia*	May – Jun	Not common but locally frequent – upland wet pasture, *on devil's bit scabious*
Pearl-bordered fritillary *Clossiana euphrosyne*	May – Jun, Aug	Uncommon, decreasing – bracken in large wood, *on violet*
Silver-washed fritillary *Argynnis paphia*	July – Sept	Widespread – large old woodland, *on violet*
Small pearl-bordered fritillary *Clossiana selene*	June – Sept	Not common, decreasing – deciduous wood, clearings and edge, bog, *on violet*

Browns

Gatekeeper *Pyronia tithonus*	July – Sept	Very common – farm, hedge, lane, *on coarse grasses*
Grayling *Hipparchia sernele*	July – Sept	Locally common – heath, cliff, dune, *on bristle bent and red fescue grasses*
Marbled white *Melanargia galathea*	July – Aug	Locally common – farm, grassland also chalk/limestone, *on grasses, esp. cock's foot, cat's tail*
Meadow brown *Maniola jurtina*	June – Oct	Very common – grassland everywhere, *on coarse grasses*
Ringlet *Aphantopus hyperanthus*	June – Aug	Common – grass near hedge, walls, lanes, wood clearings, *on coarse grasses*
Small heath *Coenonympha pamphilus*	May – Oct	Locally common – down, *on fine-leaved grasses*
Speckled wood *Pararge aegeria*	Apr – Oct	Common and widespread – wood rides and edge, *on coarse grasses*
Wall brown *Lasiomnata megera*	May – Oct	Formerly common, now uncommon – grass banks, cliff, lane, hedge, *on coarse grasses*

BUTTERFLIES	WHEN FLYING	Devon status and where found adult and *caterpillar*
Blues, Coppers & Hairstreaks		
Brown hairstreak *Thecla betulae*	Aug – Sept	Widespread, but rarely seen – Blackthorn hedge, wood edge, scrub, *on blackthorn*
Green hairstreak *Callophrys rubi*	May – July	Locally common – wood edge, heath, *on gorse, rock rose, bird's foot trefoil*
Purple hairstreak *Quercusia quercus*	July – Sept	Widespread, but rarely seen – Oak wood, hedge, *on oak*
White-letter hairstreak *Strymonidia w-album*	July – Aug	Very rare – Elm, Wych elm, hedge, wood, *on elm, wych elm*
Adonis blue *Lysandra bellargus*	May – Sept	Probably extinct – chalk/limestone grass, *on horseshoe vetch*
Brown argus *Aricia agestis*	May – Sept	Not widespread, decreasing – grass, down, meadow, *on rock rose, stork's bill, cranesbill*
Chalk-hill blue *Lysandra coridon*	July – Sept	Very rare, one colony, stray E Devon – chalk/limestone grass, undercliff, *on horseshoe vetch*
Common blue *Polyommatus icarus*	May – Oct	Locally common – chalk down, rough grass, *on bird's foot trefoil and clover*
Holly blue *Celastrina argiolus*	Mar – Oct	Common and widespread – wood, garden, *on holly, ivy*
Large blue *Maculinea arion*	July	Reintroduced, rare – Thyme/anthills grass, heather, gorse, *on thyme with myrmica ants*
Silver-studded blue *Plebejus argus*	July – Aug	Locally common – heath, down, dunes, *on gorse, bird's foot trefoil*
Small blue *Cupido minimus*	May – Sept	Very rare – chalk/limestone grassland dunes, *on kidney vetch*
Small copper *Lycaena phlaeas*	April – Oct	Widespread but rarely common – grass, down, heathland, *on sorrel, dock*
Skippers		
Dingy skipper *Erynnis tages*	May – Jun	Locally common – chalk/limestone grass, quarry, wood edge, heath, dune, *on bird's foot trefoil*
Grizzled skipper *Pyrgus malvae*	April – Jun	Uncommon – wood edge, down, *on wild strawberry, bramble and tormentil*
Large skipper *Ochlodes venatus*	May – Aug	Quite common – farm, grassland, wood edge, *on coarse grasses*
Lulworth skipper *Thymelicus acteon*	July	Rare stray, S E Devon – coastal grassland, *on brachypodium grasses*
Small skipper *Thyrnelicus sylvestris*	June – Aug	Locally common – farm, hillside, wood edge, damp meadow, *on soft grasses (e.g. Yorkshire fog)*

Some grass downland species of butterflies may be found near sea shores, on sand dunes amongst Marram grass and other dune vegetation.

Moths

When compared with our butterflies, the number of moths found in the British Isles is impressive. Moth caterpillars, like butterflies, are dependent on plants for food; almost every fern, grass, flower, bush and tree feeds one or two species of moth.

Moths are many and varied: indeed, so varied that around 2,500 species of moth have so far been found in the British Isles. They are broadly divided into two groups, the larger Macro moths and the smaller Micro moths, sometimes described as the 'outdoor clothes variety'.

Devon has up to 600 macro moths and a similar number of micro, so nearly half of all the moths recorded in Britain have also been found in Devon.

Wood – means deciduous woodland unless otherwise stated.

When flying – some female moths are flightless and two dates indicate double brooded.

Scientific names after J D Bradley 2000

SOME OF THE MOST COMMON MOTHS	WHEN FLYING	Devon status and where found – adult and *caterpillar food plant*
Lackey *Malacosoma neustria*	July – Aug	Common and widespread, hedge – caterpillars together weave a communal silken tent *on hawthorn, oak, elm, willow*
Oak Eggar *Lasiocampa quercus*	July – Aug (male only)	Common and widespread – hedge, wood border, heath, even cliff and dune, *on bramble, dogwood, hawthorn, heather*
Scalloped Hook-tip *Falcaria acertinaria*	May – Jun August	Locally common, wood, heath, *on birch*
Peach Blossom *Thyatira batis*	May – Jun Aug – Sept	Common, wood, *on bramble*
Common Lutestring *Ochropacha duplaris*	Jun – July	Common and widespread, wood, heath, *on birch, also alder, oak*
March Moth *Alsophila aescularia*	Mar – April (male only)	Common and widespread – hedge, park, garden *on hawthorn, sloe, oak*
Large Emerald *Geometra papilionaria*	Jun – July	Common wood, heath, moor *on wide variety of deciduous trees*
Blood-vein *Timandra comae*	Jun – Aug	Common and widespread – ditches, hedge bank or moist places *often on dock, sorrel*
Flame Carpet *Xanthorhoë designata*	May – June August	Common – moist woods *on low small plants*
Common Carpet *Epirrhoë alternata*	May – Jun Aug – Sept	Common and widespread – grassland, fields *on bedstraw*

SOME OF THE MOST COMMON MOTHS	WHEN FLYING	Devon status and where found – adult and *caterpillar food plant*
Phoenix *Eulithis prunata*	July – Aug	Common in gardens, hedge *on sloe, , cultivated black/red current, gooseberry*
Common Marbled Carpet *Dysstroma truncata*	May – Jun Sept – Oct	Common and widespread wood, hedge *on sallow, hawthorn, bilberry, wild strawberry*
Green Pug *Pasiphila rectangulata*	Jun – July	Common orchard, garden, hedge, *on hawthorn, apple, pear*
Willow Beauty *Peribatodes rhomboidaria*	July – Aug occ. Sept	Common and widespread, hedge, park, garden, *on ivy, hawthorn, birch, privet, rose and other shrubs*
Poplar Hawk-moth *Laothoe populi*	May – July	Common and widespread farm, park, garden, *on poplar, aspen, sallow, willow*
Iron Prominent *Notodonta dromedarius*	May – Jun Aug – Sept	Common and widespread, wood, heath, *on birch, alder, hazel, oak*
Pale Tussock *Calliteara pudibunda*	May – Jun	Common and widespread, adult often resting on bracken in woods, *on birch, hazel, oak*
Large Yellow Underwing *Noctua pronuba*	Jun – July and occ. May – Nov	Common park, garden, hedge, *on grasses and low plants*
Setaceous Hebrew Character *Xestia c-nigrum*	May – July Sept – Oct	Common and widespread *on dock, chickweed and other low plants*
Common Quaker *Orthosia cerasi*	Mar – April	Common hedge, wood, park, *on oak, birch, sallow, beech, elm*

Poplar hawk moths mating

SOME SPECIAL DEVON MOTHS	WHEN FLYING	Devon status and where found, adult and *caterpillar food plant*
Ground Lackey *Malacosoma castrensis*	July	Isolated colony at Axemouth saltings *on wild carrot, sea plantain and other plants in the saltings*
Grass Eggar *Lasiocampa trifolii*	Aug – Sept (male only)	S Devon coast only around Prawle Point *on trefoils, thrift, heather, sallow, hawthorn, bramble*
Poplar Lutestring *Tethea sp.*	June – July	Isolated colony nr Hatherleigh *on aspen*
Devon Carpet *Lampropteryx otregiata*	May and August	Fairly common in damp woods, also on Dartmoor *on marsh bedstraw*
Barred Carpet *Perizoma taeniata*	from mid July	Isolated colony nr Lynton *on mosses*
Narrow-bordered Bee Hawk-moth *Hemaris tiyus*	mid May – June	Increasingly restricted to Devon, especially Dartmoor, seems to be doing well *on devil's-bit scabious*
Jersey Tiger *Euplagia quadripunctaria*	mid July – Aug (day- flying moth)	Mainly found Plymouth to Exeter, most commonly around Torquay, Newton Abbot and Teignmouth, *on dandelion, white deadnettle, ground ivy, groundsel, nettle, plantain, elm*
Scarlet Tiger *Callimorpha dominula*	mid July – Aug	Mainly restricted to south-west *on nettle, groundsel, hound's tongue, bramble, sallow, comfrey*
Double Line *Cerastis leucographa*	mid June – July	Mainly south-west, common mid Devon, *on cocksfoot and other grasses*
White Marked *Gypsitea leucographa*	Mar – Apr	Common in Devon, Bideford to Tiverton, *on sallow, bilberry, dock, plantain*
Barrett's Marbled Coronet *Hadena luteago barrettii*	July	Special to southwest, confined to N and S coastal cliffs, *on roots of sea campion, rock spurrey*
White Spot *Hadena albimacula*	mid Jun	Isolated colony Beer and Branscombe, *on seeds of catchfly, campion*
Lead-coloured Drab *Orthosia populeti*	late Mar – April	Isolated colony nr Hatherleigh, *on aspen*
Devonshire wainscot *Mythimna putrescens*	July – Aug	First discovered Torquay, now found N and S coasts, *on grasses*
Black Banded *Polymixis xanthomista sub sp.*	Aug – Sept	N coast of Devon, *on sea thrift flowers, plantain*
Scarce Merveille du Jour *Moma alpium*	late Jun – July	Old oak woods Torridge valley, *on oak*
Morris's Wainscot *Chortodes morrisii*	Jun	S coast, Devon/Dorset border, *on tall fescue grass*
Scarce Blackneck *Lygephila craccae*	late July – Aug	N Devon coast, *on tufted vetch, sometimes wood vetch*
Bloxworth Snout *Hypena obsitalis*	Jun – Aug/Sept	First appeared in county 1990, S coast and spreading, *on nettle, pellitory*

Damselflies and Dragonflies

Damselflies and dragonflies, with their electric blues and vibrant reds, are surprisingly colourful insects, and many are masters of flight. Among the most ancient in origin of all Devon's creatures, their giant ancestors first took to the air over 300 million years ago, just after our Devonian rocks were laid down. Yet despite their fearsome appearance, these creatures are harmless to humans; they hunt much smaller prey, much as their ancestors once did when they flew around monstrous dinosaurs.

Today 39 damselflies and dragonflies are resident in Britain, while another 9 are regular migrants or rare vagrants. Nearly two-thirds of these can be regularly seen in Devon.

DAMSELFLIES	WHEN FLYING	Devon status and where found
Azure damselfly *Coenagrion puella*	mid May – mid Aug	Common – water meadow, canal, pond, ditch
Banded demoiselle *Calopteryx splendens*	late May – early Sept	Common, W and S Devon, also Slapton – slow stream, river
Beautiful demoiselle *Calopteryx virgo*	mid May – early Sept	Very common – all Devon – fast, clear stream, river
Blue-tailed damselfly *Ischnura elegans*	end May – early Sept	Very common except moors – canal, pond, slow stream, ditch
Common blue damselfly *Enallagma cyathigerum*	mid May – Sept	Very common – large lake, pond, canal
Emerald damselfly *Lestes sponsa*	mid June – end Sept	Locally common S and W Devon – canal, pond, bog
Large red damselfly *Pyrrhosoma nymphula*	late April – Aug	Very common – any slow or still, fresh water
Red-eyed damselfly *Erythromma najas*	early June – early Sept	Locally common only SE Devon – centre pond or lake
Scarce blue-tailed damselfly *Ischnura pumilio*	end May – early Sept	Scarce, locally common S&W well spread on S, C & W Dartmoor only – shallow pool, stream, bog
Small red damselfly *Ceriagrion tenellum*	late April – early Sept	Scarce, locally common – bog, heathland pool
Southern damselfly *Coenagrion mercuriale*	early June – mid Aug	Rare, SE Devon and NE Dartmoor only – heathland stream
White-legged damselfly *Platycnemis pennipes*	late May – mid Aug	Locally common river and stream, found on Tamar, Otter, Exe, Axe and Culm

DRAGONFLIES	WHEN FLYING	Devon status and where found
Black darter *Sympetrum danae*	July – early Oct	Common especially south Dartmoor and E Devon heaths – heathland and moorland bog
Black-tailed skimmer *Orthetrum cancellatum*	end May – early Aug	Locally common S Devon – pond, flooded clay pit
Broad-bodied chaser *Libellula depressa*	mid May – early Aug	Common especially in south – pond
Common darter *Sympetrum striolatum*	mid June – end Oct	Very common, also moors – pond, woodland ditch
Common hawker *Aeshna juncea*	mid July – early Oct	Fairly common – heath and moorland pool
Downy emerald dragonfly *Cordulia aenea*	mid May – early July	Scarce, SE Devon only – edge wooded lake, pond
Emperor dragonfly *Anax imperator*	end May – end Aug	Locally common – large lake, pond, canal
Four-spotted chaser *Libellula quadrimaculata*	mid May – mid Aug	Fairly common – pond, boggy pool
Golden-ringed dragonfly *Cordulegaster boltonii*	end May – mid Sept	Common – stream, also on moor river
Hairy dragonfly *Brachytron pratense*	early May – mid Jun	Scarce and local – S and E Devon only – stream, ditch, canal, pond
Keeled skimmer *Orthetrum coerulescens*	mid June – early Sept	Common – heathland and moorland bog
Migrant hawker *Aeshna mixta*	late July – end Oct	Locally common especially S and E Devon – pond, lake edge
Ruddy darter *Sympetrum sanguineum*	end June – early Sept	Rare SE Devon only – pond, marsh, ditch
Southern hawker *Aeshna cyanea*	July – mid Oct	Very common – lane, hedgerow, small pond, lake

Emperor drasgonfly egg laying

Grasshoppers and Crickets

One of the most familiar sounds of summer on a warm day, as you walk through any grassland or along a leafy lane, must surely be a chorus of insects. Like radio broadcasters, grasshoppers and crickets are better known by their voices rather than by their looks – although 'voice' is not strictly accurate, as they produce their amazing calls by rubbing legs against wings (grasshoppers) or wings together (crickets). Devon is especially rich in these creatures: 23 of the 28 species known on the British mainland can be found in the county. They are most active during summer.

Best places to look: Braunton Burrows in North Devon, Branscombe under-cliff, and the Pebblebed Commons of East Devon are recommended for enthusiasts looking for many different varieties, including some of our rarest ones. The long-winged cone-head is a new arrival, having only recently colonised some areas of the county.

BUSH CRICKETS	Devon status and where found
Bog bush-cricket *Metrioptera brachyptera*	Nationally scarce: rare outside east Devon, pebblebed commons, also colony at Chudleigh Knighton – Wet lowland heaths, moor, valley bog.
Dark bush-cricket *Pholidoptera griseoaptera*	Most common Devon bush-cricket – Wasteground, scrub, hedgerows, brambles
Great green bush-cricket *Tettigonia viridissima*	Stronghold in South Hams, colony at Braunton N coast – Coastal cliffs and scrub, bramble, parks and gardens, hedgerow
Grey bush-cricket *Platycleis albopunctata*	Nationally scarce, colony at Braunton – Coastal cliffs and scrub, sand dunes on N coast.
Long-winged Cone-head *Conocephalus discolor*	Suitable habitat south only – Wide range of habitats, coastal reedbed, grassland, urban wasteland
Oak bush-cricket *Meconema thalassinum*	Any suitable habitat in north and south Devon – Deciduous woodland, hedgerows, parks (attracted to lights)
Short-winged Cone-head *Conocephalus dorsalis*	South coast, also colonies on Taw and Torridge estuaries N Devon – Grasses in estuary salt marsh
Speckled bush-cricket *Leptophyes punctatissima*	Widespread, common parks and gardens south Devon – Scrub, bramble, gardens, open woodland

GRASSHOPPERS

TRUE CRICKETS	Devon status and where found
Wood cricket *Nemobius sylvestris*	Confined E Devon commons and Dunsford woods – Deep leaf litter in deciduous woodland borders, also heath scrub. Nationally very scarce
Scaly cricket *Pseudomogoplistes vicentae*	Endangered species, only Branscombe beach – Shingle beach

MOLE CRICKETS	Devon status and where found
Mole-cricket *Gryllotalpa gryllotalpa*	Not recorded since last century, probably extinct – Wet meadow, flood plain, damp pasture, moist soil on vegetable allotments. Endangered species.

GROUND-HOPPERS	Devon status and where found
Cepero's ground-hopper *Tetrix ceperoi*	Nationally very scarce, very localised colonies on SE and NW coasts – Wet flushes on coastal cliff, near river, dune slack, saltmarsh
Common ground-hopper *Tetrix undulata*	Most common ground-hopper, found most suitable places – Woodland ride, moist or dry bare ground with short vegetation
Slender ground-hopper *Tetrix subulata*	Generally S coast, also colonies at Braunton – Coastal, wet bare ground with short vegetation, dune slacks, often near water

GRASSHOPPERS	Devon status and where found
Common green grasshopper *Omocestus viridulus*	Common and widespread – Most grassland, especially moist unimproved lands
Field grasshopper *Chorthippus brunneus*	Common and widespread – Almost any dry sunny habitat, railway cuttings, hedge bank
Lesser marsh grasshopper *Chorthippus albomarginatus*	Rare in Devon, recently recorded from grazing marsh on Exe estuary, Clyst valley – Lowland pasture, shingle, saltmarsh, flood meadow, rough grassy areas
Meadow grasshopper *Chorthippus parallelus*	Common and widespread – Mainly coarse grassland, widespread from moor to coastal dune
Mottled grasshopper *Myrmeleotettix maculatus*	Fairly common, widespread especially on drier ground – Heath, dune, free draining soil with short turf and bare ground
Rufous grasshopper *Gomphocerippus rufus*	Nationally scarce, rare in Devon. Confined to chalk downland and cliffs, Seaton to Dunscombe – Generally rough dry calcareous grassland, sometimes near dunes
Stripe-winged grasshopper *Stenobothrus lineatus*	Rare in Devon, recently recorded from east Devon pebblebed commons – Mainly chalk and limestone grassland with short turf, some dry heath
Woodland grasshopper *Omocestus rufipes*	Nationally scarce, rare in Devon. Recently recorded from two sites in E Devon – Woodland ride and clearing, adjacent heath or scrub

Birds

[This section is best used in conjunction with the following one, 'Best Bird Sites in Devon'.]

Birds are among the most entertaining wild creatures and, at times, the easiest to watch. They sing and dance to find a mate, forage and feed at regular intervals, and come in all colours, shapes and sizes – a lot like us. Some are also international travellers, while others are resident and may seldom stray more than a few miles from home.

More than 500 birds are included on the Official British List, of which, amazingly, just over 400 have been recorded in Devon.

Passage migrant – a bird passing through on migration between summer and wintering areas.

Vagrant – a rare accidental visitor from abroad, mainly at migration time. Only a few of the most recent have been included.

Pelagic – a seabird that feeds over the ocean, not normally seen around coasts except when nesting or blown in by gale.

Locally common – widespread bird that occurs infrequently but where it does it may be found in some numbers.

Regular Devon bird – either resident or visitor.

Birds are listed alphabetically by their common name, in related groups: e.g. buntings are listed together.

BIRDS	Devon status and where found
Avocet *Recurvirostra avosetta*	Regular winter visitor – Exe estuary, some Tamar
Bittern *Botaurus stellaris*	Rare winter visitor – reed beds
Blackbird *Turdus merula*	Very common resident, winter visitor, breeds – wood, garden, farm
Blackcap *Sylvia atricapilla*	Common summer visitor, some winter, breeds – wood, garden, hedge
Bluethroat *Luscinia svecica*	Rare passage migrant – marsh, wet scrub
Brambling *Fringilla montifringilla*	Winter visitor, usually small flocks with chaffinch – wood, hedge
Bullfinch *Pyrrhula pyrrhula*	Common resident, breeds – orchard, hedge, wood
Bunting, Cirl *Emberiza cirlus*	Locally uncommon resident, breeds S coast Plymouth – Exeter farm, hedge
Bunting, Corn *Miliaria calandra*	Scarce resident, has bred – farm, grass, scrub
Bunting, Lapland *Calcarius lapponicus*	Regular passage migrant on Lundy – coast
Bunting, Ortolan *Emberiza hortulana*	Rare passage migrant on Lundy – coast

BIRDS	Devon status and where found
Bunting, Reed *Emberiza schoeniclus*	Fairly common resident, breeds – estuary, marsh, moor
Bunting, Snow *Plectrophenax nivalis*	Scarce passage migrant and winter visitor – coast, hillside
Buzzard *Buteo buteo*	Common resident, breeds – wood, farm, moor
Buzzard, Honey *Pernis apivorus*	Rare summer visitor, has bred, passage migrant – conifer forest
Chaffinch *Fringilla coelebs*	Common resident, breeds, passage migrant, winter visitor – farm, park, hedge, garden
Chiffchaff *Phylloscopus collybita*	Common summer visitor, scarce winter near coast, passage migrant, breeds – wood, hedge, garden
Coot *Fulica atra*	Resident, winter visitor, breeds – lake, reservoir, canal
Cormorant *Phalacrocorax carbo*	Resident, breeds – sea cliff, islet, lake, reservoir
Crake, Spotted *Porzana porzana*	Uncommon passage migrant, irregular visitor – marsh
Crossbill *Loxia curvirostra*	Irregular visitor, occasionally breeds – conifer wood
Crow, Carrion *Corvus corone*	Common resident, breeds – moor, farm
Crow, Hooded *Corvus cornix*	Rare winter visitor – anywhere
Cuckoo *Cuculus canorus*	Summer visitor, breeds, declining – moor, farm, reedbed
Curlew *Numenius arquata*	Resident, common winter visitor, now rare breeder – moor, upland pasture, coast, estuary
Dipper *Cinclus cinclus*	Fairly common resident, breeds – fast stream, river
Diver, Black-throated *Gavia arctica*	Winter visitor, passage migrant, annual but scarce – sheltered coastal bay
Diver, Great Northern *Gavia immer*	Fairly common winter visitor – sheltered coastal bay
Diver, Red-throated *Gavia stellata*	Annual winter visitor – sheltered coastal bay

Black-tailed godwit

BIRDS	Devon status and where found
Dotterel *Charadrius morinellus*	Rare passage migrant – Lundy, Dartmoor, S coast
Dove, Stock *Columba oenas*	Common resident and winter visitor – farm, buildings
Dove, Turtle *Streptopelia turtur*	Scarce summer visitor, some breed – farm
Dove, Collared	Common resident, breeds – farm, villages
Duck, Long-tailed *Clangula hyemalis*	Regular winter visitor, small numbers – estuary
Duck, Ruddy *Oxyura jamaicensis*	Introduced winter visitor, has bred – Slapton
Duck, Tufted *Aythya fuligula*	Regular, fairly common, winter visitor, scarce annual breeder – slow river, pond, lake, reservoir
Dunlin *Calidris alpina*	Resident, passage migrant and winter visitor, a few breed – Dartmoor, estuary
Dunnock *Prunella modularis*	Common resident, breeds – farm, garden
Egret, Little *Egretta garzetta*	Resident and passage migrant, rare breeder – estuary, marsh
Eider *Somateria mollissima*	Resident, non breeding, small numbers – estuary, coast
Fieldfare *Turdus pilaris*	Regular common winter visitor – orchard, hedge, grassland
Firecrest *Regulus ignicapillus*	Widespread passage migrant mainly autumn, winter visitor in small numbers – wood, scrub, coast and near water
Flycatcher, Pied *Ficedula hypoleuca*	Summer visitor, breeds, small numbers, regular passage migrant – oak wood
Flycatcher, Red-breasted *Ficedula parva*	Scarce passage migrant – Lundy, S coast
Flycatcher, Spotted *Muscicapa striata*	Fairly common summer visitor, breeds – park, garden, wood edge
Fulmar *Fulmarus glacialis*	Pelagic, common summer visitor, breeds – sea cliff
Gadwall *Anas strepera*	Regular winter visitor, not common, breeds – estuary, Slapton, Beesands
Gannet *Sula bassana*	Regular non-breeding visitor – coast
Garganey *Anas querquedula*	Passage migrant, occasionally breeds – marsh, pond, Slapton
Godwit, Bar-tailed *Limosa lapponica*	Winter visitor, passage migrant – estuary, coastal
Godwit, Black-tailed *Limosa limosa*	Common winter and a non-breeding summer visitor, passage migrant – estuary, coast, marsh, wet grassland
Goldcrest *Regulus regulus*	Common resident, winter visitor, breeds – conifer wood
Goldeneye *Bucephala clangula*	Regular winter visitor, small numbers – estuary, lake, reservoir
Goldfinch *Cardueljs carduelis*	Common resident, breeds – farm, hedge
Goosander *Mergus merganser*	Regular, uncommon, winter visitor – breeds on rivers. inland waters, reservoirs, rivers

BIRDS	Devon status and where found
Goose, Barnacle *Branta leucopsis*	Irregular winter visitor – estuary
Goose, Bean *Anser fabalis*	Rare winter visitor – wet grassland
Goose, Brent *Branta bernicla*	Regular winter visitor, good numbers – estuary
Goose, Canada *Branta canadensis*	Introduced resident, breeds – large pond, estuary
Goose, Greylag *Anser wiser*	Scarce feral visitor – estuary
Goose, White-fronted *Anser albifrons*	Irregular winter visitor, small numbers – wet grassland
Goshawk *Accipiter gentilis*	Resident, rare breeder – wood
Grebe, Black-necked *Podiceps nigricollis*	Scarce winter visitor – Torbay, Slapton
Grebe, Great Crested *Podiceps cristatus*	Few resident, breeds and winter visitor – lake, Slapton
Grebe, Little *Tachvhaptus ruficollis*	Few resident, breeds and winter visitor – slow river, big pond
Grebe, Red-necked *Podiceps grisegena*	Winter visitor, rare – seabird watch point, estuary
Grebe, Slavonian *Podiceps auritus*	Scarce winter visitor – estuary, coast
Greenfinch *Carduelis chloris*	Common resident, breeds – farm, garden, esp. nr. conifer trees
Greenshank *Tringa nebularia*	Fairly common passage migrant, winter visitor – estuary
Grouse, Red *Lagopus lagopus*	Scarce resident, breeds – high moor
Guillemot, Common *Uria aalge*	Common resident, breeds – Lundy, Berry Head, cliff, coast
Gull, Black-headed *Larus ridibundus*	Resident and common winter visitor – estuary
Gull, Common *Larus canus*	Common winter visitor and passage migrant – estuary, reservoir
Gull, Glaucous *Larus hyperboreus*	Scarce, irregular winter visitor – seabird watch point, coast, estuary and fish quay
Gull, Great Black-backed *Larus marinus*	Common resident, winter visitor, breeds – cliff, coast, estuary
Gull, Herring *Larus argentatus*	Common resident, breeds – cliff, coast, estuary
Gull, Iceland *Larus glaucoides*	Scarce, irregular winter visitor – seabird watch point, coast, estuary, fish quay
Gull, Lesser Black-backed *Larus fuscus*	Fairly common resident, passage migrant, occasionally breeds – seabird watch point, Lundy, estuary, reservoir
Gull, Little *Larus minutus*	Not common, regular passage migrant and winter visitor – seabird watch point, coast

Gull, Mediterranean *Larus melanocephalus*	Regular migrant, winter visitor, often with black-headed gulls – estuary
Gull, Ring-billed *Larus delawarensis*	American almost regular trans-Atlantic vagrant – Slapton, Plymouth, Barnstaple, Teign estuaries
Gull, Ross's *Rhodostethia rosea*	Rare vagrant (4 records) – sheltered bay, coast
Gull, Sabine's *Larus sabini*	Annual vagrant – seabird watch point, Slapton
Harrier, Hen *Circus cyaneus*	Regular winter visitor – marsh, moor, reed, dune
Harrier, Marsh *Circus aeruginosus*	Irregular visitor, passage migrant – estuary, marsh
Harrier, Montagu's *Circus pygargus*	Uncommon summer visitor, has bred in past – marsh, moor, young conifer plantation
Hawfinch *Coccothraustes coccothraustes*	Uncommon resident, winter visitor, occasionally breeds – hornbeam, cherry, wood, hedge
Heron, Grey *Ardea cinerea*	Common resident, winter visitor, breeds – estuary, river, pond
Heron, Purple *Ardea purpurea*	Regular vagrant – marsh
Hobby *Falco subbuteo*	Scarce summer visitor, breeds – open conifer wood, moor, heath
Hoopoe *Upupa epops*	Rare passage migrant, frequent single birds – migration watch point, Lundy
Jackdaw *Corvus monedula*	Common resident, breeds – farm, park, cliff, old buildings
Jay *Garrulus glandarius*	Fairly common resident, breeds – deciduous wood, farmland
Kestrel *Falco tinnunculus*	Fairly common resident, breeds, some passage migrants – sea cliff, quarry, farm, road side
Kingfisher *Alcedo atthis*	Widespread resident, breeds – stream, river, lake
Kite, Red *Milvus milvus*	Irregular visitor – wood, farm
Kittiwake *Rissa tridactyla*	Common resident, breeds – sea cliff, Lundy
Knot *Calidris canutus*	Fairly common winter visitor and passage migrant – estuary
Lapwing *Vanellus vanellus*	Resident and common winter visitor, some breed – estuary, marsh, moor
Lark, Shore *Eremophila alpestris*	Rare passage migrant – migration watch point
Linnet *Carduelis cannabina*	Common resident and winter visitor, breeds – farm, heath, coast
Magpie *Pica pica*	Common resident, breeds – farm, garden
Mallard *Anas platyrhynchos*	Common resident and winter visitor, breeds – freshwater, estuary

BIRDS

BIRDS	Devon status and where found
Martin, House *Delichon urbica*	Common summer visitor, breeds – farm, village
Martin, Sand *Riparia riparia*	Locally common summer visitor, breeds – riverside, sand quarry
Merganser, Red-breasted *Mergus serrator*	Regular, locally common, winter visitor – estuary, bay
Merlin *Falco columbarius*	Uncommon resident and winter visitor, breeds – moor
Moorhen *Gallinula chloropus*	Common resident, breeds – slow/still freshwater
Nightingale *Luscinia megarhynchos*	Rare summer visitor, has bred in past – scrub, wood
Night Thrush *Luscinia luscinia*	Rare vagrant – Lundy
Nightjar *Caprimulgus europaeus*	Locally common, summer visitor, breeds – heath, moor
Nuthatch *Sitta europaea*	Fairly common resident, breeds – wood
Oriole, Golden *Oriolus oriolus*	Irregular spring passage migrant, last bred Victorian times – Lundy
Osprey *Pandion haliaetus*	Rare passage migrant – raptor watch point, estuary
Ouzel, Ring *Turdus torquatus*	Uncommon summer visitor, breeds – high moor, clitter
Owl, Barn *Tyto alba*	Resident, breeds, never common – farm
Owl, Little *Athene noctua*	Resident, breeds, local not common – farm
Owl, Long-eared *Asio otus*	Irregular visitor – conifer wood, hedge
Owl, Short-eared *Asio flammeus*	Winter visitor and passage migrant – coast, estuary marsh
Owl, Tawny *Strix aluco*	Common resident, breeds – wood
Oystercatcher *Haematopus ostralegus*	Resident and common winter visitor, breeds – estuary, coast
Partridge, Grey *Perdix perdix*	Rare resident, breeds – arable farm

Barn owl

Grey plover

BIRDS	Devon status and where found
Partridge, Red-legged *Alectoris rufa*	Uncommon resident, breeds E Devon – arable farm
Peregrine *Falco peregrinus*	Resident, breeds, small numbers sea cliff, quarry, Exeter city
Petrel, Leach's *Oceanodroma leucorhoa*	Pelagic, irregular autumn/winter visitor – sea watch point
Petrel, Storm *Hydrobates pelagicus*	Pelagic, summer visitor – sea watch point, Lundy
Phalarope, Grey *Phalaropus fulicarius*	Uncommon passage migrant – sea watch point
Phalarope, Red-necked *Phalaropus lobatus*	Uncommon passage migrant – sea watch point
Pheasant *Phasianus colchicus*	Common introduced resident, breeds – farm, wood
Pintail *Anas acuta*	Fairly common, winter visitor – estuary
Pipit, Meadow *Anthus pratensis*	Common resident and winter visitor, breeds – moor, dune, rough pasture
Pipit, Rock *Anthus petrosus*	Common resident, breeds – rocky shore
Pipit, Tree *Anthus trivialis*	Summer visitor, breeds, regular but not common – heath, open wood, hillside
Pipit, Water *Anthus spinoletta spinoletta*	Scarce winter visitor – estuary, marsh
Plover, Golden *Pluvialis apricaria*	Resident, common winter visitor, passage migrant, few breed – high moor
Plover, Grey *Pluvialis squatarola*	Scarce winter visitor and passage migrant – estuary
Plover, Kentish *Charadrius alexandrinus*	Scarce passage migrant – estuary, sea shore
Plover, Little Ringed *Charadrius dubius*	Scarce passage migrant, has bred recently – sea shore, reservoir
Plover, Ringed *Charadrius hiaticula*	Resident, passage migrant and winter visitor, some breed – estuary, sea shore
Pochard *Aythya ferina*	Regular winter visitor, fairly common – estuary, Slapton
Puffin *Fratercula arctica*	Summer visitor, some still breed Lundy – Lundy
Quail *Coturnjx coturnix*	Irregular summer visitor, occasionally breeds – arable farm
Rail, Water *Rallus aquaticus*	Regular winter visitor and passage migrant, occasionally breeds – reed bed, marsh
Raven *Corvus corax*	Fairly common resident, breeds – moor, farm
Razorbill *Alca torda*	Common resident, breeds – cliff, Lundy, Berry Head
Redpoll *Carduelis flammea*	Uncommon resident and winter visitor, breeds – wood, moor. heath
Redshank *Tringa totanus*	Common visitor, a few breed – estuary
Redshank, Spotted *Tringa erythropus*	Scarce passage migrant and winter visitor in small numbers – estuary

BIRDS	Devon status and where found
Redstart, Common *Phoenicurus phoenicurus*	Uncommon summer visitor, breeds – deciduous wood
Redstart, Black *Phoenicurus ochruros*	Scarce passage migrant and winter visitor – cliffs, buildings
Redwing *Turdus iliacus*	Common winter visitor – farm, orchard
Robin *Erithacus rubecula*	Common resident, breeds, also autumn immigrant – farm, park, garden,
Rook *Corvus frugilegus*	Common resident, breeds – farm, wood
Ruff *Philomachus pugnax*	Regular winter visitor and passage migrant in small numbers – estuary, marsh, reservoir
Sanderling *Calidris alba*	Common winter visitor and passage migrant – estuary, sea shore
Sandpiper, Broad-billed *Limicola falcinellus*	Rare migrant – estuary
Sandpiper, Buff-breasted *Tryngites subruficollis*	Regular American vagrant in southwest – Thurlestone links
Sandpiper, Common *Actitis hypoleucos*	Summer and winter visitor, common passage migrant, rare breeder – estuary, river, reservoir
Sandpiper, Curlew *Calidris ferruginea*	Uncommon passage migrant – estuary, sea shore, reservoir
Sandpiper, Green *Tringa ochropus*	Regular winter visitor and passage migrant in small numbers – estuary, flood meadow, river, stream
Sandpiper, Pectoral *Calidris melanotos*	Vagrant – most common American wader – Lundy
Sandpiper, Purple *Calidris maritima*	Locally common winter visitor, small numbers – estuary, rocky shore
Sandpiper, Wood *Tringa glareola*	Regular passage migrant in small numbers – estuary, marsh, reservoir
Scaup *Aythya mania*	Scarce winter visitor – estuary, lake
Scoter, Common *Melanitta nigra*	Regular summer and winter visitor, non breeding, fair numbers – sheltered bay
Scoter, Velvet *Melanitta fusca*	Uncommon, regular winter visitor – sheltered bay
Serin *Serinus serinus*	Vagrant, has bred – park, garden, coast
Shag *Phalacrocorax aristotelis*	Common resident, breeds – sea cliff, islet, Lundy, estuary
Shearwater, Balearic *Puffinus mauretanicus*	Pelagic, scarce passage migrant – sea watch point
Shearwater, Cory's *Calonectris diomedea*	Pelagic, rare autumn passage migrant – sea watch point
Shearwater, Great *Puffinus gravis*	Pelagic, rare autumn passage migrant – sea watch point
Shearwater, Manx *Puffinus puffinus*	Pelagic, summer visitor breeds Lundy – sea watch point
Shearwater, Sooty *Puffinus griseus*	Pelagic, scarce autumn passage vagrant – sea watch point

BIRDS	Devon status and where found
Shelduck *Tadorna tadorna*	Common resident, breeds and winter visitor – estuary, coast
Shoveler *Anas clypeata*	Winter visitor – estuary, lake
Shrike, Great Grey *Lanius excubitor*	Irregular winter visitor – heath, wood edge, moor
Shrike, Red-backed *Lanius collurio*	Scarce passage migrant, used to breed – heath, scrub, coast
Siskin *Carduelis spinus*	Fairly common resident and winter visitor, breeds – conifer wood, garden
Skua, Arctic *Stercorarius parasiticus*	Passage migrant, small numbers – estuary, sea watch point
Skua, Great *Stercorarius skua*	Scarce passage migrant – sea watch point
Skua, Pomarine *Stercorarius pomarinus*	Scarce passage migrant – sea watch point
Skylark *Alauda arvensis*	Less common resident and winter visitor, breeds – moor, farm, marsh, dune
Smew *Mergus albellus*	Irregular winter visitor, small numbers – Exe estuary, Slapton, reservoir. lake
Snipe, Common *Gallinago gallinago*	Resident and common winter visitor, breeds – marsh, bog, estuary
Snipe, Jack *Lymnocryptes minimus*	Winter visitor and passage migrant, small numbers – marsh, bog, estuary
Sparrow, Tree *Passer montanus*	Rare visitor – farm
Sparrow, House *Passer domesticus*	Locally common resident, breeds – farm, village, town
Sparrowhawk *Accipiter nisus*	Resident and passage migrant, breeds – farm, park, wood
Spoonbill *Platalea leucorodia*	Few, mainly winter visitor – estuary
Starling *Sturnus vulgaris*	Formerly common resident, breeds, common winter visitor – farm, garden, reed
Stint, Little *Calidris minuta*	Regular, uncommon passage migrant – estuary, reservoir
Stonechat *Saxicola torquata*	Locally common resident, breeds – moor, heath, coast
Swallow *Hirundo rustica*	Common summer visitor and passage migrant, breeds – farm, reed

Curlew sandpiper   *Manx shearwater*

BIRDS

BIRDS	Devon status and where found
Swan, Bewick's *Cygnus columbianus bewickii*	Occasional winter visitor, small numbers – marsh, lake
Swan, Mute *Cygnus olor*	Common resident, breeds, not uplands – freshwater, estuary
Swan, Whooper *Cygnus cygnus*	Occasional winter visitor, small numbers – marsh, estuary
Swift *Apus apus*	Common summer visitor, breeds – old buildings
Teal *Anas crecca*	Resident and winter visitor, occasionally breeds – pond, lake, estuary
Tern, Arctic *Sterna paradisaea*	Scarce passage migrant – estuary, offshore
Tern, Black *Chlidonias niger*	Regular passage migrant – estuary, reservoir, lake
Tern, Common *Sterna hirundo*	Regular passage migrant – estuary, offshore
Tern, Little *Sterna albifrons*	Scarce passage migrant – estuary, coast
Tern, Roseate *Sterna dougallii*	Rare passage migrant – estuary, coast
Tern, Sandwich *Sterna sandvicensis*	Common passage migrant – estuary, coast
Tern, White-winged Black *Chlidonias leucopterus*	Summer vagrant – coast, reservoir, lake
Thrush, Mistle *Turdus viscivorus*	Common resident, breeds – park, farm, garden
Thrush, Song *Turdus philomelos*	Common resident and winter visitor, breeds – farm, garden
Tit, Bearded *Panurus biarmicus*	Rare winter migrant, has bred – reed bed
Tit, Blue *Parus caeruleus*	Common resident, breeds – wood, hedge, garden
Tit, Coal *Parus ater*	Common resident, breeds – wood, hedge, garden
Tit, Great *Parus major*	Common resident, breeds – wood, hedge, garden
Tit, Long-tailed *Aegithalos caudatus*	Common resident, breeds – wood, hedge, heath
Tit, Marsh *Parus palustris*	Fairly common resident, breeds – wood, hedge
Tit, Willow *Parus montanus*	Rare resident, breeds – wet thicket
Treecreeper *Certhia familiaris*	Common resident, breeds – wood, hedge
Turnstone *Arenaria interpres*	Passage migrant, common winter and non-breeding summer visitor – estuary, sea shore
Wagtail, Grey *Motacilla cinerea*	Common resident, breeds – stream, buildings, wetland
Wagtail, Pied *Motacilla alba yarrellii*	Common resident and passage migrant, breeds – farm, garden, buildings
Wagtail, White *Motacilla alba alba*	Scarce passage migrant, has bred Lundy – coast

| --- | --- |
Wagtail, Yellow *Motacilla flava*	Scarce summer visitor, annual passage migrant, has bred – nr water, marsh, farm
Warbler, Cetti's *Cettia cetti*	Mainly resident, breeds – reed bed, swamp
Warbler, Dartford *Sylvia undata*	Once rare, increasing, resident, breeds – heath and coast with heather & gorse
Warbler, Garden *Sylvia bonn*	Widespread summer visitor, breeds – wood, scrub
Warbler, Grasshopper *Locustella naevia*	Locally fairly common summer visitor, breeds marsh, hedge, water meadow, heath
Warbler, Icterine *Hippolais icterina*	Rare passage migrant – migration watch point
Warbler, Marsh *Acrocephalus palustris*	Vagrant in summer – migrant watch point, marsh
Warbler, Melodious *Hippolais polyglotta*	Rare autumn passage migrant – migrant watch point
Warbler, Reed *Acrocephalus scirpaceus*	Locally common summer visitor, breeds, and passage migrant – reed bed
Warbler, Sedge *Acrocephalus schoenobaenus*	Locally common summer visitor, breeds – reed bed, swamp
Warbler, Willow *Phylloscopus trochilus*	Common summer visitor and passage migrant, breeds – scrub, wood
Warbler, Wood *Phylloscopus sibilatrix*	Locally common summer visitor, breeds – wood – oak, beech
Waxwing *Bombycilla garrulus*	Irregular winter visitor – hedge, garden
Wheatear *Oenanthe oenanthe*	Locally common summer visitor, breeds – moor, dune, coast
Whimbrel *Numenius phaeopus*	Passage migrant, locally common – estuary, coast
Whinchat *Saxicola rubetra*	Fairly common resident and migrant, breeds – moor, scrub, coast (migrant)
Whitethroat *Sylvia communis*	Common summer visitor, breeds – farm, scrub, bramble
Whitethroat, Lesser *Sylvia curruca*	Summer visitor, scarce breeder – farm, scrub, trees, hedge
Wigeon *Anas penelope*	Common winter visitor – estuary, lake, reservoir
Woodcock *Scolopax rusticola*	Common winter visitor, occasionally breeds – wet wood
Woodlark *Lullula arborea*	Scarce resident, breeds – hillside, farm
Woodpecker, Great Spotted *Dendrocopos major*	Widespread resident, breeds – wood, hedge, park
Woodpecker, Green *Picus viridis*	Common resident, breeds – decid wood, park, farm
Woodpecker, Lesser Spotted *Dendrocopos minor*	Uncommon resident, breeds – orchard, open wood
Woodpigeon *Columba palumbus*	Common resident, breeds and large number of winter visitors – farm, park
Wren *Troglodytes troglodytes*	Common resident, breeds – farm yard, hedge, wood, scrub
Wryneck *Jynx torquilla*	Scarce passage migrant – garden, migration watch point
Yellowhammer *Emberiza citrinella*	Common resident, breeds – farm, hedge, heath, moor, coast

BIRDS

Best Bird Sites in Devon

Star rating: *   Limited local interest
                   **   Can be good
                   ***   Consistently best

Wildfowl include: teal, wigeon, mallard, shoveller, tufted duck, pochard, goldeneye and maybe scaup as well as long-tailed duck.

Sea duck include: common scoter, also red-breasted merganser, scaup, eider, maybe velvet scoter.

Seabirds include: herring and greater black-backed gull, fulmar, cormorant, shag, guillemot, razorbill, passing gannet, manx shearwater.

Waders include: curlew, greenshank, redshank, oystercatcher, little stint, common sandpiper, dunlin, ruff, ringed plover, grey plover and turnstone.

Winter thrushes: North European migrants, mainly redwing and fieldfare with blackbird and song thrush joining local birds.

Resident and visiting birds at individual **Sites** are in addition to the **Habitat** residents and visitors.

Habitat and Site	Best Time	Best Season	Main birds
ESTUARY MUDFLATS – edge, salt marsh and flying over	mid tide	All – resident	Cormorant, shag, grey heron, shelduck, oyster-catcher, little egret
Axe Estuary**	mid tide	Mar – May Nov-Feb	Sand martin, redshank Wigeon, teal, green sandpiper, wader rarities
Otter Estuary *	mid tide	Nov – Feb Mar -May	Divers, grebes, gulls, wildfowl & waders, merganser, peregrine, coot, kingfisher. Little grebe, fulmar, sand martin, sandwich tern
Exe Estuary *** (Especially from Topsham, Exmouth, Turf Lock, Dawlish Warren)	mid tide	Nov – Feb Mar – May Jun – Jul Aug – Oct	Gulls, wildfowl & waders incl. avocet, brent geese, grey plover, godwits, slavonian grebe, pintail Wheatear, terns, whimbrel, sandpipers, Sandwich tern Terns, osprey
Kingsbridge Estuary **	mid tide	Nov – Feb	Divers, grebes, gulls, wildfowl & waders, peregrine, coot, kingfisher.
Plym Estuary (Plymouth) **	mid tide	Dec – Feb Aug – Nov	Gulls, wildfowl & waders, merganser, goosander, peregrine Good for rare gulls, waders (from Saltram)

Habitat and Site	Best Time	Best Season	Main birds
ESTUARY MUDFLATS – edge, salt marsh and flying over	mid tide	All – resident	Cormorant, shag, grey heron, shelduck, oyster-catcher, egret
TaMar – Tavy **	mid tide	Nov-Feb	Wildfowl & waders incl. avocet
Taw-Torridge Estuary *	mid tide	Dec – Feb	Wildfowl & waders, kingfisher, snow bunting, spoonbill
		Mar – May	Whimbrel, wheatear, terns,
		Aug – Nov	Swallows, martins, first waders, peregrine, merlin, hen harrier, spoonbill (Isley marsh)
Yealm/Erme*	mid tide	All – Resident	Little egret
FLOOD MEADOW (grazing marsh)	high tide	Dec – Feb	Waders and wildfowl
	any	Mar – May	Waders, garganey, little grebe, swallow and martin
	any	Aug – Nov	Terns, gulls, waders
South Huish (Thurlestone) **	high tide	Dec – Feb	Wildfowl & waders, gulls, peregrine,
	any	Mar – May	Godwit, whimbrel, garganey, wheatear
Exe: Bowling Green Marsh***	high tide	Dec – Feb	Wildfowl & waders, black-tailed godwits brent geese, little egret
	any	Mar – May	Waders on migration
	any	July – Oct	Waders on migration, whimbrel
Exminster marshes ***	high tide	Dec – Feb	Wildfowl & waders incl. brent geese, curlew, field-fare, redwing, kingfisher, Cetti's warbler (on canal side), short-eared owl, merlin, water rail
	any	Mar – June	Breeding lapwing, redshank, wildfowl, Cetti's warbler, reed bunting
LAKES, POOLS AND RESERVOIRS	any	All – Resident	Mallard, heron, coot, kingfisher, mute swan, sometimes water rail
Arlington Lake (N Devon) *	any	Mar – May	One of Devon's largest heronries
Beesands Ley **	any		Similar to Slapton Ley but smaller
Burrator Reservoir **	any	All – Resident	Wildfowl, buzzard, raven, dipper
Slapton Ley ***	any	Dec – Feb	Great crested grebe (resident), wildfowl, gulls, cormorant, great northern diver, grebes, gadwell, ruddy duck
	evening		
		Mar – May	Migrant gulls, marsh harrier, swallow, martin, swift
		Jun – Jul	Young great crested grebe, gadwell
		Aug – Nov	Swallow, martin & other migrants
Tamar Lakes ***	any	Dec – Feb	Wildfowl, little grebe
		Mar – May	Green, wood and common sandpipers, ringed plover, greenshank and sometimes black tern
		Aug – Nov	Wader migration, terns
Wistlandpound Reservoir (N Devon coast) *	any	Dec- Feb	Diving duck and other wildfowl
		Aug – Nov	Greenshank, green sandpiper

Habitat and Site	Best Time	Best Season	Main birds and comments
LOWLAND HEATH	any	All – Resident	Sparrowhawk, buzzard, redpoll, reed bunting, merlin, woodcock, snipe, redwing, fieldfare, siskin, Dartford warbler, stonechat
		Dec – Feb	Cuckoo, hobby, tree pipit, warblers
		Mar – May	Turtle dove, nightjar
			breeding birds most active
		Jun – July	Hobby
Chudleigh Knighton Heath **	any	May – Aug	
East Devon Commons ***	any	Resident	Dartford warbler, stonechat
		Oct – Mar	Brambling, great grey shrike, possible peregrine, merlin
		Apr – Sep	Curlew, stonechat, sand martin, wheatear, hobby, cuckoo, tree pipit, warblers, turtle dove, nightjar, grasshopper warbler
Haldon ***	any	Oct – Mar	Woodcock, snipe
		Apr – Sep	Cuckoo, tree pipit, Dartford warbler, nightjar, turtle dove, also hobby, possible honey buzzard and occasional other migrant raptors, stonechat
MIGRATION WATCH POINT 1: Good passerines – small birds	early am	All – Resident	Herring & great black-backed gull, oystercatcher, raven, rock pipit
Berry Head***	am	All – Resident	Stonechat, rock pipit, shag
		Dec – Feb	Divers, common scoter, auks
		Mar – May	Manx shearwater, fulmar, wheatear, chiffchaff and other warblers
		Jun – Jul	Auks, fulmar, gannet, kittiwake, shearwater, common scoter all offshore, and on heath, warblers, curlew, nightjar, turtle dove
		Aug – Nov	Arctic & great skua, fulmar in Sept/Oct, chats, warblers, flycatchers Aug/Sep then black redstart, winter thrushes, pipits and finches Oct/Nov with raptors, grey wagtail
		Oct – Nov	Firecrest and rare warblers

Habitat and Site	Best Time	Best Season	Main birds and comments
MIGRATION WATCH POINT 1: Good passerines – small birds	early am	All – Resident	Herring & great black-backed gull, oystercatcher, raven, rock pipit
Dawlish Warren***	early am	All – Resident	Stonechat, rock pipit
		Dec – Feb	Hen harrier, merlin, divers, common scoter,
		Mar – May	Manx shearwater, fulmar, wheatear, chiffchaff and other warblers and by end of month, curlew, nightjar, turtle dove
		Jun – Jul	Fulmar, kittiwake, shearwater, common scoter all off-shore, and on heath, warblers, curlew, nightjar, turtle dove
		Aug – Nov	Arctic & great skua, fulmar in Sept/Oct, chats, warblers, flycatchers Aug/Sep then black redstart, winter thrushes, firecrest, pipits and finches Oct/Nov with raptors, grey wagtail
Hartland Point **	am	All – Resident	Barn owl, stonechat, rock pipit, grey wagtail, shag
		Dec – Feb	Hen harrier, merlin, divers, common scoter, auks
		Mar – May	Manx shearwater, fulmar, wheatear, chiffchaff and other warblers, auks, fulmar, gannet, kittiwake, shear-water, common scoter all offshore
		Aug – Nov	Arctic & great skua, fulmar in Sept/Oct, chats, warblers flycatchers Aug/Sep then black redstart, winter thrushes, pipits and finches Oct/Nov with raptors
Prawle Point *** and Start Point **	am	All – Resident	Sparrowhawk, buzzard, stock dove, little owl, green woodpecker, stonechat, reed, cirl bunting
		Dec – Feb	Occasional eider, divers, common scoter, passing off-shore – gulls, gannet, auks, kittiwake onshore – golden & grey plover, turnstone, curlew, purple sandpiper, peregrine, black redstart, finch & lark flocks
		Mar – May	Goldcrest, firecrest, chiffchaff, wheatear, black red-start, occasional hoopoe, migrant raptors, most small migrants Apr/May, shearwater, storm petrel, puffin, divers, eider, common scoter, merganser, bar-tailed godwit, skuas sandwich tern, whimbrel
		Jun – Jul	Offshore feeding parties – shearwaters, storm petrel, fulmar, gannet, breeding shag, kittiwake, shelduck, sandwich tern
		Aug – Nov	Most seabird movement – shearwaters, skuas small migrant birds, swallows & martins, occasional short eared owl, then black redstart, winter thrushes, ducks, divers, firecrest, rare warblers
Soar Area **			Similar to above, but not seabirds

Habitat and Site	Best Time	Best Season	Main birds and comments
MIGRATION WATCH POINT 2: Raptors – birds of prey can only soar from mid-morning as land warms	mid day	All	
Haldon raptor viewpoint *	mid day	May	Hobby, possible honey buzzard and other passage migrants
		Aug – mid Oct	As above also occasional osprey
MOORLAND Open moor, bog and wood		All – resident	carrion crow, raven, red grouse, buzzard, grey wagtail, dipper
Cranmere Pool/N Dartmoor ***	any	Dec – Feb	Very quiet
		Mar – May	Summer visitors return – wheatear, ring ouzel, skylark, meadow pipit, whinchat, golden plover, lapwing, dunlin, maybe common sandpiper, snipe and occasional passing dotterel
		Jun – Jul	Breeding birds finish song/display by July
		Aug – Nov	Young and adults depart, occasional peregrine, merlin, harrier and flocks of golden plover
Soussons/Postbridge area **	any	All – resident	Kestrel, stock dove, goldcrest, coal tit, crossbill, grey heron
		Nov – Feb	Merlin, hen harrier, woodcock, snipe, occasional short eared owl, great grey shrike, finches incl. brambling, also fieldfare, redwing, starling
		Mar – Jul	Breeding snipe, curlew, lapwing, wheatear, ring ouzel, cuckoo, whinchat, redstart, followed by redpoll, siskin
		Aug – Oct	Most summer migrants gone by end Aug, but some ring ouzel, wheatear in Oct
Fox Tor Mire (nr. Princetown) *	any	Dec – Feb	Very quiet
		Mar – May	Summer visitors return – wheatear, skylark, meadow pipit, whinchat, lapwing, snipe breeding
		Jun – Jul	Birds finish song/display by July
		Aug – Nov	Young and adults depart, occasional merlin, and peregrine
Tavy Cleave**	any	Mar – May	Wheatear, ring ouzel, skylark, meadow pipit, whinchat

Habitat and Site	Best Time	Best Season	Main birds and comments
OPEN GRASS – golf course Do not enter without permission, views can be obtained from adjacent paths.	any but early am is best	All – Resident	Kestrel, stonechat, green woodpecker, sparrowhawk as well as a few waders, wagtails and pipit
Dawlish Warren – golf course*	any	Mar – May	Meadow pipit, skylark begin breeding, first wheatear arrive, small migrants pass through
		Jun – Jul	Summer breeding
		Aug – Nov	Passage migrants
Little Haldon – golf course *	any	All – resident	Buzzard,
		Mar – May	Meadow pipit, skylark, wheatear
Thurlestone – golf course *	any	Mar – May	Wheatear, meadow pipit, skylark, cirl bunting, occasional hoopoe
		Aug – Nov	Passage migrants, buff-breasted sandpiper
REED BED	any evening	All – Resident	Reed bunting, possibly water rail
		Apr – Aug	Reed and sedge warbler
		Aug – Sept	Swallow and martin – roosts (not all reed beds)
		Oct – Feb	Starling – roost (not all reed beds), water rail, sometimes bearded tit
Beesands *	any		As above + Cetti's warbler
Exe Estuary: Dawlish Warren *	any		As above
Exminster Marsh-Topsham **	any		As above
Hallsands *	any		As above
Otter Estuary *	any		As above
Slapton Ley ***	any	All – Resident	Cetti's warbler
	evening	Nov-May	Occasional bittern
	evening	Aug – Sept	Swallow, martin, wagtail – best roost + hobby
		Oct-Feb	Starling – good roost + raptors
South Milton Ley (Thurlestone) ** view from NT car park	evening evening	All – Resident	Cetti's warbler,
		Aug – Sept	Swallow, martin, wagtail – roost
		Oct-Feb	Starling – best roost

Habitat and Site	Best Time	Best Season	Main birds and comments
SAND DUNE Dawlish – people disturbance in summer, best visited early am. Braunton – beware military exercises.	high tide	All – Resident Dec – Feb Mar – May Jun – Jul Aug – Nov	Grey heron, stonechat, sparrowhawk, reed bunting, some barn owl (not Dawlish) Occasional short-eared owl, waders Wheatear, harrier Meadow pipit, skylark, whitethroat Waders along shoreline
Braunton Burrows (Taw-Torridge) **	high tide		As above
Dawlish Warren **	high tide	Aug – Feb	Waders on roost and along shore
SEABIRD BREEDING COLONY	any	All – Resident Mar – Jul	Sparrowhawk, green woodpecker, rock pipit, stonechat, raven, shag, Most gulls and auks collecting and breeding
Berry Head **	any		As above (best for auks)
Budleigh Salterton-Ladram Bay *	any		As above
Heddons Mouth (N Devon) **	any		As above
Hope's Nose *	any		As above
Lundy ***	any		As above
Start Point and Hallsands**	any	Mar – Jul	Large kittiwake colony at Hallsands and Start Point
SEABIRD WATCH POINT Berry Head*** Capstone, Ilfracombe (N Devon coast) * Exe Estuary: Langstone Rock, Dawlish Warren ** Hartland Point *** Hope's Nose *** Morte Point (N Devon coast) * Prawle Point *** Start Point **	any	All – Resident Dec – Feb Mar – May Jun – Jul Aug – Nov	Sparrowhawk, green woodpecker, rock pipit, stonechat, raven, shag, Divers, grebes, gulls, sea ducks, waders Seabirds, gulls, auks, migrant warblers, terns Breeding seabirds, passage shearwaters, storm petrels Passage shearwaters, terns, skuas, warblers
SEA COAST – Sheltered bay Exe Estuary in/offshore – Dawlish Warren and Exmouth *** Torbay *** Start Bay *** Plymouth Sound **	any, unless onshore wind	All – Resident Dec – Feb Mar – May Jun – Jul Aug – Nov	Great black-backed gull, shag, rock pipit Divers, grebes, sea duck and a few waders Fulmar, auks, Manx shearwater Breeding cliffs busy, few birds on water Shearwaters, first divers and grebes

Habitat and Site	Best Time	Best Season	Main birds and comments
SHINGLE BEACH Beesands * Northam Burrows (Taw-Torridge) * Slapton **	early am	Dec – Feb Mar – May Aug – Nov	Divers, grebes, shag, eider, scoter all offshore gulls, dunlin may roost Migrant gulls, whimbrel, auks offshore, hoopoe on sandy turf Terns, skuas, migrant gulls offshore, snow bunting
WOODLAND **Coniferous** Bellever, Dartmoor (Soussons, Postbridge area) * Burrator * Hennock *	any	All – Resident Dec – Feb Mar – Jul Aug – Nov	Buzzard, sparrowhawk, kestrel, goldcrest, coal tit, crossbill, redpoll, siskin Woodcock, finches, roosting wood pigeon Breeding residents, tree pipit Occ. peregrine and passing hobby or harrier
Fernworthy **	any	May – Jul	As above, and nightjar
Haldon Woods ***	any	May – Jul	Nightjar, turtle dove, whinchat, redstart, siskin
WOODLAND **Mixed and** **Deciduous** Chapel Wood, Spreacombe (N Devon coast) * Dartington ** Dunsford Wood Okement Woods * Stoke Woods ** Tarr Steps, Exmoor **	any	All – Resident Dec – Mar Apr – May Jun – Jul Aug – Nov	Most common woodland birds plus buzzard, sparrowhawk, kestrel, woodpeckers, stock dove, tawny owl, grey wagtail, goldcrest, possible raven Woodcock, brambling, siskin, redpoll, Cuckoo, tree pipit, blackcap, whitethroat, garden warbler, wood warbler Residents and visitors breeding Redwing, fieldfare from Oct, mixed tit flocks
Plymbridge *	any	May – Jul	As above (peregrine watch point, wood warbler)
Yarner Wood ***	any	Apr – Jul	As above, and redstart, pied flycatcher
FARMLAND – Cirl **bunting areas** Berry Head** Coast between Erme and Yealm* Cockington* Maidencombe** Mansands area* Prawle Point to Start** Snapes Pt*	any	All – Resident	Cirl bunting and other farmland birds

Mammals

Not including ourselves, just over 100 different mammals are recorded as living wild in and around the British Isles. Less than half are considered native and resident, the rest being escapees and introductions, vagrant bats and visiting seals. There are 17 kinds of whale and dolphin which are regularly seen off Britain's shores, and 23 species in all have been recorded from British waters.

Devon has 43 breeding mammals recorded living in the wild, from the smallest shrew to the biggest deer and massive bull seal, as well as 10 regular marine visitors.

Common and scientific names are as used in the *Handbook of British Mammals*, (ed) Southern.

INSECTIVORES	Devon status and where found
Hedgehog *Erinaceous europaeus*	Common but not abundant – wood, garden, hedgerow
Mole *Talpa europaea*	Common everywhere except heath
Common shrew *Sorex araneus*	Common everywhere – grass, scrub
Pygmy shrew *Sorex minutus*	Locally very common, especially moor, also Lundy
Water shrew *Neomys fodiens*	Locally common, especially leat, stream

BATS (Chiroptera)	Devon status and where found (approx time of emergence after sunset)
Barbastelle bat *Barbastella barbastellus*	Not common – wooded river valley *Summer* – hollow tree, building (variable, sometimes before sunset) *winter* – cave
Brown long-eared bat *Plecotus auritus*	Fairly common – farmland *Summer & winter* – sheltered wood, buildings
Daubenton's bat *Myotis daubentoni*	Locally common – open wood, park, farm, near or over water *Summer* – building, hollow tree (30 mins) *Winter* – cave
Leisler's bat *Nyctalus leisleri*	Rare in Devon – woodland (0-5 mins) *Summer* – hollow tree, building *Winter* – hollow tree, building
Greater horseshoe bat *Rhinolophus ferrumequinum*	Nationally rare, locally common limestone caves in Devon – wooded valley, farm *Summer* – loft, barn (30 mins) *Winter* – cave, building

CHIROPTERA (continued)	Devon status and where found (approx time of emergence after sunset)
Lesser horseshoe bat *Rhinolophus hipposideros*	Locally common – wooded valley, farm Summer – (20 mins) Winter – cave, building
Natterer's bat *Myotis nattereri*	Fairly common – open wood, park, farm Summer – tree, building (1-5 mins) Winter – cave
Noctule bat *Noctula noctula*	Common – wood, farm, park Summer – hollow tree, (before or <20 mins) Winter – building, tree
Pipistrelle bat *Pipistrellus pipistrellus*	Most common bat in Devon – anywhere not windy, feeds over water and meadow Summer – buildings, tree (20 mins) Winter – small spaces building, tree
Serotine bat *Eptesicus serotinus*	locally fairly common E Devon – open wooded park, farm Summer – hollow tree (15-20 mins) Winter – tree, building
Whiskered bat *Myotis mystacinus*	Fairly common – wood, farm, hedge Summer – tree, building (1-5 mins) Winter – cave

HARES & RABBITS	Devon status and where found
Brown Hare *Lepus europaeus*	Widespread but no longer common everywhere – open farmland
Rabbit *Oryctolagus cuniculus*	Common and widespread everywhere, numbers can fluctuate with outbreaks of myxomatosis disease.

RODENTS	Devon status and where found
Bank vole *Clethrionomys glareolus*	Common but numbers can fluctuate from year to year – hedge, wood
Black rat *Rattus rattus*	Possibly present around ports
Brown rat *Rattus norvegicus*	Very common on farmland and near water courses, especially where household waste is available
Dormouse *Muscardinus avellanarius*	Widespread but not common, becoming more scarce – hedge, hazel coppice, wood
Grey squirrel *Scirius carolinesis*	Common N. American alien introduced in 19th C. – park, garden, woodland, hedge
Harvest mouse *Micromys minutus*	Locally common in and around cereal crops, reed beds and other tall marshy vegetation
House mouse *Mus musculus*	Common around buildings
Red squirrel *Sciurus vulgaris*	Extinct in Devon by mid-1950s
Short-tailed vole *Microtus agrestis*	Very common in rough pasture and fields but numbers can fluctuate from year to year
Water vole *Arvicola amphibius*	Formerly common, now rare if not extinct in Devon – waterways
Wood mouse *Apodemus sylvaticus*	Very common – wood, hedge

CARNIVORES	Devon status and where found
Fox *Vulpes vulpes*	Common and widespread, even seashore
Stoat *Mustela erminea*	Not common, mainly farm, heath, wood
Weasel *Mustela nivalis*	Widespread probably more common than stoat – farm, wood
Mink *Mustela vison*	Introduced alien common – freshwater
Polecat *Mustela putorius*	Probably extinct in Devon by 1960s
Badger *Meles meles*	Very common across county except high moors
Otter *Lutra lutra*	1960 almost extinct in England now increasing – lake, river, estuary, coast, even water courses in urban areas
Grey Seal *Halichoerus grypus*	Fairly common, resident populations around Lundy, rocky coast, occasionally in estuaries

DEER (Artiodactyls)	Devon status and where found
Fallow deer *Dama dama*	Reintroduced, becoming common – wood, conifer plantation, others kept in parks
Muntjac deer *Muntiacus spp*	Introduced, becoming more common, spreading – farm, wood
Red deer *Cervus elephus*	Native, common on and around Exmoor and present on Dartmoor
Roe deer *Capreolus capreolus*	Native, widespread and common – farm, wood, plantation
Sika deer *Cervus nippon*	Introduced, common Lundy and elsewhere – wood, moor edge
Wild goat *Capra hircus*	Feral herds on Lundy and N. Devon cliffs

WHALES & DOLPHINS (Cetaceans)	Devon status and where found
Bottle-nosed whale *Hyperoodon ampullatus*	Occasional stranding
Minke whale *Balaenoptera acutorostrata*	Most commonly seen large whale
Common porpoise *Phocoena phocoena*	Most commonly seen porpoise, regular off Hartland Point and Berry Head
Killer whale *Orcinus orca*	Occasionally seen offshore and around Lundy
Pilot whale *Globicephala melaena*	Not uncommon
Bottle-nosed dolphin *Tursiops truncatus*	Most common dolphin seen off Devon, especially Torbay and Lyme Bay
Common dolphin *Delphinus delphis*	Fairly common, usually seen bow riding
Risso's dolphin *Grampus griseus*	Uncommon, usually solitary or small groups
Striped dolphin *Stenella coeruleoalba*	More common in SW waters than rest of British Isles
White beaked dolphin *Lagenorhynchus albirostris*	May be fairly common
Fin whale *Balaenoptera physalus*	Second largest animal on earth. Mainly deep water; may be more common than sightings suggest.

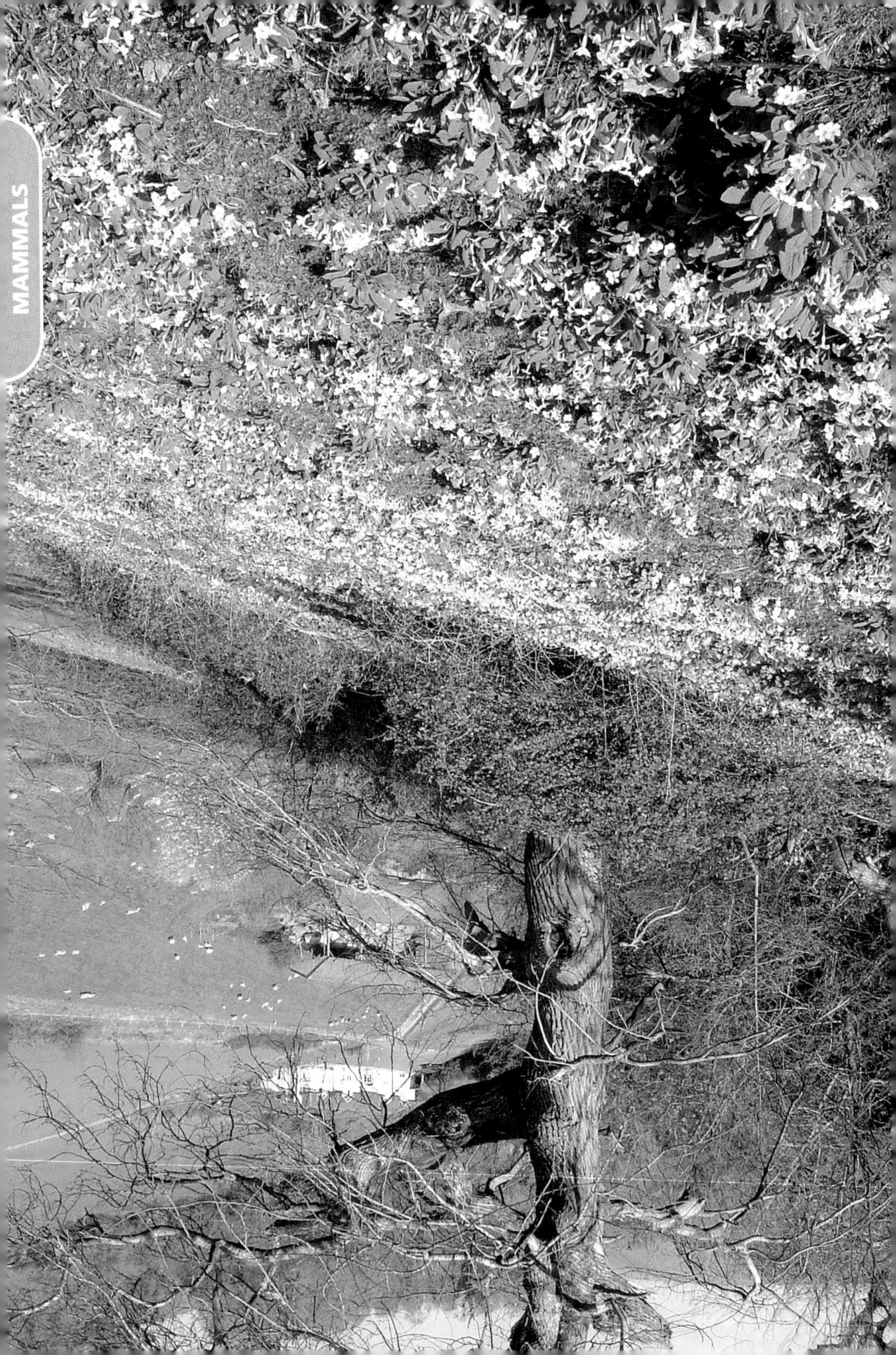

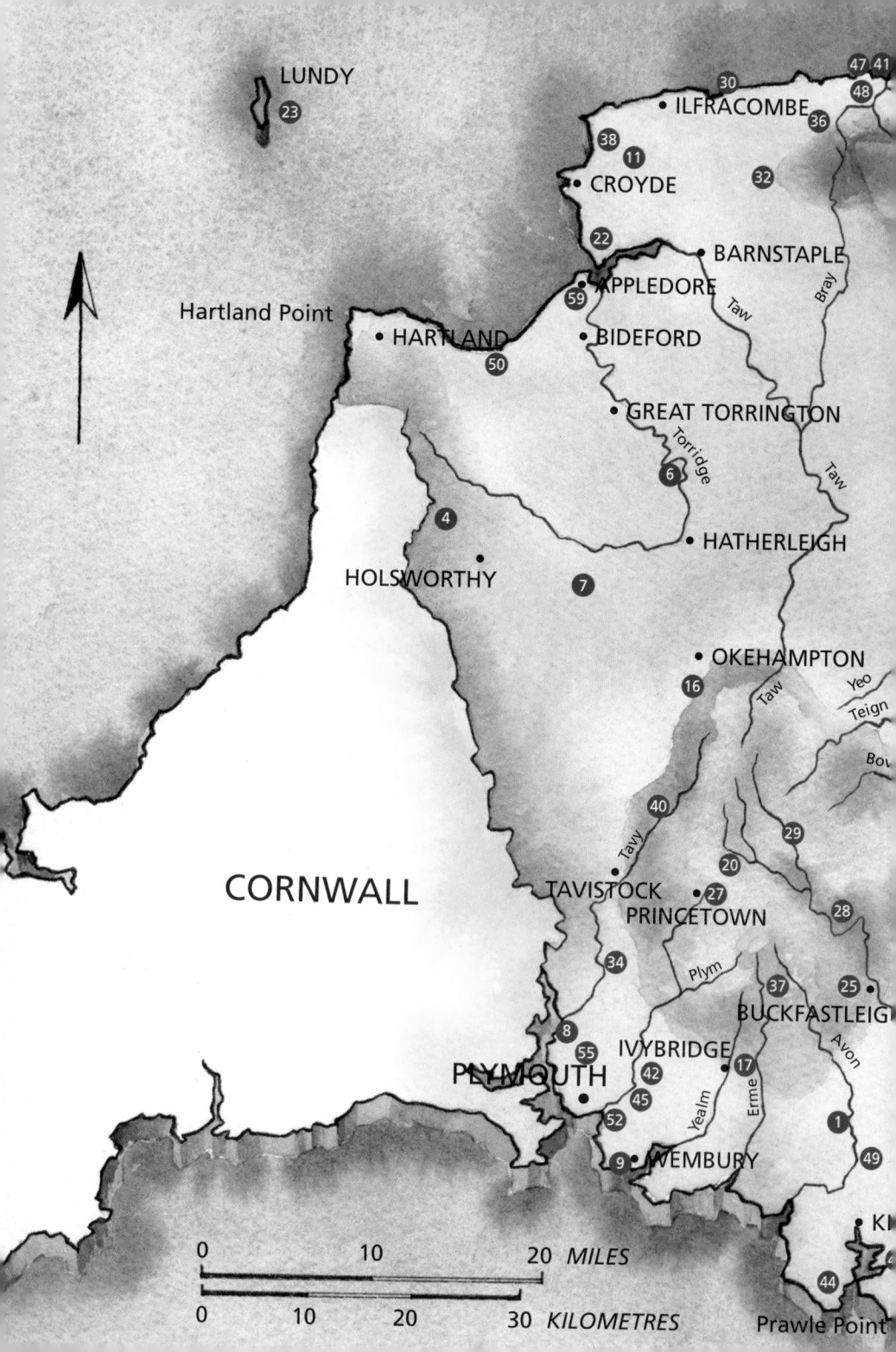

SOMERSET

DEVON

TIVERTON
57

Exe

Creedy

Culm

Clyst

Otter

Axe

DORSET

39
EXETER
TOPSHAM

LYME REGIS

18

5

35

53

MORETON-
HAMPSTEAD

54

21

6

2

BOVEY TRACEY

60

56

58

24

TORQUAY

TOTNES

Dart

BRIXHAM

15

46

DARTMOUTH

BRIDGE

19

Start Point

51

33

SIDMOUTH

AXMOUTH

10

12

3

BUDLEIGH SALTERTON

EXMOUTH

13

DAWLISH

SHALDON

NEWTON ABBOT

Recommended

Devon
Wildlife
Sites

see pages 208–241 for details

Where to See

For great wild days out in Devon, here are some of the best nature reserves and wildlife sites in the county.

Devon has large areas of woodland, heathland, moorland and wetland, as well as extensive and important coastal, geological and marine interests. The county is rich in the quantity and variety of its wild animal and plant life.

The Devon Wildlife Trust **(DWT)** manages over 40 prime nature reserves, and the RSPB has 3 principal bird reserves. There are 17 Natura 2000 sites that are internationally important for their wildlife and natural features, 200 Sites of Special Scientific Interest **(SSSI)**, six groups of National Nature Reserves **(NNR)** covering woodland, Culm grassland, coastal and moorland habitat, and England's only Marine Nature Reserve around Lundy, as well as 18 Local Nature Reserves **(LNR)** and one Unesco Biosphere reserve. These represent the 'jewels in the crown' of the county's wildlife and natural features. Local authorities and other charitable organisations in the county also manage some good wildlife areas. The National Trust owns and manages many of the county's great historic estates, and also the famed Coastal Footpath. The Woodland Trust also maintains many good sites.

Nature reserves and wildlife-rich locations with the best access and/or good facilities nearby are detailed below. The exception is the Great Undercliff, which is only for the physically able and not for the faint-hearted, but is well worth the effort.

Wildlife Sites

DEVON WILDLIFE TRUST

THE wildlife TRUSTS

Devon

(DWT) NATURE RESERVES

The Devon Wildlife Trust manages more than 3,300 acres (over 1,300 hectares) of the county. Most are freely open for public access all year round. The best and easiest to see are listed below. Most DWT reserves are accessible by bicycle. Public transport is not easily available in the countryside, although some reserves are on bus routes. Parking may also be limited on some of the smaller reserves. For a full list of Devon Wildlife Trust's reserves and county-wide events, please contact the Trust directly.

1 Andrew's Wood SSSI

DEVON WILDLIFE TRUST
Tel: 01392 279244
www.devonwildlifetrust.org
Nearest town: Kingsbridge
OS Map: SX 713 520

A total of 70 acres (28 ha) of wet woodland and wet acidic grassland. This site was once a system of agricultural fields. Abandoned 100 years ago, it now has a mix of woodland and grassland clearings. It hosts one of Britain's largest populations of dormice, and is one of only five sites in the UK where heath lobelia grows.

Wild highlights	Dormice, dense populations of woodland birds, heath lobelia, yellow bartsia, marsh orchid, various butterflies including the marbled white, silver-washed fritillary and purple hairstreak.
Best time	Spring time or August to see the heath lobelia, but open all year.
Access	A sloping track from the car park leads through a wet uneven field into the woodland. From here the ground is mostly flat with some steps, bridges and boardwalks. An easy place for young families to explore.
How to find it	From the A38 take the B3196 following the signs to Loddiswell. Andrew's Wood is on the right, 250m beyond Coldharbour Cross before Loddiswell village.
Parking	There is a car park at the entrance for 6 cars.
Facilities	Leaflet available. Information board. 2 waymarked trails. WC and pub are at California Cross or in Loddiswell.
Time to see	1.5 hours to complete the longest circular walk
Short visit	Stroll to the first meadow or take the short 40-minute waymarked trail.
More	Andrew's Wood was once called Stanton Moor; it was sold to DWT on the condition that the name was changed in memory of the former owner's son who was killed in a car accident. Located in the South Hams, this is a popular area for beaches, camping and cream teas!

NATURE RESERVES

② Bovey Heathfield
SSSI, LNR, SAM

DEVON WILDLIFE TRUST
Tel: 01392 279244
www.devonwildlifetrust.org
Nearest town: Bovey Tracey
OS Map: SX 824 765 and SX 824 768

This 50 acre (23.5 ha) reserve is an important component of the Bovey Basin heaths. It is home to many threatened heathland birds, butterflies and insects.
   Bovey Heathfield is now a Local Nature Reserve, but before Devon Wildlife Trust's purchase of the site in 2002, the heathland suffered from fly-tipping and unauthorised off-road scrambling. DWT, with the help of the local community, aims to restore the heath.

Wild highlights	Three types of heather, bog myrtle, dragonflies and grayling butterflies, various insects including the bog-bush cricket, solitary bees, birds including stonechat, nightjar and Dartford warbler, slow worms, lizards and adders.
Best time	Late summer to see the heathland in bloom.
Access	The main part of the reserve has a circular path rising to a view point. The ground is compact with some loose stones. An ideal site for a family visit.
How to find it	From the A38 take the A382 towards Bovey Tracey. At the traffic lights turn right, take the second left into Cavalier Road. Turn left into Dragoon Close. The gravel track on the right leads to the reserve.
Parking	Parking is along the roadside in Dragoon Close.
Facilities	Leaflet available, information board, waymarked trail, benches, information hut. WC and other facilities are in Bovey Tracey.
Time to see	1 hour
Short visit	A stroll to the view point overlooking Hay Tor on Dartmoor will take about half an hour.
More	A battle took place here during the English Civil War in 1646; the rare earthwork has been declared a Scheduled Ancient Monument. Close access to Dartmoor National Park and Bovey Tracey.

③ Bystock SSSI

DEVON WILDLIFE TRUST
Tel: 01392 279244
www.devonwildlifetrust.org
Nearest town: Exmouth
OS Map: SY 033 844

This 67 acre (27 ha) reserve is part of a larger SSSI,
the East Devon Pebblebed Heaths. It includes both wet and dry heath, woodland,
scrub, grassland, small pools and a man-made reservoir.

Wild highlights	Three types of heather: ling, bell heather and cross-leaved heath. Sphagnum moss and marsh violets. It is an important site for dragon-flies, damselflies and butterflies.
Best time	Visit in June to see the grassland teeming with butterflies. The heath-land is at its most colourful in late summer. A great site for a visit at any time of year.
Access	An easy access path leads onto the reserve, with views over the reser-voir. This track is suitable for pushchairs and wheelchairs. Paths across the rest of the reserve vary, as they are unsurfaced. An ideal place for the family to explore.
How to find it	Take the A376 from Exeter to Exmouth and the B3179 through Woodbury. Take the first turning on the right as you leave the village, signed Exmouth. At the end of this road turn right onto the B3180. Once you pass the turning for Exmouth (to the right) take the left turn a few hundred metres down the road. The reserve entrance is on the left by the reservoir.
Parking	A large parking area can be found beyond the entrance on the right.
Facilities	Refreshments and WC at Bundles Garden Centre on the road to Exmouth, or head into East Budleigh or Exmouth.
Time to see	1 hour.
Short visit	A 15-minute walk next to the reservoir.
More	This area is part of the East Devon Area of Outstanding Natural Beauty. It is a popular tourist area with the south coast and Exmouth nearby.

NATURE RESERVES

④ Dunsdon NNR SSSI

DEVON WILDLIFE TRUST
Tel: 01392 279244
www.devonwildlifetrust.org
Nearest town: Holsworthy
OS Map: SS 295 078 and SS 307 083

Dunsdon National Nature Reserve is one of the best Culm grassland sites in Britain. Grazed by red ruby cattle during summer, these pastures are also home to one of the rarest and most spectacular displays of wild flowers and butterflies in the country. Snipe and woodcock are the reserve's main winter visitors when the ground is wet and boggy, and this is when short-eared owl and barn owl may sometimes be seen.

Wild highlights	Wild flowers, especially orchids, and a rare opportunity to see good numbers of rare marsh fritillary butterfly in fine weather. So far 26 different butterflies recorded on the reserve. A spring visit is a good time to see the heronry just beyond the viewing platform.
Best time	Early summer but open all year.
Access	A rough, wet and boggy reserve at the best of times, hence the special wheelchair access – 400 metres of woodland board walk with a viewing platform across the Culm grassland.
How to find it	Taking the B3072 from Holsworthy towards Bude, turn right to Pancrasweek. One mile past the church, turn right again and follow the lane. The reserve entrance is on the left just before Gains Cross.
Parking	There is a large car park with capacity for more than 25 cars.
Facilities	Leaflet available. Information boards. WC next to the main car park in Holsworthy.
Time to see	Up to 2 hours to fully appreciate the reserve.
Short visit	Walk along woodland path on the boardwalk to the viewing platform which overlooks the Culm grasslands.
More	Close to North Devon coast, beaches and historic Bude canal. Tamar lakes birdwatching and picturesque Clovelly not too far away, hence many campsites, B&B and other accommodation available.

⑤ Dunsford SSSI

DEVON WILDLIFE TRUST
Tel: 01392 279244
www.devonwildlifetrust.org
Nearest town: Moretonhampstead
OS Map: SX 805 883 (Steps Bridge) and
SX 784 893 (Clifford Bridge)

140 acres (57 ha) of river valley woodland, flood plain grassland and scrub with rocky slopes and heath, part of a larger SSSI.

Dunsford has few rivals to match its diversity of plants and animals. This is mainly due to the rich mixture of habitats within its 57 ha: large areas of oak, ash and hazel with grassy clearings, bracken-covered slopes and a series of exposed rocky outcrops. Dunsford is most famed for its spectacular spring display of thousands of wild daffodils. The reserve has been leased by the Devon Wildlife Trust since 1965 and is owned by the National Trust. It lies within the Dartmoor National Park and is part of the Teign Valley SSSI.

Wild highlights	Otter, deer, badger, dormouse, dipper, buzzard, pied flycatcher, salmon, dark green, high brown and pearl-bordered fritillary butterflies, wood cricket, bluebell, old sessile oak trees and wild daffodil.
Best time	Open all year. Daffodil season March – April.
Access	Footpath and bridleway follow river. An ideal location for a family visit. Level access along valley floor, suitable for both pushchairs and wheelchair users from Steps Bridge.
How to find it	There are two entrances: one at Steps Bridge, the other not far from Clifford Bridge. The main entrance at Steps Bridge lies on the Exeter to Moretonhampstead road about 3 miles (5 km) from Moretonhampstead. This reserve is on a main bus route.
Parking	Next to Steps Bridge Inn, Dartmoor National Park car park at SX 802 883, or in lay-by at Clifford Bridge end.
Facilities	Leaflet available. Information boards. Benches. Facilities at Strawberry Hill tea rooms (on the main road just outside Dunsford) and in Dunsford village.
Time to see	Up to 2.5 hours.
Short visit	Just wander along the edge of the river.
More	It was once a flower picker's paradise where hundreds of people used to come to collect daffodils for business and pleasure. Now they are left for everyone to enjoy.

NATURE RESERVES

⑥ Halsdon

DEVON WILDLIFE TRUST
Tel: 01392 279244
www.devonwildlifetrust.org
Nearest town: Great Torrington
OS Map: SS 554 131 (Ashwell car park)
and SS 560 117 (Quarry car park)

140 acres (57 ha) of river valley woodland and riverside pasture, part of a larger SSSI.

The river Torridge lies at the heart of 'Tarka the Otter' country which was immortalised in Henry Williamson's classic novel. Halsdon nature reserve is one of the Devon Wildlife Trust's largest and most spectacular reserves, offering a beautiful riverside walk with magnificent views to Dartmoor. A stretch of river and wood of more than two miles provides a home for a rich variety of wildlife.

Wild highlights	Otter, deer, badger, dipper, kingfisher, buzzard with pied flycatcher, sand martin and wood warbler from mid-summer. Carpets of bluebells in spring. Watch for good populations of white-legged damselflies, and from late summer signs of salmon rising. There is also a small area of rare Culm grassland with wavy St John's wort flowers in July and August.
Best time	Spring and summer but open all year.
Access	The southern entrance (Quarry car park) has a compact path suitable for pushchair and wheelchair users. Some riverside access is restricted. The woodland's tracks are steeper and uneven in places. A great location for children to explore with their families.
How to find it	Taking the A377 from Exeter to Crediton, onto the Morchard road and turn left onto the B3220. 5 miles beyond Winkleigh turn left to Dolton. In Dolton drive up Fore Street and down West Lane. Turn right at the crossroads. From Torrington take the B3220 beyond Beaford and follow signs to Dolton. Turn right to Halsdon; the reserve is 1.5 miles signed on the right.
Parking	Parking for 4 cars is available in the lay-by at the Quarry car park and for 12 cars at Ashwell car park.
Facilities	Leaflet available. Information boards. 4 waymarked trails. Benches. WC and refreshments available in Dolton.
Time to see	Up to 2 hours to follow the longest circuit.
Short visit	Walk through the woodland to the river edge. Or choose one of the 4 circular waymarked walks.
More	The long distance Tarka Trail (180 miles) passes many of the places in the book. See the DWT annual events programme for guided walks.

⑦ Halwill Junction

DEVON WILDLIFE TRUST
Tel: 01392 279244
www.devonwildlifetrust.org
Nearest town: Okehampton/Holsworthy
OS Map: SS 443 004

Halwill Junction is a disused railway line with a variety of habitats. The Devon Wildlife Trust has managed the site for its wildlife value since purchasing it from British Rail in 1990. Now the National Cycle Network Route 3 runs through the reserve making it accessible to everyone.

Wild highlights	In the wet areas angelica, meadowsweet, ragged robin, and broad leaved helleborine, in July marsh orchids. Various birds including green woodpecker, tits and warblers. Some interesting butterflies such as wood white, and dragonflies.
Best time	Mid-summer for the wildflowers and butterflies.
Access	The new cycle path through this reserve is flat, compact and smooth, making access easy for everyone. The wooded path that branches to the left is unsurfaced but mostly dry underfoot.
How to find it	The village of Halwill Junction lies between Okehampton and Holsworthy on the B3079. At the roundabout in the village centre, take the road past the shops. The reserve can be found at the far end of Beechings Close, past the Junction Inn on the left. This reserve is on a main bus route.
Parking	The best place to park is in the village car park (behind the shops); from here walk through the houses into Beechings Close.
Facilities	There are various facilities in Halwill Junction and toilets in the Junction Inn when open.
Time to see	45 minutes.
Short visit	20 minutes to the end of the surfaces path and back.
More	The cycle network route runs through the reserve and is close to Cookworthy Forest.

⑧ Warleigh Point SSSI

DEVON WILDLIFE TRUST
Tel: 01392 279244
www.devonwildlifetrust.org
Nearest town: Plymouth
OS Map: SX 447 610

Warleigh Point has accessible coastal sessile oak woodland with magnificent views over the Tamar and Tavy estuary. Over half of this 84 acre (33.8 ha) reserve lies below the high tide line and provides ideal feeding ground for wading birds. The woodland and glade are well worth a visit, providing a special atmosphere of peace and tranquillity.

Wild highlights	Both ancient and young woodland with wet acid mire flushes. Carpets of bluebells in spring. Wild service trees. Woodland birds including tawny owls, great spotted woodpecker and a rookery. A good mix of wading bird species, also great crested grebe and little egret.
Best time	Excellent all year round.
Access	An easy access track leads to the Point, or a circular route can be taken to the far side of the reserve although this can be narrow, muddy and steep in places. A great reserve for children to explore with their families.
How to find it	From the village of Tamerton Foliot, just north of Plymouth on the B3373, the reserve is signposted with a brown tourist sign. The road follows the tidal creek to the reserve, found at the dead end about 2 miles from the village.
Parking	There is room for roadside parking for 4 cars at the dead end.
Facilities	Leaflets available. Information board. Nearest WC in Tamerton Foliot.
Time to see	45 minutes to follow the circular walk.
Short visit	A 30-minute walk to the glade or point and back.
More	On the edge of the city of Plymouth and the river estuary. Cornwall can be seen from the reserve, along with the small villages that spill onto the water edge. A popular area for local boating activities and crab tiling.

9 Wembury

VOLUNTARY MARINE CONSERVATION AREA
DEVON WILDLIFE TRUST
Tel: 01752 862538
www.devonwildlifetrust.org
Nearest town: Plymouth
OS Map: SX 518 484

4 miles of coastline from Bovisand just outside Plymouth to Yealm Head and off shore to a depth of 10 metres. This reserve offers sandy beaches, great rock pooling and cliff top walks.

It is one of the best places for a chance to see the rare cirl bunting and explore rock pools at low tide. Beautiful views from the cliffs.

Wild highlights	Rock pool life with furrowed and porcelain crabs, squat lobster, shrimps, blenny, goby, pipefish, wrasse, cushion and spiny starfish, sea urchin, sea anemone and sea spider. Keep a watch for cirl bunting and peregrine.
Best time	Something to offer at any time of the year, but consult local tide times if you want to go rock pooling. Visitor centre usually open Easter to Oct, 9am – 5pm weekdays and 10am – 6pm at weekends and school holidays.
Access	Good coastal footpath, but can be muddy in places. The visitor centre has wheelchair access and has displays and activities that appeal to everyone. An ideal location for a family day out. Access to the beach is a little more limited, with wide tarmac steps.
How to find it	Well signposted. Taking the A379 from Plymouth to Kingsbridge, follow signs to Wembury. On reaching the village follow more signs to the beach. Walk via the South-west Coast Path from Plymouth or take a no. 48 bus from the city depot.
Parking	Large National Trust car park for over 300 cars. While it is free for NT members, a charge is made for non-members (£3 spring to autumn).
Facilities	Leaflets available. Good little visitor centre with children's activities available, WC with disabled access. Café and holiday accommodation nearby with good village pubs in the surrounding areas. DWT events, walks and talks from April to end Sept. See the DWT events programme.
Time to see	Allow up to 5 hours to walk the full circuit of some 8 miles.
Short visit	A quick visit to the Visitor Centre next to the car park, followed by a stroll along the shore and cliffs for some wonderful sea views in good weather.
More	The National Marine Aquarium in Plymouth is Britain's biggest and Europe's deepest. It is a great place to learn about marine life before you go hunting in the wild. At Wembury the Great Mewstone island offshore attracts large numbers of seabirds in summer. Although it is closed to public access the birds can be seen flying to and fro – shag, cormorant and herring gull nest in large numbers.

NATURE RESERVES

RSPB NATURE RESERVES

The Royal Society for the Protection of Birds is the UK charity working to secure a healthy environment for birds and wildlife, helping to create a better world for all of us.

⑩ Aylesbeare Common
SSSI, SPA

RSPB South West England Regional Office
Keble House, Southernhay Gardens,
Exeter EX1 1NT
Tel: 01392 432691
www.rspb.org.uk
Nearest town: Exmouth
OS Map: SX 057 897

Part of the East Devon Pebblebed heaths, this reserve is the place to see Dartford warblers and heathland wildlife in Devon.

Wild highlights	This heathland reserve in East Devon is important for Dartford Warbler, Nightjar and Stonechat. Its sheltered woods fringe streams and ponds which are alive with butterflies, dragonflies and damselflies during summer. The reserve is open at all times, and is the place to see Dartford warblers and heathland wildlife in Devon.
Best time	All year. Best time to see heathland wildlife is spring and summer.
Access	Two nature trails: 3 miles and 0.75 miles. One farm track crosses the reserve and is suitable for wheelchairs and pushchairs.
How to find it	8 miles/12.8 km east of Exeter. 6 miles east from the M5 on the A3052. Travel 0.5 miles/0.8 km past the Halfway Inn, turn right towards Hawkerland and the car park is immediately on the left. Buses: Half-hourly 52 and 52A Exeter to Sidmouth service. Request stop at Joneys Cross.
Parking	Large car park at Joneys Cross.
Facilities	Trails and information board.
Time to see	At least 2 hours each to fully appreciate the reserve.
Short visit	A walk around the shorter trail offers the chance of seeing Dartford warblers.
More	Regular events throughout the year to see Dartford warblers, nightjars, snakes and dragonflies. Opportunities to volunteer.

⑪ Chapel Wood SSSI

RSPB South West England Regional Office
Keble House, Southernhay Gardens,
Exeter EX1 1NT
Tel: 01392 432691
www.rspb.org.uk
Nearest town: Barnstaple
OS Map: SS 483 415

This small, remote North Devon reserve consists of mixed woodland.

Wild highlights	Good variety of woodland and hill birds including buzzard, grey wagtail and woodpeckers.
Best time	All year. Woodland birds best in spring and early summer
Access	Single nature trail of up to 1.5 miles.
How to find it	1.5 miles/2.4 km west of the A361 and 2 miles/3.2 km north of Braunton. The reserve is a remote location. Please be aware that you may need to pull in for cars on the narrow lane.
Parking	Restricted to a single parking space on the road.
Facilities	Trail and information board.
Time to see	At least 1 hour to fully appreciate the reserve.
Short visit	Can be seen briefly in 30 minutes.
More	Also remains of an old hill fort and historic chapel with a well.

⑫ Exe Estuary

SSSI, SPA, RAMSAR

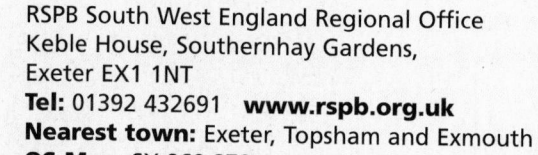

RSPB South West England Regional Office
Keble House, Southernhay Gardens,
Exeter EX1 1NT
Tel: 01392 432691 **www.rspb.org.uk**
Nearest town: Exeter, Topsham and Exmouth
OS Map: SX 960 870

The RSPB Exe Estuary reserves consist of two separate areas of coastal grazed marsh on opposite sides of the estuary: Exminster Marshes and Bowling Green Marsh in Topsham.

Wild highlights	Very good for birds. In spring, look for breeding lapwings and red-shanks: over half Devon's lapwings breed on Exminster Marshes. In winter, during floods and at high tide, you can see thousands of ducks and geese and wading birds roosting and feeding, such as curlews, lapwings, black-tailed godwits and wigeons. One of the most important wintering sites for avocets in Britain. Seals are commonly seen in the estuary.
Best time	All year. Most wildfowl and waders Sept – March.
Access	A short walk along road to Bowling Green Marsh hide. Wheelchairs can be driven to entrance of hide. There is also a viewing platform overlooking the estuary. At Exminster Marshes there is easy access to footpath from the main car park, but it can be muddy in winter.
How to find it	Exminster Marshes is east of Exminster village; Bowling Green Marsh is on the outskirts of Topsham. Both 5 miles/8 km south of Exeter on either side of the river. Exminster Marshes is accessible from the A379 Dawlish road. There is a regular bus service. Bowling Green Marsh is signposted from the Holman Way car park in Topsham. There is a regular bus service from Exeter. Topsham is a station on the Exeter to Exmouth railway, known as *The Avocet Line*.
Parking	Parking is available in Holman Way, a short walk from the reserve. Large free car park available at Exminster Marshes.
Facilities	Bowling Green Marsh: hide and viewing platform with information boards. Pubs, shops, accommodation and toilets available in Topsham. Exminster Marshes: information boards, leaflet, trails. Two pubs adjacent to the reserve (Turf Locks & Swan's Nest Inn).
Time to see	At least 2 hours each to fully appreciate the reserves.
Short visit	Bowling Green Marsh hide at high tide: thousands of birds roost here.
More	The RSPB arrange avocet cruises during the winter from Topsham, Exmouth and Starcross – the best way to get really close to the 25,000 wintering waterbirds. Public footpaths serve both reserves, and the hide at Bowling Green Marsh is always open. A foot ferry is sometimes available from Topsham across the Exe estuary linking the two reserves. There are also regular opportunities to volunteer on the reserve.

LOCAL NATURE RESERVES

13 Dawlish Warren

NNR, SSSI, LNR

TEIGNBRIDGE DC / DEVON WILDLIFE TRUST
The Wardens, Dawlish Warren NNR,
Teignbridge District Council, Forde House,
Brunel Road, Newton Abbot TQ12 4XX
Tel: 01626 863980 / 215754
www.devonwildlifetrust.org
www.dawlish.gov.uk/leisure
Nearest town: Dawlish **OS Map:** SX 983 788

West bank of Exe estuary: sand spit across Exe estuary mouth. Along with the estuary this is one of the most important places for wildfowl and wading birds in the south-west of England.

Wild highlights	Mile-long sand spit, dune vegetation, ponds and small reedbed. Salt marsh on the estuary side. Well positioned for migrant birds in spring and autumn. In winter the roost is excellent for wildfowl and waders, including Brent geese. High tide roost attracts up to 3,000 oystercatchers, 2–3,000 dunlin, hundreds of bar-tailed godwit, and good numbers of other waders; while on the seaward side, divers, sea duck and grebe (including Slavonian) can be seen offshore. In autumn look also for Skuas, which can occasionally be seen chasing terns. The Exe estuary area is very good for birds and is an especially important wintering ground for avocet.
Best time	All year. Most wildfowl and waders Sept – March. Sand crocus early April, most other wild flowers May – July.
Access	Easy access from main car park to visitor centre but sand paths beyond. No access permitted across golf course. Dogs must be kept on leads, banned past groyne 9.
How to find it	From A379 Exeter – Dawlish road follow signs. Turn first left after tunnel under railway line. Regular bus service between Exeter and Newton Abbot stops at Dawlish Warren.
Parking	There is a large car park with capacity for hundreds of cars. Can be busy in holiday season.
Facilities	Leaflets available. Information boards. Visitor centre. Hide. Public WC, café and holiday accommodation nearby. Good pubs in Cockwood.
Time to see	At least 3 hours to fully appreciate the reserve.
Short visit	Pop into the visitor centre to see what you will miss by not staying longer! Walk along sea wall.
More	To see most birds on the roost from Sept – March, check tide tables and arrive at least one hour before high water.

⑭ Prawle Point

DEVON BIRDWATCHING & PRESERVATION
SOCIETY / SOUTH HAMS DC
Mrs J. Vaughan, 28 Fern Meadow,
Okehampton. Devon EX20 1PB
Nearest town: Kingsbridge
OS Map: SX 741 373

Picturesque coastal headland south of the village of East Prawle. Devon's most southerly point, great views. Recognised as one of the region's top bird migration watchpoints. Worth the walk for the coastal scenery alone.

Wild highlights	Well known migration watch point for land and sea birds. Good record of rarities. Cirl bunting breed in the area.
Best time	Spring and autumn especially for seabird migrants, summer for breeding birds.
Access	Good paths, but can be rough and steep in places. Reserve area only for DBPS members, but otherwise free access to footpaths.
How to find it	From A379 Dartmouth–Kingsbridge road, follow signs on minor roads via East Prawle.
Parking	Free parking.
Facilities	Information board.
Time to see	2–3 hours depending on weather.
Short visit	Just appreciate the superb cliff and coastal views in good weather.
More	Start Point not far away. Lighthouse can attract migrant birds after dark.

NATIONAL NATURE RESERVES

ENGLISH NATURE (EN) – DEVON

English Nature champions the conservation of wildlife, geology and wild places in England. It is a Government agency funded by the Department of Environment, Food and Rural Affairs (DEFRA). Working with the people of Devon for a future where wildlife thrives and natural features are valued and enjoyed, is the vision of the **English Nature** team for Devon.

English Nature is responsible for 10 National Nature Reserves in Devon, 17 Natura 2000 locations and more than 200 Sites of Special Scientific Interest (SSSIs) which cover over 30,000 ha and more than 1900 SSSI owners and occupiers. The Devon team works with these vital land managers and wildlife charities to help maintain the county's wealth of wildlife.

Berry Head to Sharkham Point

NNR, SSSI, COUNTRY PARK

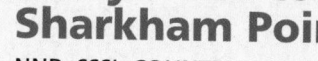

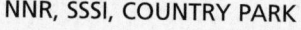

TORBAY COAST AND COUNTRYSIDE TRUST
Gillard Road, Brixham, Torquay TQ5 9AP
Tel: 01803 882619
www.countryside-trust.org.uk
Nearest town: Brixham   **OS Map:** SX 941 562

Torbay's most important wildlife site. Contains several nationally rare and threatened limestone plants. Important seabird colony, trails and great forts. More information in main chapters under *Limestone & Chalk* and *Sea Cliffs*.

Wild highlights	Dramatic limestone headland. Guillemot colony on cliffs below Southern Fort is the largest colony on south coast. Many gulls, fulmar and sometimes peregrine also nest here. Rare limestone flowering plants and ferns. Many orchids. Important bird migration watch point. Greater horseshoe bat caves. Basking sharks seen from cliff tops.
Best time	All year. Spring – summer for breeding guillemots, May – August wild flowers.
Access	Easy access from car park to visitor centre and forts. Cliff-top paths good in places, single track and less easy the further you get from visitor centre. Dogs allowed under close control.
How to find it	Follow signs for Berry Head from Paignton to Brixham A3022 road; narrow access for big vehicles. Bus service No. 12 from Torquay to Brixham town centre. Then pleasant 40-minute walk along King Street towards harbour, then Berry Head road to Berry Head Hotel. Follow signs for the Coast Path or continue along road to car park.
Parking	There is a large pay-and-display car park but can be busy in holiday season.
Facilities	Leaflets available. Information boards. Visitor centre with CCTV during guillemot breeding season. Centre open April–October (10.00–17.00) Public WC. Café open from Easter–October. Plenty of holiday accommodation in surrounding area.
Time to see	At least 3 hours to fully appreciate the reserve.
Short visit	1 hour if you do not want to explore all the site has to offer.
More	Two fine 18th-century Napoleonic forts, Scheduled Ancient Monuments. Great views over Torbay and coastline.

⑯ Black-a-Tor Copse

NNR, SSSI

ENGLISH NATURE
Level 2, Renslade House, Bonhay Road,
Exeter EX4 3AW
Tel: 01392 889770
www.english-nature.org.uk
Nearest town: Okehampton
OS Map: SX 562 918

This 29 hectare reserve is situated some 380 metres up on Dartmoor. It is one of the best examples of a small high altitude oak wood in Britain.

Wild highlights	Its trees and rocks are festooned with a nationally important variety of mosses and lichen. Provides a rare habitat for some moorland birds.
Best time	All year for mosses and lichens. Mid-April – August for moorland birds. Mosses and lichens are at their best after rain. Please remember this is a fairly remote NNR, so good weather is important to enjoy the reserve at its best.
Access	This is a high altitude site where winter and early spring weather can be severe and highly changeable even in summer. Adequate clothing and footwear essential.
How to find it	The reserve is some six miles south-west of Okehampton. Follow signs to Meldon Reservoir. The wood is less than one and a half mile walk across the open moors. The nearest bus stop is at Hughslade on the B3260, just north of Meldon.
Parking	The nearest public car park is at Meldon Reservoir.
Facilities	Leaflet available about the reserve from English Nature's Okehampton office. There is an information sign on the reserve itself. Public toilets are available at the South West Water car park at Meldon Reservoir, along with picnic tables. Café facilities can be found at the Betty Cottles Inn on the B3260.
Time to see	At least 3 hours to fully appreciate the reserve and surrounding moors.
Short visit	Not really possible unless you literally walk there and back quickly!

⑰ Dendles Wood NNR, SSSI

ENGLISH NATURE
Level 2, Renslade House, Bonhay Road,
Exeter EX4 3AW
Tel: 01392 889770
www.english-nature.org.uk
Nearest town: Ivybridge
OS Map: SX 615 620

Important 30 hectare oak-beech woodland, formerly wood pasture with coppice, located in a narrow gorge of the River Yealm. This reserve is used for long-term monitoring of changes in the woodland environment.

Wild highlights	Woodland is rich in ferns, mosses and lichens. Good bluebells and woodland bird life.
Best time	All year. Mid-April – mid-June for bluebells and birds.
Access	Public access is limited to permit holders only for health and safety reasons. Applications for permits should be sent to the Site Manager, English Nature, Yarner Wood, Bovey Tracey TQ13 9LJ. Tel: 01626 832330. Dendles Wood is situated 2 miles north of Cornwood, on the south edge of Dartmoor. There is no disabled access to the site.
How to find it	Take the signs to Cornwood off A38 or from Ivybridge. Nearest bus stop is in Cornwood, Mon–Sat only.
Parking	The nearest car park is in Cornwood.
Facilities	The nearest facilities to the site are located in Cornwood.
Time to see	At least 3 hours to fully appreciate the reserve.
Short visit	Not really worthwhile.

⑱ Great Underscliff

NNR SSSI

ENGLISH NATURE
Part of Jurassic Coast World Heritage Site
Coast path maintained by E. Devon
Countryside Service
Tel: 01395 517557
www.english-nature.org.uk/speciallink
Nearest town: Axmouth/Lyme Regis
OS Map: SY 256 896 – SY 323 913

The largest self-sown ash woodland in Britain. Sheep once extensively grazed the Undercliff but this came to an end in the 1920s with the import of New Zealand lamb. The majority of the biggest trees are therefore less than a century old. The Coastal Path can be muddy and very slippery when wet. The beaches are boulder-strewn and rough. There is no formal access to the reserve from the Coast Path. The trail itself is well marked and an amazing experience in fine weather, but be wary of ticks during spring and summer. Use a plastic sheet to sit on if intending to take a picnic (from personal experience!). Mist is a common hazard, and knowledge of tides is essential if beach walking.

BEWARE: DUE TO HIDDEN CLIFFS AND DEEP FISSURES IT IS DANGEROUS TO LEAVE THE COASTAL FOOTPATH. A PERMIT IS REQUIRED FROM ENGLISH NATURE IF YOU WISH TO DO SO.

Best time to visit March – mid-June for woodland birds, March – late May for spring flowers.

Best time to see all Walk via coastal footpath is about 7 miles from end to end with lots of steps.

Best access is from Lyme Regis, and these are some of the main features to look out for:

Ware Fields SY 335 917. Owned and managed by the National Trust, these fields are rich in wildflowers. Numerous fissures and landslips can be seen across the fields, especially to the west. The views over the West Dorset coast are magnificent. A well known feature on the Devon Dorset border is a large crab apple tree, so big that it has fallen across the path and must be propped by large timbers.

Underhill Farm SY 327 915. Famed for one of its past residents: this is where John Fowles lived when he wrote his famous novel *The French Lieutenant's Woman*. The Undercliff features large in his classic romantic story involving the encounter between a Victorian gentleman and amateur fossil collector, Charles Smithson, and Sarah Woodruff, who lived locally. Still a private property, it is sadly abandoned as landslips have severely damaged the house.

Ravine Pond SY 324 912 (approximate grid reference.). A pool of water formed in a ravine from a portion of cliff top that slipped sometime in the past. If evidence were needed that the area is still moving, look no further: in the winter of 2001 its waters suddenly drained away before mysteriously filling again the following year.

NATURE RESERVES

Pinhay Cliffs SY 317 908. There is evidence of land movement here where the Coast Path joins a track to Pinhay Pumping Station. A cliff fall in the high chalk face here took place in 2000, and numerous other fissures, cracks and pressure ridges can be seen all along the road. Indeed this stretch of land, at least one and a half miles in length from Ravine Pond through to the Pumping Station and beyond, is still moving.

Pinhay Pumping Station SY 318 909. A spring issued from the cliffs and formed a pond here before the pumping station was installed. The area is now a turning circle. The water supply is reliable and pure, but the ground around is still on the move. The water company was forced to abandon the site in 2000.

Mrs Gappers Cottage SY 298 898 (approximate grid reference). The house is now unmarked and very difficult to see. It is amazing to think that until the 1950s a cottage stood here and teas were sold in the garden. Its location must have been stunning, looking straight out over the sea. There was never a road here, so all the food had to be carried to the cottage on foot. As if you need an example of how quickly vegetation can grow in the Undercliff, a nearby sheep wash was discovered in the late 1980s but it is now rapidly being reclaimed by nature.

The Badgers Drinking Trough SY 285 895 (approximate grid reference.) An avenue of trees marks this spot. One trunk is split near ground level and a small pool of water is often present. Animal tracks leading up to the water prove its popularity.

Goat Island SY 275 893. This is one of the few places where the path comes out of the woodland. The high cliff is the face of Goat Island, the largest historical landslip anywhere along the Undercliff. It took place over Christmas in 1839, when a huge chasm opened up detaching about a large area of land estimated at over 8 million tonnes of rock. Marooned from the rest of the cliff, it now forms Goat Island.

Haven Cliffs SY 266 897. The views from here to Beer Head are magnificent. Emerging from the woodland again, the Coast Path runs along the edge of a field. In the late 1990s the whole area started slipping, and now large wedges of land are breaking away and sliding into the Undercliff.

⑲ Slapton Ley NNR, SSSI

WHITLEY WILDLIFE CONSERVATION TRUST /
FIELD STUDIES COUNCIL
Slapton Ley Field Centre, Slapton,
Kingsbridge TQ7 2QP
Tel: 01548 580685
www.slnnr.org.uk
Nearest town: Kingsbridge
OS Map: SX 824 421 (car park at Torcross)

Spectacular sheltered east-facing bay. Large shingle beach with freshwater lagoon behind.

Wild highlights	Three mile shingle ridge. Extensive reed bed and open water. Major wintering site for wildfowl. Summer wetland bursting with life: fish, birds, damselflies and dragonflies. Evidence of otter relatively easy to find, mink easier to see. Very good wetland and coastal flora. Great crested grebe and Cetti's warbler breed. Good for kingfisher.
Best time	All year. Most wildfowl in winter when everywhere else is frozen. Calm conditions best for sea ducks and divers offshore. Good spring and autumn bird migration. May – July for wild flowers. Swallow roost in Torcross reed beds late August. Huge starling roost all winter.
Access	Easy access from car park to waterside hides and view points. Paths around inland edge not suitable for wheelchair access. Good 'jungle' paths for children and pond-dipping courses run from Field Study Centre.
How to find it	On the main A379 between Dartmouth and Kingsbridge.
Parking	There are large car parks at Torcross and on Slapton ridge. Small area near Slapton Bridge for a few cars. All can be busy in holiday season.
Facilities	Leaflets available. Information boards. Field Studies Centre run excellent wildlife courses. Hides. Public WC and café at Torcross, plenty of holiday accommodation in surrounding area.
Time to see	At least 3 hours to fully appreciate the reserve.
Short visit	Watch from Slapton Bridge or visit the bird hide at Torcross.
More	Slapton can easily be combined with a day visit to Prawle and Start point.

Wistmans Wood
NNR, SSSI, ESA

ENGLISH NATURE
Site Manager, Yarner Wood NNR,
Manaton Rd, Bovey Tracey,
Newton Abbot TQ12 9LJ
Tel: 01626 832330
www.english-nature.org.uk
Nearest town: Princetown **OS Map:** SX 612 774

A remarkable small upland oak wood surrounded by granite tors and moorland. The entire reserve extends over a large area of 170 hectares. The contorted and stunted trees have to be seen to be believed!

Wild highlights	Its trees and rocks are festooned with a nationally important variety of mosses and lichen. Provides a rare habitat for some moorland birds.
Best time	All year for mosses and lichens. Mid-April – August for moorland birds. Mosses and lichens are at their best after rain. Please remember this is a fairly remote NNR, so good weather is important to enjoy the reserve at its best. It can be hazardous to visit in bad weather, especially in winter.
Access	This is a high altitude site where winter and early spring weather can be severe and highly changeable even in summer. Adequate clothing and footwear essential. There is no disabled access to the site.
How to find it	Wistmans Wood is approximately 1 mile north of Two Bridges Hotel on Dartmoor, barely two miles from Princetown. Two Bridges is situated on the intersection of the B3357 Tavistock to Ashburton and B3212 Moretonhampstead to Yelverton roads. They are the only main roads across central Dartmoor. There is also a summer bus service which passes the hotel.
Parking	The nearest car park is at Two Bridges.
Facilities	Leaflet available from English Nature's Exeter office on request and also from Yarner Wood. The nearest public toilet and refreshment facilities are situated in Postbridge and Princetown.
Time to see	At least 3 hours to fully appreciate the reserve and surrounding moors.
Short visit	Not really possible, unless you literally walk there and back quickly!

21 Yarner Wood NNR, SSSI

ENGLISH NATURE
Yarner Wood NNR, Manaton Rd,
Bovey Tracey, Newton Abbot TQ12 9LJ
Tel: 01626 832330
www.english-nature.org.uk
Nearest town: Bovey Tracey
OS Map: SX 786 788

Part of East Dartmoor NNR group, comprising Trendlebere Down and Bovey Valley woods. Upland woods and heath on the southern edge of Dartmoor. Best place to see uncommon woodland birds and wood ants in summer.

Wild highlights	Oakwood and heathland excellent for breeding birds. Pied flycatcher, redstart, wood warbler, tree pipit, dipper, raven and buzzard. Good for wood ant nests.
Best time	All year. Spring and summer (mid-April – mid-June) best for breeding woodland birds, April – July for heathland birds and mid-July – mid-August for butterflies. September – November is good for woodland fungi.
Access	Good paths but can be muddy and steep in places.
How to find it	The Reserve is located within Dartmoor National Park approximately 2 miles north-west of Bovey Tracey on the B3344 Manaton Road. It is well signed, left off bend.
Parking	Free parking for several cars between 08.30–19.00 or dusk if earlier.
Facilities	Leaflets available. Information board. Nature trail and hide. WC usually available during open hours. Good food and accommodation available in and around Bovey Tracey.
Time to see	At least 3 hours to fully appreciate the reserve.
Short visit	Various well marked woodland walks.
More	Trendlebere Down above the woods is good for Dartford warbler. It has a good car park adjacent to the Manaton Road.

BIOSPHERE RESERVE

(22) Braunton Burrows
BIOSPHERE RESERVE, SSSI, SAC

N DEVON COAST AND COUNTRYSIDE SERVICE
Bideford Station, East-the-Water,
Bideford EX39 4BB
Tel: 01237 423 655
www.devon.gov.uk/ndccs
Nearest town: Barnstaple/Braunton
OS Map: SS 464 326

Braunton Burrows is one of the richest parts of this newly enlarged 3,120 hectare reserve, which also includes Northam Burrows, the Taw-Torridge estuary and Braunton Marshes with Great Fields, Kipling Tors and Croyde Dunes. This is one of the largest sand dune systems in Britain, containing around 500 different flowering plants, some very rare. It is one of only two UK sites for the water germander, and has a wide range of rare orchids. The new designation means it now ranks alongside Mount Vesuvius in Italy and Ayers Rock in Australia. The Biosphere Reserve has a core area centred on Braunton Burrows which is owned by the Christie Estate. They manage the site with the MOD.

Wild highlights	Huge sand dunes, rocky foreshore, mud and sand flats, saltmarsh of various types, grazing marsh, coastal heath, back-shore marsh, lowland farmland and woodlands. Rarities include water germander, great sea stock, sand toadflax and several scarce orchids. Abundance of wild flowers attracts many insects including 41 different butterflies. Good for common lizard and banded snails.
Best time	Open all year. April – July wildflowers, April – June breeding birds, spring and autumn for migrant birds and winter for wildfowl and waders.
Access	Numerous tracks and trails, many on soft sand in the dunes. Part of the area is also a military training area, so watch out for red flags flying on firing days and other manoeuvres. Summer guided tours are available into the sand dunes and other wildlife-rich areas with the warden. Crow Point and the toll road are easily accessible with convenient parking. Great place for children to explore, but mind they don't get lost – the place is vast.
How to find it	Braunton Burrows is located to the west of Barnstaple: follow the signs.
Parking	Car parking available at all main sites. Can be busy July & August.
Facilities	Leaflets available. Information boards. Benches. Good facilities at nearby towns and villages. Popular tourist area.
Time to see	A great day out in the summer: sand, sea and wildlife.
Short visit	Just wander a short distance from the Braunton Burrows car park.
More	A popular holiday destination with plenty to see and do. Saunton and Croyde beaches nearby.

MARINE NATURE RESERVE

㉓ Lundy SSSI, MNR

LANDMARK TRUST / NATIONAL TRUST
Wildlife Warden, Lundy Island,
Bideford EX39 2LY
Tel: 01237 431831 **www.lundyisland.co.uk**
Nearest town: Ilfracombe/Bideford
Tel bookings: 01271 863636
OS Map: SX 135 465

Dramatically beautiful island off North Devon coast in the Bristol Channel. The Marine Nature Reserve extends to around 14 square kilometres of sea and seabed surrounding the island up to the highwater mark. It includes sea caves, sandbanks, and some of the best reef in the UK. There is also a No Take Zone covering part of the area which prohibits the taking of any marine life.

Wild highlights	Many seabirds including kittiwake, kerring gulls, Manx shearwater and a few puffin. Grey seal, basking shark and Sika deer. Also see Lundy chapter for more on marine life.
Best time	All year. Most seabirds and flowers April – August. Winter can be spectacular, especially when big seas are running.
Access	By boat from Ilfracombe and Bideford on the MS Oldenburg running 4 times a week between April – October. Helicopter service available during winter. Flight 12 noon, check-in one hour ahead. Dogs are not permitted.
How to find it	25 miles off North Devon coast. Contact: Lundy Shore Office, The Quay, Bideford, Devon, EX39 2LY.
Parking	Public parking available near town quays.
Facilities	Plenty of information available on island jetty, also Marisco Tavern and island shop. Public toilets are available. Good accommodation available.
Time to see	A day visit cannot do justice to the beauty and tranquillity of the island. Try a long weekend or a week is even better, especially if you dive.
Short visit	Day trips available.
More	The history of Lundy is as fantastic as it is fascinating.

OTHER RECOMMENDED NATURE RESERVES & WILDLIFE SITES

24 Kents Cavern SSSI, ANCIENT MONUMENT

KENTS CAVERN LTD,
Cavern House, Ilsham Road, Torquay TQ1 2JF
Tel: 01803 215136 **www.kents-cavern.co.uk**
Nearest town: Torquay **OS Map:** SX 934 641

Kents Cavern is the oldest Scheduled Ancient Monument in Britain. The hillside, woodlands and the internal landscape of the caves are designated a Site of Special Scientific Interest. The name Kent is thought to be from the Celtic name for a headland, and for many centuries it was known as Kent's Hole. Privately owned by the Powe family since 1903, it is one of the most popular tourist attractions in the region. Kents Cavern is now recognised as the most important Palaeolithic cave system in Northern Europe, containing evidence of human occupation since the Stone Age. It contains beautiful and spectacular cave formations and significant finds of prehistoric bones and stone implements over half a million years old.

Wild highlights	A large cave system with impressive geological formations, prehistoric stone tools and animal bones from a period much colder than today.
Best time	Open all year except Christmas Day.
Access	Easy level access and suitable for young children. Special arrangements are made for wheelchair users and other disabilities. Tours start at 10am with tours running regularly throughout the day – last tour runs from 3.30–5pm depending on the time of the year. Please check www.kents-cavern.co.uk or by phone for current charges, special arrangements and for special evening opening times and events.
How to find it	Well signposted in and around Torquay. Ilsham Road is off the Torwood Street – Babbacombe Road, a few minutes drive from the inner harbour.
Parking	There is a large free car park.
Facilities	Leaflets and information about the geology and archaeological excavations available. A popular visitor attraction with good facilities for all ages. New 100 seat licensed restaurant, café and WCs.
Time to see	At least 2 hours to fully appreciate the caves and displays.
Short visit	45 minutes – just go on a guided tour.
More	Special evening visits, corporate entertainment and educational groups.

㉕ Pengelly Caves SSSI

PENGELLY CAVES TRUST / DEVON WILDLIFE TRUST
Pengelly Caves, Russets Lane, Buckfastleigh TQ11 0DY
Tel: 01752 700293
www.pengellytrust.org.uk
Nearest town: Buckfastleigh **OS Map:** SX 743 664

The Pengelly Trust is named after William Pengelly. He was the Victorian pioneer of serious cave research and the proper archaeological excavation of bone deposits discovered in Devon's limestone caves during the 19th Century.

Several caves make up the extensive Buckfastleigh cave system. Joint Mitnor cave was discovered by three young cavers: Joint, Mitchel and Northey. Extensive excavations were carried out in 1939–41 by the Torquay Natural History Society, who discovered remains of hippopotamus and other warm climate animals, now preserved in Torquay Museum. The cave is small, and no special skills are required as steps lead into the cavern. Just inside the entrance is a chamber containing a cone of earth and bones known as a talus mound, covered by stalagmite. Now partly excavated, it has revealed over 4,000 bones of animals, including hippopotamus, bison, hyaena and elephants dating from around l00,000 years ago.

Wild highlights	An extraordinary opportunity to see remains of prehistoric creatures where they fell. This is the richest collection of mammalian remains from the last Interglacial yet found in a British cave – a period warmer than today.
Best time	Summer.
Access	May – Sept for pre-booked group visits only. August: Wednesdays open 11am – 2pm for public guided walks. Cost £4.00. Relatively easy access for adults and children along quarry footpath and steps. Not suitable for many disabled or for wheelchair access.
How to find it	Joint Mitnor cave is to be found in Higher Kiln Quarry, Buckfastleigh. Leave the main A38 Exeter Plymouth at Buckfastleigh and take road towards the town. Soon after Russet Lane will be seen on right. Short drive to Cave centre.
Parking	There is a small free car park.
Facilities	Leaflets and other information available in the small museum attached to the Study Centre. The museum is normally open by arrangement or on public access days during summer and usually includes a slide show. WC. Overnight accommodation also available for prebooked student groups only.
Time to see	Up to 2 hours to fully appreciate the caves.
Short visit	Guided walks only available.
More	Nearby the Rift Cave is an important bat colony.

NATURE RESERVES

DARTMOOR NATIONAL PARK

www.dartmoor-npa.gov.uk

26 Haytor Information Centre
Tel: 01364 661520
Open Easter – end October, 10am – 5pm
At the lower car park on the main road. Toilets with disabled access.

27 The High Moorland Visitor Centre
Tavistock Road, Princetown, Devon PL20 6QF
Tel: 01822 890414
Very good interpretation and information available.

28 Newbridge Information Centre
Tel: 01364 631303
Open Easter – end October and winter weekends. 10am to 5pm throughout the peak season, 10am – 4pm winter weekends. Riverside Car Park with toilets.

29 Postbridge Information Centre
Tel: 01822 880272
Open Easter – end October, 10am – 5pm.
On B3212, large car park and toilets with disabled access.

EXMOOR NATIONAL PARK

www.exmoor-nationalpark.gov.uk/traditional

While most of Exmoor National Park is in Somerset, the western edge lies in North Devon, with visitor centres at Combe Martin and County Gate.

30 Combe Martin Information Centre
Cross Street, Combe Martin
Tel: 01271 883319
Offers the services of both a Tourist Information Centre and a National Park Visitor Centre. Open Monday to Saturday, 10.30am – 12.30pm.

31 County Gate Information Centre
At County Gate on A39 at Countisbury on Devon-Somerset border
Tel : 01598 741321
Open 20th March to 31st October. Good information available. Large free car park, including disabled spaces. Toilets available.

Local Information Points

Barbrook Post Office Stores
Challacombe Post Office
Parracombe Stores

NATIONAL TRUST RESERVES

www.nationaltrust.org.uk/regions/devoncornwall

32 Arlington Court
Arlington, Barnstaple EX31 4LP
Tel: 01271 850296
Ancient woodland, lakes, parkland.

33 Branscombe, Salcombe Regis & Sidmouth
Killerton House, Broadclyst, Exeter EX5 3LE
Tel: 01392 881691
Shingle, woodland, heath, mining bees, fritillary butterflies, blue gromwell.

34 Buckland
Yelverton PL20 6EY
Tel: 01822 853607
Woodland, sessile oak, marshland, valerian.

35 Castle Drogo & Teign Valley Woods
Drewsteignton, Exeter EX6 6PB
Tel: 01647 433306
Buzzard, ancient woodland, heathland, grayling.

36 Heddon Valley
Heddon Valley Shop, Parracombe, Nr Barnstaple EX31 4PY
Tel: 01598 763402
Beautiful coastal and woodland walks.

37 Hentor, Willings Walls, Trowlesworthy Warrens & Goodameavy
Killerton House, Broadclyst, Exeter EX5 3LE
Tel: 01392 881691
Status: National Park
Highlights: Moor, bog asphodel, quarries, woodland.

38 Ilfracombe & Lee to Croyde
Killerton House, Broadclyst, Exeter EX5 3LE
Tel: 01392 881691
Cliff, coast, sand dunes, autumn lady's tresses.

39 Killerton
Killerton House, Broadclyst, Exeter EX5 3LE
Tel: 01392 881691
Woodland, forest, heath.

23 Lundy (see page 233)
Landmark Trust, Lundy, Bristol Channel EX39 2LY
Tel: 01237 431831
Marine Nature Reserve, island, seabirds.

NATIONAL TRUST RESERVES (continued)

40 Lydford Gorge
The Stables, Lydford Gorge, Lydford, Okehampton EX20 4BH
Tel: 0182282 441 / 320
National Park. Ravine, woodlands, ferns, pink purslane.

41 Lynmouth: Foreland Point, Countisbury Hill and Watersmeet
Killerton House, Broadclyst, Exeter EX5 3LE
Tel: 01392 881691
National Park. Woodland, cliff, heath, gorse, grassland.

42 Plym Bridge Woods
Killerton House, Broadclyst, Exeter EX5 3LE
Tel: 01392 881691
Oak woodland, quarry, wild garlic, primrose.

43 Salcombe East: Mill Bay to Prawle and Woodcombe Point
Killerton House, Broadclyst, Exeter EX5 3LE
Tel: 01392 881691
Cliff, estuary, grassland, heath, thorn scrub, cirl bunting, dark-green fritillary butterfly.

44 Salcombe West: Bolt Head to Hope Cove
Killerton House, Broadclyst, Exeter EX5 3LE
Tel: 01392 881691
Coast, sea birds, rocks, scree slopes, ants, whitethroat.

45 Saltram Park
Plympton, Plymouth PL7 3UH
Tel: 01752 336546
Parkland, estuary, woodland.

46 Southdown Cliffs, Coleton Fishacre, Dartmouth and the Dart Estuary
Killerton House, Broadclyst, Exeter EX5 3LE
Tel: 01392 881691
Beach, coast, coppice oak woodland, sea birds.

47 Watersmeet
Lynmouth, Lynton EX35 6NT
Tel: 01598 53348
Status: SSSI, AONB. Heath, river, woodland.

9 Wembury Bay and the Yealm Estuary (see page 217)
Killerton House, Broadclyst, Exeter EX5 3LE
Tel: 01392 881691
Voluntary marine nature reserve. Estuary, farmland, woodland, cliffs, grassland.

48 West Exmoor Coast: Heddon Valley and Woody Bay
Killerton House, Broadclyst, Exeter EX5 3LE
Tel: 01392 881691
National Park. Moor, cliff, woodland, sea birds, meadow, high-brown fritillary.

WOODLAND TRUST RESERVES

Woodland Trust, Autumn Park, Grantham, Lincs NG31 6LL
Tel: 01476 581111   www.woodland-trust.org.uk

49 Avon Woods, Woodleigh
OS Map: SX 732 490
AONB Ancient wood, car parking can be difficult.
Good for field maple, crab apple.

50 Buck's Wood, Buck's Mills
OS Map: SS 352 235
Walks link to the North Devon coast path.
Colour on both sides of valley in Autumn, great views.

51 Core Hill Wood, Sidmouth
OS Map: SY 113 911
AONB
Woodland, Scots pine, beech.

52 Hardwick Wood, Plymouth
OS Map: SX 530 556
Circular walk and good views down River Plym.

53 Hisley Wood, Lustleigh
OS Map: SX 778 803
SSSI, National Park
Good paths with views, rich in moss and lichen.

54 Shaptor & Furzeleigh Woods, Bovey Tracey
OS Map: SX 811 805
Dartmoor National Park
Ancient woodland, oak, wood warbler, redstart.

55 Whitleigh Wood, Tamerton Foliot
OS Map: SX 478 601
Good views and wildlife, limited parking nearby.

COUNTRY PARKS

www.devon.gov.uk/country_parks

These are designated areas for people to visit and enjoy a countryside environment. They are not formal parks as found in urban areas, nor are they remote wild places. They tend to be located where visitors can enjoy a public open space with an informal atmosphere, often close to built-up areas. They usually have more formal facilities than nature reserves, such as a car park, toilets, café or kiosk, paths and trails, and some information for visitors. Some also have much more, with museums, visitor centres, historic buildings and educational facilities.

Most Country Parks are managed by local authorities, although other organisations and private individuals may also run them. There is not necessarily any public right of access to Country Parks, and visitors are usually subject to by-laws when they enter the park. Some charge for car parking, others are free.

Country Parks vary tremendously, and really have only their purpose in common: to provide easy access to the countryside for those living in towns and cities. They do not necessarily have any great nature conservation interest, although many often do. The best in Devon include Stover, Grand Western Canal and Berry Head.

15 Berry Head SSSI, NNR (see page 224)
Nearest town: Brixham
Torbay Coast & Countryside Trust, Gillard Road, Brixham, Torquay TQ5 9AP
Tel: 01803 882619   www.countryside-trust.org.uk
Visitor centre with CCTV, seabird colony, wild flowers, trails, ancient monuments – great forts. More information in main chapters under *Limestone & Chalk* and *Sea Cliffs*.

56 Decoy Country Park
Nearest town: Newton Abbot
Teignbridge District Council, Forde House, Newton Abbot
Tel: 01626 61101 x 2705 www.teignbridge.gov.uk/countryside
Woodland with lake side walk. Level, easy access for disabled and young children.

57 Grand Western Canal Country Park
Ranger Service, The Moorings, Canal Hill, Tiverton EX16 4HX
Tel: 01884 254072 www.devon.gov.uk/grand_western_canal
Located in the heart of beautiful Devon countryside, the Grand Western Canal runs between Tiverton and Holcombe Regis in northeast Devon.

Birds such as Kingfishers are a regular sight feeding along the canal and otters are making a comeback to the area. There is an abundance of plant life along the canal flowering from early spring to late autumn, providing food and shelter for many insects. The towpath is flat, well surfaced in most areas and popular with walkers and cyclists. Other popular recreational activities include fishing and boating.

Canal boat permits can be bought at various sites along the canal, or you can contact the address above.

COUNTRY PARKS (continued)

58 Maidencombe Farm
Nearest town: Torquay/Shaldon
Torbay Coast & Countryside Trust,
Cockington Court, Cockington, Torquay TQ2 6XA
Tel: 01803 606035 www.countryside-trust.org.uk
This 150-acre farm is a stronghold for the rare Cirl bunting. Footpaths, outstanding scenery and dramatic cliffs. The Trust looks after the village green, car park and beach café. Walks and leaflets available.

59 Northam Burrows SSSI, AONB & United Nations Biosphere Reserve
Nearest town: Appledore/Bideford.
Burrows Centre, Northam Burrows, Northam, Bideford EX39 1LY
Tel: 01237 479708 www.torridge.gov.uk/index
Northam Burrows Country Park lies at the western edge of the Taw Torridge Estuary. Contains some 253 hectares of grassy coastal plain with salt marsh, sand dunes and generally unimproved grasslands. It provides a major access point for the one and a half miles of the Westward Ho! Beach.

The Park is open to walkers at all times but there are restrictions on vehicles. The Burrows Visitor Centre is open end of May to early September and the toilet facilities from Easter to the end of October. Northam Burrows can be accessed from Northam or Westward Ho! The latter has a visitor centre and bird hide with easy access for wheelchairs. Take the B3231 for one mile and turn left at Sandy Lane.

60 Stover Country Park
Stover, Newton Abbot TQ12 6QG
Tel: 01626 835236 www.devon.gov.uk/stover_country_park
Stover contains over 114 acres of woodland, heathland, grassland, lake and marsh and a substantial variety of wildlife. There is also a wealth of historical interest. The site provides all the information you need to know before visiting with an educational or local interest group, or making a private trip. Stover Country Park is owned and managed by Devon County Council.

The most exciting project recently completed at Stover is an aerial walkway. It enables visitors to gain a bird's eye view of the woodland and ponds below. The walkway is unique to the South-west and follows a 90-metre long route through the lower canopy of the wood where you may be lucky enough to see marsh tit, spotted or pied flycatcher, all three woodpeckers and, in the evening, a wide range of bats including Daubenton's, Noctule and the rare greater horseshoe bat. Tawny owl are often heard and sometimes even barn owl seen. But perhaps the walkway's best attraction is the close-up views it provides of insects such as the elusive purple hairstreak butterfly, which are seldom seen at ground level.

Carved wooden boards give visitors greater insight into what they are observing. The walkway is open dawn till dusk every day of the year. It is wheelchair-friendly and has level sections with benches. Good for young families. Bird feeders, bird and bat boxes enhance its wildlife value.

Visitor Attractions
owned by wildlife conservation charities

Living Coasts Penguins, seals, diving ducks and much more.
Torquay Harbourside, Beacon Quay, Torquay, Devon TQ1 2BG
Tel: 01803 202470. www.livingcoasts.org.uk

National Marine Aquarium Britain's biggest, Europe's deepest.
Rope Walk, Coxside, Plymouth PL4 0LF
Tel: 01752 600 301 www.national-aquarium.co.uk

Paignton Zoological and Botanical Gardens
& Whitley Wildlife Conservation Trust
Paignton Zoo Environmental Park, Totnes Road, Paignton TQ4 7EU.
Tel: 01803 697500 www.paigntonzoo.org.uk

Further Information

Organisations

Devon Wildlife Trust (and Devon Biodiversity Record Centre)
Tel: 01392 279244
www.devonwildlifetrust.org

Royal Society for the Protection of Birds (RSPB)
South West England Regional Office, Keble House, Southernhay Gardens,
Exeter EX1 1NT
Tel: 01392 432691 www.rspb.org.uk

Devon Bird Watching and Preservation Society (DBWPS)
Mrs J. Vaughan, 28 Fern Meadow, Okehampton EX20 1PB

Amateur Entomologist's Society
P.O. Box 8774, London SW7 5ZG
www.ex.ac.uk/bugclub/aes

Botanical Society of the British Isles
BSBI, 41 Marlborough Road, Roath, Cardiff CF23 5BU
www.bsbi.org.uk

British Butterfly Society
Manor Yard, East Lulworth, Wareham, Dorset BH20 5QP
www.butterfly-conservation.org

British Dragonfly Society
Dave Smallshire, 8 Twindle Beer, Chudleigh, Newton Abbot TQ13 0JP
www.dragonflysoc.org.uk

Devon Moth Group
36 Paradise Road, Teignmouth TQ14 8NR
www.devonmothgroup.org.uk

Mammal Society
2B Inworth Street, London SW11 3EP
www.abdn.ac.uk/mammal

Books & Guides

For the author's latest top 50 recommended wildlife books, please see his website: www.wildlink.org

FSC AIDGAP British Wildlife Guides, Field Studies Council. Fold-out identification guides to trees, flowers, insects, birds – even seaweeds, crabs etc.

Highly recommended, accurate, laminated fold-out guides are available from:

Devon Wildlife Trust Shop, Harlequin Centre, Exeter

Natural History Book Service, 2-3 Wills Road, Totnes, Devon TQ9 5XN
Tel: 01803 865913 www.nhbs.com

BIRDS

Collins Field Guide to the Birds of Britain and Europe by Roger Tory Peterson, Guy Mountfort and PAD Hollom, Harper Collins, ISBN 0007192347

Collins Wild Guide: Birds of Britain and Ireland by Peter Holden, Harper Collins, ISBN 0007177925

BUTTERFLIES AND MOTHS

Britain's Butterflies by David Tomlinson & Rob Still, Wildguides, ISBN 1903657016

Collins Field Guide to the Butterflies of Britain and Europe by Tom Tolman and Richard Lewington, Harper Collins, ISBN 0007189915

Moths of Devon: An Account of the Pyralid, Plume and Macromoths of Devon by Roy F McCormick, John Walters, ISBN 095402561X

DRAGONFLIES

Britain's Dragonflies by Dave Smallshire and Andy Swash, Wildguides, ISBN 1903657040

GRASSHOPPERS AND CRICKETS

A field guide to the grasshoppers and crickets of Britain and northern Europe by Heiko Bellman, Collins, ISBN 0002198525

INSECTS

Collins Field Guide to the Insects of Britain and Northern Europe by Michael Chinery, Harper Collins, ISBN 0002199181

Collins Wild Guide: Insects of Britain and Europe by Bob Gibbons, Harper Collins, ISBN 000717795X

MAMMALS

Collins Wild Guide: Wild Animals of Britain and Europe by John A Burton, Harper Collins, ISBN 0002200082

WILD FLOWERS AND TREES

The Mitchell Beazley Pocket Guide to Wild Flowers of Britain and Europe by Peter Moore, Mitchell Beazley, ISBN 1840002719

Collins Wild Guide: Flowers of Britain and Ireland by John Akeroyd, Harper Collins, ISBN 0007177933

Collins Wild Guide: Trees of Britain and Ireland by Bob Press, Harper Collins, ISBN 0002200090

Index

Next in the series:

Secret Nature of

Isles of Scilly

to be published early spring 2006

Secret Nature of

Cornwall

to be published late spring 2006